Touching the Soul
of Islam

Sharing the Gospel in Muslim Cultures

BILL A. MUSK

MONARCH
BOOKS

Oxford, UK & Grand Rapids, Michigan, USA

First published in 1995 by
Monarch Books, under the MARC imprint.
This edition published in 2004 by Monarch Books,
(a publishing imprint of Lion Hudson plc),
Mayfield House, 256 Banbury Road, Oxford OX2 7DH
Tel: +44 (0)1865 302750 Fax: +44 (0)1865 302757
Email: monarch@lionhudson.com
www.lionhudson.com

UK ISBN 1 85424 652 6
US ISBN 0 8254 6075 1

Distributed by:
UK: Marston Book Services Ltd, PO Box 269,
Abingdon, Oxon OX14 4YN;
USA: Kregel Publications, PO Box 2607
Grand Rapids, Michigan 49501.

Unless otherwise stated, Scripture quotations are
taken from the Holy Bible, New International Version,
© 1973, 1978, 1984 by the International Bible Society.
Used by permission of Hodder and Stoughton Ltd.
All rights reserved.

Qur'ânic references are taken
from A. Yusuf Ali, *The Glorious Qur'an*,
American Trust Publications, 1977.

British Library Cataloguing Data
A catalogue record for this book is available
from the British Library.

Cover photos: AA World Travel Library

Book design and production for the publishers by
Bookprint Creative Services
P.O. Box 827, BN21 3YJ, England.
Printed in Great Britain.

Peter and Jeremy
In Memoriam

CONTENTS

FIGURES

ILLUSTRATIONS

ACKNOWLEDGEMENTS

My thanks are due to several people for their reflection upon the developing manuscript: Diana Adcock (née Fakhouri), Ruth Allen, Colin Chapman, Elsie Maxwell and Vivienne Stacey especially. I hope that their comments and suggestions have resulted in a clearer and more mature publication.

I am indebted to the librarians at Maghull Library for obtaining a variety of materials for me.

I am delighted with the artistic contributions of Tobias and Damaris Schultz. Their pen drawings illustrate so well various aspects of the themes described in the following pages.

I have appreciated the encouragement and patience of Tony Collins of Monarch Books as I have sought to write and rewrite whilst also fulfilling my role as vicar of a lively church.

My wife Hilary and our daughters have been very patient with me, allowing me time during holidays, late evenings and days off for the writing of this book. Hilary has also read the whole manuscript through and offered her insights and suggestions.

Inspiration comes out of friendships with Middle Easterners – Muslim and Christian – and others across various cultural divides. It derives also from getting to know friends who, in differing contexts, have lived out the kind of insightful humility and conviction promoted here. The tension between being faithful to one's missionary calling and yet learning to appreciate and respect the cultural heritage of others is not easy to sustain. I am thankful for the fellowship enjoyed (and missed) with those on similar journeys to my own.

Bill A. Musk

INTRODUCTION TO THE SECOND EDITION

A friend and I were lamenting recently that, although we did not really agree with Huntington's "clash of civilisations" thesis, too many contemporary events were seemingly proving the American professor right, and us wrong! Samuel P. Huntington, a Harvard University political scientist, outlined in the 1990s his theory about international relations in the post-Cold War era, eventually giving it popular form in a book entitled *The Clash of Civilizations and the Remaking of World Order*.[1]

In this important volume, Huntington argues that the world today can be divided into six or seven major cultural zones, or "civilisations". In almost every civilisation, religious convictions have a strong bearing on the ethos or outlook of the people concerned. Huntington's prediction is that international affairs will increasingly be determined by relations between these six or seven zones – and the religions that motivate them. A major preoccupation in Huntington's analysis is with the "clash" between the Islamic and the Western worlds. His conviction about Islamic civilisation is that wherever it comes up against other civilisations, including that of the West, "Islam has bloody borders". Religious motivations, he contends, give the recent Islamic "Resurgence" a popular base, fanning bigotry and encouraging the use of unbridled force. In his book, the professor thankfully backs down a little from earlier assertions about Islamic resurgence always being equated with violence. He admits that the movement embraces far more than just the agenda of militant extremists. His theorising has, however, helped to confirm an incipient hostility towards Islam and Muslims within his Western readership. Whatever the nuance of his less sweeping judgement of Islamic resurgence, the message is quickly perceived thus: the Soviet Union was the "Bad Guy" during the Cold War era; now Islam or Muslims constitute the "Bad Guy" – and all Muslims are of course fundamentalists or terrorists at heart.

It doesn't help that certain radical groups within the contemporary, widespread movement of Islamic resurgence manage to catch the attention of the world's media – radical groups of angry, bigoted, religious people seemingly intent on conquering the world or blowing it up.

Not that that's never been a caricature of Western nations also! The trouble today, it seems, is that there is no one strong or foolish enough to shame the West at international level except wealthy Saudi Arabian exiles and their suicide-willing disciples. Why don't the moderate Muslims stand up more and shout against such aberrant, radical extremists? In large part, I think, because there is considerable sympathy among many moderate Muslims for the extremists' diagnosis of the ills of the modern world. After all, America's agenda for the world community is perceived, as per Huntington's thesis, as religiously motivated, especially by Muslims who have read about the New Christian Right's connections with the state of Israel. Outstanding issues of international injustice seem to be heavily weighted in terms of ignoring Muslims' concerns. It appears not to be in America's national self-interest to see them resolved; that is the conclusion widely drawn.

In consequence, negative stereotypes of Muslim and Westerner prevail within each respective "civilisation". Muslims and Islam on the one hand, and Westerners and the Christian faith on the other, are given a bad press by each other's media. It is hard to break down the resulting prejudice.

My experience – and my friend's – of being hosted by generous, family-focused Muslim Middle Easterners does not really hit the headlines, even though it is a far truer approximation of the focus of life and energy for a majority of Muslims. Our experiences of being thus hosted certainly altered our perceptions of such fellow humans at a level deeper than headlines can upstage. I hope something of my debt to Muslims will become apparent in the chapters of this book. Sojourn in their midst makes it easy to proceed from the consideration of cultural themes of Muslim societies to the realisation that one has gained some unexpected insight into Old and New Testament texts. We can grow in Christian faith and discipleship through getting to know ordinary Muslims!

I have been gratified that the first edition of *Touching the Soul of Islam* has proved beneficial to many readers, especially Western Christians working among Muslims. This expanded text follows the same overall pattern of the first edition, only it takes investigation into the various themes a step further.

In many ways, the core of this book lies within Chapter 4, in the middle of the exposition. My gut feeling is that the honour/shame tension is central to the manner in which many Muslim communities and cultures cohere – and fundamentally alien to the way that most Westerners function. This central cultural theme is like a will-o'-the-wisp; you think you begin to get some measure of it and then it dances away, not fully graspable! In so many areas, reference to honour and shame seems unavoidable: in the consideration of family, of space, of "face", of gender roles, of sin, of careerism, of community and language and so on.

There are rich pickings for those who seriously try to understand the powerful and normative functioning of shame and honour themes in Muslim societies. Hope begins to grow that seemingly inexplicable or "hard to swallow" facets of the Old and New Testaments might become more comprehensible when read through this lens. Certainly the honour/shame tension appears central to Scripture: from the naked ashamedness in Eden as delineated in Genesis to the honouring prostration before Jesus so movingly described in the book of Revelation. The Bible strongly expresses the nature of divine/human and inter-human relatedness in terms of shame and honour. Maybe also, relationships between divine Father and Son might be appreciated more insightfully when approached from this angle? Jesus' thoughts certainly turn in this direction when he comes to contemplate his impending death. He prays: "I have brought you glory on earth by completing the work you gave me to do. And now, Father, glorify me in your presence with the glory I had with you before the world began" (John 17:4, 5). Glory, or honour, is central to the fellowship between Father and Son. We may evidently learn something more of God himself from a deeper appreciation of our Muslim friends!

Bill A. Musk

Introduction

A society's culture is a reflection of its soul.
President Havel of Czechoslovakia

CHAPTER ONE

TO SAVE A SOUL

Knowledge comes, but wisdom lingers.
Alfred, Lord Tennyson

Was it a word? Was it a picture? Was it a doodle? Whatever Jesus traced in the dust beneath the angry gaze of religious bigots inflamed with bloodlust, it gave him space to sort out his own response to the tricky problem of "a woman taken in adultery". Eventually looking up, he uttered a single sentence and waited for the rules of Sanhedrin decision-making to break down: "If any one of you is without sin, let him be the first to throw a stone at her" (John 8:7). The older men, notables who normally reserved their power of veto until after the younger rulers had committed themselves, on this occasion broke with precedence and voted first. They walked away, shamed. It was not for them to claim sinlessness. How could they remain, allowing themselves to be exposed for wanting to stone to death one half of the guilty pair simply in order to score a political point? The younger accusers gradually caught on and they too slipped away, one by one, shamed into withdrawal. The thoughtful pause of a crouching Christ had ramifications beyond the expectations of furious critics and sobbing woman.

When Paul picked up the theme of the "unknown god" in the respected Athenian council of the Areopagus, he latched onto a basic anxiety among the Greeks. They had to cover all the philosophical angles and here was one indeed! Beyond the fullness of the pantheon lay the mists of supernatural possibility: what if there were a god unknowable, unrecognisable in the Greek mythological tradition? A safety net was extended to placate and honour that god also, and Paul found his way into the vacuum inside their hearts: " . . . what you worship as something unknown I am going to proclaim to you" (Acts 17:23). The apostle had chosen the right local altar in which to take interest!

The Bible bears testimony to many simple statements, questions and deeds that acted on their audiences like today's "passwords" on computer programs. If you correctly type in the appropriate characters, a secret world is opened to you; you are taken to a new level. So, in Genesis for example, God is walking in the garden in the awful silence after that first crisp bite of human disobedience and a question ripples through the vegetation: "Adam, where are you?" Goodbye, Paradise! Centuries later, a man in a boat stage-manages a blockbuster of a fishing expedition and the first mate falls on his face in the bilge: "Get out of my filthy life, Lord!" Hello, holy Messiah! Christians are surviving, fighting, winning, losing, rejoicing and suffering in towns on the western seaboard of Asia Minor at the end of the first century, and "angels" mediate messages which touch the nerve of each community: "I know your deeds"; "I know your afflictions"; "I know where you live". Listen, proclaims each angel to each church, give heed and change, or die!

Getting under the surface

The "chemistry" is such that when God mixes with humankind, a reaction takes place. The Lord knows all the elements that make up the human predicament. As he interjects divine resources into human lives, the latter can never be the same again. God is an agent of change *par excellence*. He sees the real issues and speaks to them. Unfailingly, he gets through to the souls of men and women. All of us have experienced the effect of a dream, a sentence in a song, a glimpse of another dimension in nature, a rescue from an impossible situation that has changed our attitudes, melted our hearts, strengthened our weak wills and given us renewed hope and sustenance.

A doodle in the sand, a passing glance at an altar with a difference, the smell of the aroma of apple – each indicates a searching for insight. Discerning the undisclosed thoughts and intentions of the human heart, and addressing them directly or through his friends, is a considerable part of God's business on earth.

Christians who share the good news of Christ's kingdom with

others are also, as God's friends, agents of change. The New
Testament word for such a person (*apostolos*) carries the connotation
"sent for a purpose". To be sent by Christ, as he was sent by the
Father, is to be sent with a mission. The point of sharing the gospel
is that a kingdom might come on earth, that allegiances might alter
in human hearts, that nothing be the same again. If the call to repentance and faith is heeded, no one can predict the possible
ramifications in the lives and communities of those turning to Christ.

To woo or to wound?

One recurring, critical issue in the sharing of the gospel by God's
friends revolves around the matching or mismatching of messenger
and recipient. The former bears a wonderful, liberating proclamation
but the latter often fails to hear it. All too frequently, other facets of
the messenger's presence (his cultural "baggage") drown out the
story he comes to bring. The history of Christian missions is full of
such sadness: evangelist unwittingly nullifying the evangel he is
announcing.

It is not only in a missions context that such mismatching of
ambassador and host community has occurred. The "ugly American"
of eastern Asia is a caricature of numerous agents of change who
have not appreciated that a wholesale imposition of one set of
cultural norms upon another society is totally inappropriate.[2]
However well intended, the judging of one culture by the tenets of
another has historically led to much ill-will between people and
nations. At the turn of the second millennium, we live with the
results of continuing cultural and economic imperialisms in a world
that has largely renounced direct political or military colonisation.
Those results are expressed in a widespread, angry impatience with
a Western cultural norm that is still generally perceived as being the
dominant force in the world today.

Such contemporary impatience with the West seems to me to be
to a considerable extent justified. Many peoples of the world feel that
the only interest the West shows in them is as a potential market for
Western technology, as a potential source for much needed energy
and as a potential supporter of the West's agenda in global politick-
ing. What interest does the West, especially the United States of
America, really have in international or regional issues of justice?

The recent Iraq war has dramatically emphasised that the USA, Britain, Spain and Italy at least, will seek regime change in the Middle East outside the aegis of the United Nations. Preemptive warfare, when there is only a single global superpower, is a very one-sided affair. The foreign policy of the USA in the 21st century is perceived as highly selective and hypocritical. Does that critical perception not accurately reflect a huge cultural gap between Westerners and other peoples of today's world? One can hardly avoid noticing the negative perceptions of Arabs, Palestinians, Algerians, Iranians, Pakistanis, Muslims, in many Western nations today. Issues to do with the accommodation of refugees and asylum seekers – many of them Muslim – plus the high profile terrorist acts of certain extremist Muslim groups have inflamed an incipient and historical antipathy towards "foreigners" who are seen as displacing poorer members of indigenous Western communities in the scramble for housing and other benefits. The electoral gains in recent years of the British National Party reflect this disturbing trend.

Western perceptions of others that arise out of ignorance or prejudice occur as much in Christian circles as in the secular worlds of international politics and commerce. The secular media's focus upon the more unpalatable expressions of contemporary Islam is mirrored by the vogue among Christians for referring to Islam or the Islamic world as the last remaining "giant" to be conquered or tamed. The previous Goliath of communism is perceived as being rendered powerless in the changes that swept through the former USSR and its satellite countries in the 1990s. Now, efforts in prayer and mission to address the "giant" of Islam are increasingly on the agendas of denominations and mission groups throughout the Christian world.[3] That is quite acceptable so long as the ascription of "giant" doesn't allow only negative connotations. Too often, Muslims or Islam are mistaken for "the enemy". Recent and continuing negative pronouncements by national Christian figures – especially in the United States – concerning Prophet Muḥammad or the religion of Islam do little to help ordinary Christian believers in the West abandon a hostile view of Muslims whether at home or abroad.

Standing in others' shoes

The paragraphs of this book are offered in this context or climate, in which passions and maybe even bloodlust – secular and Christian – run high. They constitute a doodle, an aid to understanding "souls" very different from ourselves. Attention is focused upon some of the important themes found in many contemporary Muslim cultures, especially Arab ones. It is my conviction that Muslim cultures are as positive and strong, as evil and sad, as Western secular humanist cultures. Muslim cultures cohere in specific ways, different from Western ones. That the two kinds of cultures are different is no licence for condemning one and assuming that the other is beyond reproach.

Some aspects of Muslim cultures derive specifically from their Islamic inheritance. They result from the impact that the Qur'ân and Islamic law have had on different societies as that faith expanded geographically and came to be consolidated politically. Other significant aspects of Muslim cultures derive from concepts of reality that predate Islam and that have survived its intrusion. In fact, the cultures of many Christians in the developing world share far more themes and assumptions about reality with Islamic cultures than with Western ones. There need not be anything intrinsically upsetting about that fact.

Controlled experiments in chemistry take seriously the nature of the various elements being put together. A similar seriousness is incumbent upon those of us who seek to share Christ across cultural boundaries, whether overseas or within pluralist Western societies. My concern in these pages is to help Western Christians discern more carefully how Muslim cultures (and especially Arab cultures) cohere.

The approach adopted in this investigation of Muslim culture draws heavily on insights from the discipline of cultural anthropology. It is recognised, naturally, that such an avenue of inquiry is only one of many possible courses. In books of introduction to Islam, however, it remains an approach comparatively little utilised. Jacques Jomier, for example, in his important volume entitled *How to Understand Islam*, includes a few hints of cultural themes in a chapter on "The Law of Islam and Social Life".[4] In *Ishmael My Brother*, four themes common to Muslim cultures are briefly described in a chapter on "Islam as Culture".[5] Similar summaries of a few of the more significant cultural themes of Muslim societies are offered in passing in various introductory explorations of "Islam" or "Islamic culture", but few authors look at those themes in depth.[6] For Christians actually engaged with Muslims, it is non-understanding of these themes that seems most often to confuse their relationships with Muslims and to prejudice their interaction with them.

Neither is it sufficient simply to supply Western Christians with a list of guidelines as to the customs and etiquette of Muslims (helpful though such contributions can be). Rather, an understanding of the assumptions about reality that lie behind such surface behaviour is needed. Communication too often fails to get off the ground or develop appropriately precisely because different assumptions are being made about what is going on in the relationship between Western Christian and non-Western Muslim. One can learn appropriate words and gestures – surface customs – but remain ignorant of what lies behind them, what makes sense of them.

At a deep level in the West, for instance, we value the freedom of the individual, the right to self-expression, the primary importance of wealth-creation, efficiency, love and personal security. We construct our societies around such basic convictions, including the belief that we are free to manage ourselves however we want.[7] Muslim cultures function very differently. Other values at that deeper level are revered and preserved at all costs. Other norms have precedence. Other goals fire people's imaginations.

In the chapters that follow, we are invited to look more deeply into the complex world of Arab and other (mostly) Middle Eastern cultures. We will see how life for such people makes sense, how various themes reinforce and validate one another. We will feel the strengths of such perspectives and identify some of their weaknesses. "Themes in tension" will disclose varying contradictions with which some of our fellow humans have daily to live. Examples of success in communicating the gospel within various Muslim cultures will illustrate how an appreciation of such themes and tensions might well be applied.

If we are wishing to communicate at the level of spirit or soul, we need to learn how the Middle Easterner's spirit or soul functions. I have quoted quite extensively from various Muslim authors in order to allow something of that deeper level of human self-awareness to come across. For the most part, such authors are composers of fiction. Their fiction, however, carries weight within the various communities from which they speak precisely because it is reflective of reality. Muslim authorship and participant observation by Westerners and others provide the material from which I have distilled the major themes of Muslim cultures described in these pages. Sometimes I have focused on a particular society in order to illustrate a point. Sometimes I have spoken more broadly about "Middle Easterners" or even "Muslims". That there are generalisations sometimes being made as a consequence, I accept.[8] That there may be errors of interpretation I also acknowledge.[9] For the most part, however, I have tried to let the original sources speak for themselves. My (Western) mind has contributed a framework around which to organise and analyse the ensuing story.

That story needs to be read and received with discernment. In utilising its insights, the Western missionary (especially) needs to bear in mind the possibility of subcultural variation, the influence of Western thought and education, the effects of materialism and urbanisation and so on. Ultimately, each Muslim friend is a separate individual with a unique mix of accumulated experience and inner motivation. He or she needs to be respected as such. Appendix 1 accordingly provides some questions to help the reader assess where in the mix of "themes in tension" his particular friends or hosts might be standing.

Nevertheless, Muslim cultures as investigated here do appear to manifest some prevailing norms. Those norms have to do with gender interaction, the relationship between individual and family, the weightiness of honour and shame, the contrast between hospitality and violence, and so on. Such norms function at least as a continuing frame of reference, even if their influence today does not seem to be quite so uniformly evident as in previous generations.

The themes in tension described in these pages, then, are of both a general and foundational nature. They feature somewhere (in the background if not in the foreground) in the inherited outlook of many contemporary Muslims.

My prayer is that, as a result of this book, the "giant" of Islam will not seem so large or so alarming as it is often portrayed in both the Christian and secular media. Perhaps many of the Muslim's qualities will come to be accepted, even admired. Hopefully, we will come to appreciate the Bible (nearly completely Semitic in style and thought-form) more deeply. Eventually, maybe, our apostolic mission will be more suitably fulfilled as we learn to express it in ways appropriate to human spirits very different from our own.

Themes in Tension

CHAPTER TWO

MALE AND FEMALE

Don't show the woman the white of your tooth,
or she will show you the red of her buttocks.

If you smile at your wife, she will take advantage of you! The health warning offered to new bridegrooms in this proverb from Arabia illustrates in a humorous way one very important issue in most Muslim cultures. Men and women are seen as completely different "animals" from one another. Between them a huge gulf is fixed.

Outside or inside?

Male and female "live" in distinct universes. To some considerable extent, in most Muslim countries the great "outside", the public world, is the domain of men. Even within the home, rooms that the outside world might infiltrate are carefully managed so that women will only be found in them when no strange males are visiting. If a woman needs to pass through the outside world on some errand or visit, she does so by making herself inconspicuous: she veils herself in varying degrees of anonymity. The woman's world is the darker "indoors", the private world – the world, mind you, where men as well as women need physical and emotional sustenance. Figure 1 summarises the major differences between the two universes.

To confuse the two universes is to court disaster. I well remember the embarrassment I felt when living in Istanbul in 1971. A close female relative of mine came to visit me. In the West it was the age of the miniskirt and my visitor had packed several! As I showed her the sights and sounds of Istanbul, she was spat on and

29

cursed, propositioned and pinched. The only kind of female who could be so publicly fleshy was a type despised by most Turkish women and lusted after by some Turkish men. My relative was confirming a common stereotype held by Turks concerning the West: all Western women are prostitutes at heart. Either that, or Westerners have got their universes mixed up.

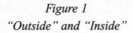

Figure 1
"Outside" and "Inside"

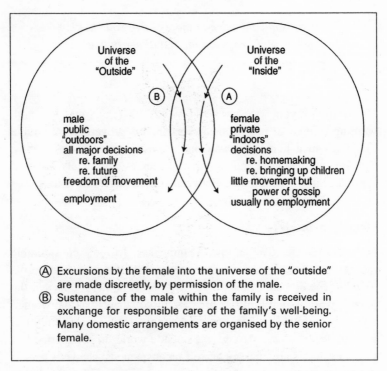

Ⓐ Excursions by the female into the universe of the "outside" are made discreetly, by permission of the male.
Ⓑ Sustenance of the male within the family is received in exchange for responsible care of the family's well-being. Many domestic arrangements are organised by the senior female.

It is in the nature of things Islamic that male and female occupy different worlds. The two sexes are constructed differently:

> Men are the protectors
> And maintainers of women
> Because God has given
> The one more (strength)
> Than the other, and because

They support them
From their means.
Therefore the righteous women
Are devoutly obedient, and guard
In (the husband's) absence
What God would have them guard.

(Sura 4:34)

Gentlemen only

Both sexes have rights. Both sexes have duties. Ideally, neither sex should dominate the other (see Figure 2).[10] Indeed, male and female believers are supposed to be protectors of one another (Sura 9:71). In some commentators' view, the rights of the wife are defined with considerable precision because, as the party that can be easily oppressed, she is more in need of protection than the husband. Precisely named rights include those of being consulted about her marriage and being asked for her consent. The Prophet said: "A previously married woman has a better right to decide for herself than her guardian [*wali*] has to decide for her. A virgin is to be asked for her consent, and if she says nothing she has consented."[11]

Figure 2
Male and female: qur'ânic implications

Verse	Principle
"Behold thy Lord said to the angels: 'I will create a vice-regent on earth'." (Sura 2:30)	God appointed humankind as his successors on earth in two sexes
"It is He Who hath produced you from the earth and settled you therein." (Sura 11:61)	God called upon both sexes equally to build the earth
"Say: 'I am forbidden to worship those – others than God – whom ye call upon'." (Sura 6:56)	God called upon them both equally to worship God on earth

Another precisely delineated right is that of divorce at her own request. It is often contended that in its new view of females, Islam had an enlightening effect on the treatment normally dished out to women in Arabia during the early days of its establishment:

> Islam raised women from nothingness to existence, from a hypothetical humanness to one that was fully recognised, from legal incompetence to full legal competence.[12]

Traditions originating from Prophet Muḥammad emphasise the mutuality intended by God in male/female relationships. In his farewell speech at Arafat in AD 632, the Prophet said, "You have rights over your wives and they have rights over you. You have the right that they should not defile your bed and that they should not behave with open unseemliness . . . If they refrain from these things

Ladies' work

they have the right to their food and clothing with kindness."[13] Men, for their part, are blessed with social and political authority plus the freedom to move at will in the world. Along with such privileges, they have the duty of supporting their families completely. Women's primary responsibilities are the maintenance of the home and the bringing up of the children. In the home, the woman largely rules as queen and a Muslim male is in some senses a guest of his wife. According to this ideal perspective, a balanced mutuality is intended in relationships between males and females:

> From the Islamic point of view the question of the equality of men and women is meaningless. It is like discussing the equality of a rose and jasmine. Each has its own perfume, colour, shape and beauty.[14]

For some couples, life reflects this balanced mutuality as Umm Mustafa, a woman living in Cairo's City of the Dead, bears witness:

> During my twenty-eight years that I was married I rarely left my husband's house. He provided me everything I needed. I was completely safe and secure inside the house and never had to face the hubbub of the streets. It was a pleasant life and I'm proud that I lived this way.[15]

Fatima Mernissi, an outspoken Moroccan sociologist, acknowledges that Islam affirms the potential equality of men and women but, she claims, "there is a fundamental contradiction between Islam as interpreted officially and equality between the sexes".[16] That contradiction occurs, she claims, because of Islam's theological perspective on male and female. Official Islam is bound to promote inequality between the sexes because it condones and promotes a certain view of sex itself:

> Sexual equality violates Islam's premise, actualised in its laws, that heterosexual love is dangerous to Allah's order. Muslim marriage is based on male dominance. The desegregation of sexes violates Islam's ideology on women's positioning in the social order; that women should be under the authority of their fathers, brothers or husbands. Since women are considered by Allah to be a destructive element, they are to be spatially confined and excluded from matters other than those of the family. Female access to non-domestic space is put under the control of males.[17]

Women are seen as intrinsically dangerous or tempting, in a sexual sense. Men must be protected from their wiles! Not all commentators are so despairing. Nevertheless, in the lived reality of many families, it seems, the duties expected of women tend to emphasise the superiority of men, for the latter are the judges of whether the womanly duties are adequately being fulfilled. Ibn al-Ḥajj, a puritanical fourteenth-century North African scholar, produced a treatise on Islamic behaviour in which he claimed that according to a *ḥadîth* or tradition, the equivalent of *jihâd* (holy war) for women is for them to please their husbands. That is their religious duty! Haifaa Jawad, a contemporary female Muslim theologian, angrily quotes the Council of Ulema of South Africa for their statement in the 1990s on "the pious woman":

> She (the wife) should mould herself to wholeheartedly submit to his whims and fancies. His likes must become her likes and his dislikes, her dislikes. She should step out of her way to comfort him and to console him in his worries and distress. Her wishes and desires are subservient to his wishes and orders . . . The Shariah has accorded the husband the highest degree of authority over his wife . . . men are the rulers of women and they have a superior rank . . . (as such) it is the husband's right and role to dominate and dictate (and) it is the duty of the wife to submit and serve.[18]

Jawad sees such "misinformation" as contradictory of the ideal and equal partnership detected by her in the Qur'ân.[19] Leila Ahmed agrees with Jawad, commenting (concerning Sura 33:35) on the fact that women are explicitly addressed in several passages of the Qur'ân.[20] This, in her view, is a radical and positive development.

Ashghar Ali Engineer probably offers the most fair-minded commentary on what the Qur'ân says about the status of male and female:

> There are verses of the *Quran* which emphasise equal status for both the sexes as well as verses indicating differences and even inequalities. There are also verses which together indicate equality of the sexes as well as the superiority of man over woman to some extent.[21]

Figure 3 gives an example from the Qur'ân of each of these possible interpretations.

Figure 3
Status of male and female according to the Qur'ân

Equal status for both sexes – Sura 33:35
"For Muslim men and women, for believing men and women, for true men and women, for men and women who are patient and constant, for men and women who humble themselves, for men and women who give in charity, for men and women who fast (and deny themselves), for men and women who guard their chastity, and for men and women who engage much in God's praise – for them has God prepared forgiveness and a great reward."

Inequalities between male and female – Sura 4:34
"Men are the protectors and maintainers of women, because God has given the one more (strength) than the other, and because they support them from their means. Therefore the righteous women are devoutly obedient, and guard in (the husband's) absence what God would have them guard. As to those women on whose part ye fear disloyalty and ill-conduct, admonish them (first), (next) refuse to share their beds, (and last) beat them (lightly); but if they return to obedience, seek not against them means (of annoyance): for God is Most High, great (above you all)."

Equality and inequality for male and female – Sura 2:228
"Divorced women shall wait concerning themselves for three monthly periods. Nor is it lawful for them to hide what God hath created in their wombs, if they have faith in God and the Last Day and their husbands have the better right to take them back in that period, if they wish for reconciliation. And women shall have rights similar to the rights against them, according to what is equitable; but men have a degree (of advantage) over them. And God is Exalted in Power, Wise."

Amongst Muslims, male and female, there are considerable differences of view concerning the interrelationship of the two sexes. By and large, however, the reality of "non-ideal" relating appears to be the norm worked out in everyday living. Even Engineer admits as much. "Though there is nothing in the *Quran* to the effect that women must remain subservient to their husbands and do everything to please them," he says, "this became the norm in later Islamic society."[22] Even so, such allegedly non-ideal relating cannot simply be prejudged as wrong or inferior by external Western observers. A variety of perspectives is allowed by the Qur'ân; one of those perspectives, it would seem, has come to be the most commonplace in Muslims' experience. We need to understand why this might be.

Good enough for the group?

While relationships between the sexes are matters of individual choice for Westerners, within most Muslim communities such relationships are permitted or proscribed according to a different rationale. It is not so much a question of what the individuals concerned would like, but what the group decides is "good". Westerners, looking from afar into a Muslim community, quickly conclude that women must be deemed inferior to men because of the imbalance in permitted and proscribed behaviour as applied to the two sexes. They observe that the men can basically live as they please, making decisions concerning wife and children without consulting them. The women, meanwhile, are concealed at home or behind a veil, with all kinds of restrictions upon their socialising with people other than certain relatives.

It comes as a bit of a shock when we discover that many of the people publicly demonstrating for a return to more traditional customs in Iran or Egypt or Pakistan or Algeria have been women. Many Muslim women prefer to wear the veil, for instance, because it gives a secure sense of place and identity in the public, "outside" world. For several years my family lived in Egypt. Our home-help in Cairo came from Imbaba, a district renowned for being a hotbed of Islamic "fundamentalism". While with us, she took to wearing the veil out of pride and pragmatism. She could travel safely on the public transport system, being referred to deferentially as "sister" in a way not guaranteed to an uncovered woman. She could also buy the "fundamentalist" clothing outfit at a discounted price! The demands of group identity in such situations easily override any inclination towards individual freedom and choice.

What then does the "group" so strongly demand? What ordering of male and female universes is required at all costs?

Above all, the group prizes men, sustainers of life and custom. Such prizing seemingly comes with qur'ânic encouragement: "Wealth and sons are allurements of the life of this world" (Sura 18:46). Although in context this verse is actually warning against the vanity and intoxication found in those two aspects of power represented by riches and sons (reminders of the pre-Islamic outlook), it tends nevertheless to confirm in the popular mind the inestimable value of male progeny. Baby boys, potential men, are demanded of wives. A newly married couple is frequently congratulated with the phrase: "We wish you prosperity and sons." An Iraqi proverb gives the sense: "A crazy boy (*majnûn*) is preferable to a girl destined even to become a famous woman (*khâtûn*)."[23] The threat of divorce or upstaging by a second wife pursues a Muslim woman who can only produce baby girls. My wife gave birth to three girls while we lived in the Middle East. The first was born in Lebanon; the other two in Egypt. Fortunately in Egypt, unlike most of the Middle East, the birth of a child of either sex makes possible the male parent's transformation from "bridegroom" to "father" – for most situations in the Arab world, a son is required! One of our daughters was born in a private clinic on an island in the Nile. Various Arabs from the Gulf brought their wives to the same clinic for childbirth. Above the door in the waiting room outside the delivery suite were two naked light-bulbs. I asked what was the significance of the contrasting colours: green and red. I was told that if a girl was born the red bulb was turned on; if a boy, the green one. At a red light, the waiting husband is liable to walk away upset; at a green light he is extravagant in his joy. In her revealing book *Princess*, the unidentified Saudi Arabian author describes the gifts of car, jewellery and cash lavished on a British obstetrician and nursing team who had been airlifted to the Kingdom to superintend the birth of her baby. Fortunately it turned out to be a boy! The Saudi prince got his son and heir and the ex-patriates went home amply rewarded.[24] A contrasting emotion is recorded by a sympathetic Christian health visitor as she observed what giving birth to a girl meant for a Muslim woman from an Asian home in Britain:

> She had felt so certain it would be a boy; special prayers had been said and a holy man consulted. A celebration had been planned, but now there were to be no guests, no special food, no special clothes. The grandparents obviously favoured the boy cousin born a few weeks before. Now there was just the anticipation of saving money for three dowries, preparing for the heartbreak of giving away her precious daughters to other families and being bereft of the comfort of a son who would stay with her in her old age. She feared that a fourth child might only add to the distress by being another girl.[25]

Jan Goodwin records that a female obstetrician at a high-tech Arab hospital in one of the Gulf states told her that they never inform a pregnant woman of the sex of their baby-to-be after an ultrasound: "We find they can cope much better and longer with labor pains if they don't know they are giving birth to a girl."[26]

Young males, especially, are marked as members of the "group" through the rite of circumcision. Interestingly, this rite has no privileged status in a theological sense; it is part of the *sunna*, not urged as essential in the Qur'ân. It is thus more a practice of Muslims than a requirement of the Islamic faith. The Tunisian sociologist Abdelwahab Bouhdiba says of the festivities surrounding circumcision that they are "in fact ceremonies by which young children are admitted to the group. Hence the relatively advanced age at which it is practised".[27] Circumcision introduces a male child to the world of adults, with its concomitant responsibilities. Focus is centred upon the joyful prospect of future progeny – but that focus involves blood and pain. Bouhdiba quotes a traditional song celebrated at Tunisian circumcision parties. The song well illustrates this emphasis on fecundity for the all-important male line:

> You begin with circumcision and you end in marriage,
> And still your horse neighs in the forest.
> You begin with circumcision and you end in youth,
> And still your horse neighs among the bachelors.
> Let us call quickly for his mother,
> Let us call quickly for his aunt,
> Let them come quickly and throw money on the procreative rod.[28]

Hope is expressed for a full, great, durable genetic life in this sexually euphemistic song.

The stages of growth through which a male child proceeds are carefully marked (see Figure 4). Weaning – as well as circumcision – occurs quite late and at some point the male child will be removed from the skirts of his mother to join the adult male world. The stage of *kuttâb* or initial religious education traditionally went alongside apprenticeship in a trade. A child is expected to learn much of the Qur'ân during these years and to pray the formal prayers of the faith. From the age of thirteen or fourteen years, a boy enters the state of *taklîf* or legal responsibility. Now he is expected to engage regularly in formal prayer, almsgiving, fasting, pilgrimage if possible and *jihâd* if necessary. From puberty until the time that his beard is fully formed a male is called *fatâ'* or young man – this is the stage of *futûwa* where he learns a trade or gets educated or "grows up". From his late teens until about 40 years of age, a male is in the *shabâb* or "youth" state. At 40, a man reaches the age of reason (*ᶜaql*). Adulthood lasts from the ages of 40 to 60. Prophet Muḥammad recorded his first revelation at the age of 40 and his last revelation at around the age of 60. Prior to that, during his *futûwa* and *shabâb* stages, he engaged in trade.[29] It can be seen from this summary that Islamic societies do not have a strong concept of "youth", certainly not of independent, individually minded teenagers.

Figure 4
Stages of childhood and youth in Arab culture

Stage	Involves	Age
infancy	nurture by mother	0–5
kuttâb	religious education at mosque school; task apprenticeship under male supervision	6–13
taklîf	legal responsibility; expectation to pray, fast, give alms, go on *ḥajj*, participate in *jihâd*	13 or 14
futûwa	establishing a work ethic	14–18
shabâb	work to support family	up to 40
adulthood	maturity	40–60

What does the "group" expect of males, from the age of *taklîf* or legal responsibility? Primarily, it expects them to uphold and advance the group's good name. An Egyptian proverb posits that "A man's shadow does more for a home than the shadow of a wall". The responsible males of a household or clan determine the kind of reputation that the community holds of that family:

Arab masculinity (*rujulah*) is acquired, verified and played out in the brave deed, in risk-taking, and in expressions of fearlessness and assertiveness. It is attained by constant vigilance and willingness to defend honour (*sharaf*), face (*wajh*), kin and community from external aggression and to uphold and protect cultural definitions of gender-specific propriety.[30]

The male patrilineal relative of an extended family is economically, legally and morally responsible for his kin, whatever his marital status. We shall consider in Chapter 4 some of the implications of this emphasis on men's "responsibility for reputation" on behalf of the group.

What the "group" prizes in women is chastity. Female circumcision, still widely practised in some Muslim countries, is intended to guarantee the virginity of a girl until marriage. Such an operation is commonly deemed necessary because, as we have noted, women are mistrusted as oversexed and liable to cause problems for men. Haifaa Jawad passes on a conversation on this subject in which she took part during April 1994; it occurred in a health centre in Yemen:

> "It is important that all girls be made to undergo circumcision so that they would keep their purity." "All our girls have to be circumcised – there is no exception," said an Egyptian nurse working in a medical centre in Sanaa. "I agree with her – if I have a daughter I will definitely circumcise her – it is crucial that we attenuate our daughters' sexual desires and protect their chastity," commented an Egyptian doctor working at the same medical centre.[31]

Nawal El-Saadawi well expresses, in autobiographical form, the experience of circumcision to a bewildered, young daughter.[32] Other less drastic but careful conventions have the preservation of a girl's virginity as their major aim. The goal of such conventions (veiling at puberty, for example) is that the future bride might bring to her new family, on behalf of her old family, her chastity. Her purity is proof of the care with which her male relatives have preserved their investment in her. In other words, men's honour depends to a considerable degree on the behaviour of the women in the extended family. Premarital chastity in sisters and daughters, marital fidelity on the part of a wife and sexual abstinence by widows and divorcees (daughters or sisters) come largely to be the overriding principles on which the reputation and status of a family depend. In an autobiographical novel, Algerian novelist Djanet Lachmet describes her growing childhood hesitation in playing "bride and bridegroom", equivalent to Western children's "mummies and daddies":

> I wouldn't play those games any more. I didn't want to be dishonoured. If I played at being a bride, I would lose my virginity. Like that poor girl from the mountains who played with her cousin when she was small, and when she got married properly she wasn't a virgin. Her in-laws were furious and disowned her. They put her on a donkey facing towards its tail, with her head shaved and her arms tied, and they took her back to her family. Her elder brother stabbed her to death because she'd dishonoured the family.[33]

Marriage itself is in essence a contract between representatives of the "group". There are different views as to what constitutes the ultimate focus of that contract. Fatemeh Moghadam, writing from the perspective of a "liberated" Iranian woman in post-Khomeini Iran, describes marriage in terms of the sale of sexuality:

> The various passages of the Qur'an that deal with marriage in essence treat female sexuality as a tradeable object. In a Muslim marriage the buyer (the man) and the seller (the woman or her guardian) should agree voluntarily on the terms of the contract and the price for female sexuality, *mehr* (dowry).[34]

In many Muslim cultures, marriage choices are the ultimate scorecard by which a family is judged successful in creating a respected public image, so the focus of concern in the selection of mates often becomes that of group honour. "Love" marriage goes against this means of evaluating male/female relationship; it is invested with connotations of irrationality and is very suspect. It implies that a couple has succumbed to personal preference and physical attraction instead of submitting to a careful examination of the potential union by the group. The possibility of sexual activity by unchaperoned lovers is never far from peoples' minds in those kinds of relationships. The normal approach to marriage protects the couple from any such association. The bridegroom generally accepts the wisdom of the group with regard to the choice of the bride. The bride may not be consulted by the group as to her future mate. In some extreme cases, she may not even see him until the wedding service is completed.[35]

"Love grows, along with respect, as you live together. It is the commitment which makes the marriage work," comments one happily married
middle-aged Pakistan-born Muslim woman who met her husband-to-be
twice only before they married. They were only left alone for half an
hour each time. "If I had objected, they would not have forced me to
marry him. But we got on well and we have made it work. Love has
grown."[36]

After marriage, a woman maintains her husband's honour by living
above all reproach. A married man is dependent upon and vulnerable through the women of his household. So a wife must remain
chaste and free from any suspicion of unfaithfulness throughout her
married life. All men who are not within the woman's circle of
mahram relationships (i.e. those with whom sexual relationships
would be considered incestuous) are potential sexual threats. Access
has therefore to be carefully controlled so that no such threat, real or
imagined, could possibly become a reality.

In healthy marital relationships, sexuality is usually understood in
terms of male fulfilment. Males may even experiment in sexual relationships outside the home, especially if there are extenuating
circumstances, such as being away on a business trip, studying
abroad or whatever. The group understands that need. A real man,
after all, is expected to lead an active sexual life, or at least to behave
as if he did. Boasting on the subject is commonplace. The separation
of male and female into different worlds from the time a young boy
is too old to be around undressed mother or sisters has major consequences for such a youth's view of women. It becomes difficult for
him to imagine any form of relationship other than a sexual one with
a woman who is not a member of his family. Homosexuality among
males is hardly publicly admitted but occurs. Traditionally, the possibility of homosexuality has been openly acknowledged in the
celebrated taste of aristocrats and wealthy or influential leaders of
society for young boys. More recently, Naguib Mahfouz has included
homosexual characters in several of his novels. The passive partner,
the "woman" in the male-to-male relationship, is usually seen as an
abnormal male. Frédéric Lagrange gives a detailed account of male
homosexual characters as depicted in modern Arabic literature.[37] In
that literature, for the most part, homosexual relationships are
presented as substitutes for heterosexual ones. The shortage of avail-

able women or the difficulty of accumulating the money for a bride-price means that marriage gets delayed for many men and some of them seek substitute relationships with members of their own sex. Males should be able to experience sexual fulfilment.

An equivalent need for sexual fulfilment on the part of a woman is hardly, if ever, acknowledged. Alifa Rifaat surely speaks for many contemporary Muslim wives as she describes what sexual intercourse has come to mean for the unnamed woman in her short story *Distant View of a Minaret*:

> Through half-closed eyes she looked at her husband. Lying on his right side, his body was intertwined with hers and his head bent over her right shoulder. As usual at such times she felt that he inhabited a world utterly different from hers, a world from which she had been excluded. Only half-aware of the movements of his body, she turned her head to one side and stared up at the ceiling, where she noticed a spider's web. She told herself she'd have to get out the long broom and brush it down.[38]

The commitments of male and female are miles apart in this "mature" sexual relationship. Afternoon siesta time sees the same scene replayed, day by day. In it, over time, the husband has proven himself unable and unwilling to comprehend the needs that his wife had tried to express earlier in their marriage. Now, sexual fulfilment is nowhere near the surface for her own agenda in life. She is simply a body for her husband's pleasure. She is detached, resigned. When he finishes his physical self-gratification, he washes, then sleeps. So the process has repeated itself throughout their lives. One afternoon, after the usual routine, he dies in bed. By this time, the wife's personal feelings are so deeply submerged that the ending of her husband's life is treated in the same casual and unemotional manner as that which she has come to exhibit in their sex life. She discovers him dead, shrugs and makes coffee. The practice of female circumcision helps to underscore this male-oriented, or husband-focused, concept of sexual fulfilment. A young girl is scarred to prevent her from expressing herself sexually prior to marriage. Then, within marriage, her obligatory passivity serves to confirm that she has not been promiscuous.

One of the most well-known myths of origin in the Arab world is that supplied by al-Kisa'i, a writer of the eleventh century. His "story of the creation of Adam" is followed by the "story of the introduction of the spirit into Adam's body". Then follow three further tales describing the angels' obeisance to Adam, outlining how Adam named everything in his own language and summarising Adam's preaching. God is very pleased with Adam's performance and while Adam sleeps, exhausted, the Lord devises a special reward:

> While Adam slept Allah Most High created Eve from one of the ribs of his left side, namely that crooked rib. She is called Eve (*Hawwa'*) because she was created from a live person (*hayy*). This is as Allah has said (IV, 1): "O ye people, show piety towards your Lord, who created you from a single person, and from that person created his spouse." Eve was of the same height as Adam and equally splendid and beautiful. She had seven hundred locks of hair intertwined with jacinth and sprinkled with musk, was auburn haired, of even stature, with wide black eyes, thin skinned, white complexioned, with henna-dyed palms, and hanging locks so long you could hear their rustling. She had ears pierced for earrings, was so plump her thighs chafed as she walked, and was of the same form as Adam save that her skin was more tender, her colouring lighter, her voice sweeter, her eyes wider and darker, her nose more hooked, her teeth whiter. When Allah Most High had created her He sat her by Adam's head . . .[39]

Lucky Adam! Interestingly, as the creation myth continues, the fall of Adam is blamed quite squarely on the vine (by whose fruit Adam was seduced) and on Adam's own rebellious disobedience. Eve escapes lightly, her only "punishment" being that Adam did not approach her for a hundred years. The message of the story is that Adam, the male, is special in God's eyes. Eve is there as his reward for pleasing his Creator. She is presented to him for his pleasure.

The male response to any hint of female involvement in extra-marital relationships can be very severe. Such severity is condoned by the "group". Hanan al-Shaykh, in a book that is widely thought to be autobiographical, describes a frightening confrontation between a middle-aged man, Ibrahim, and his young daughter, Zahra. Ibrahim is a conductor on a tram in Beirut. His wife, Fatme, is pursuing a secret liaison with another man. She is in the habit of taking her child Zahra along with her when she visits her lover in order to protect herself from gossip. Ibrahim gradually suspects that Fatme is involved in an extra-marital affair. One day, his anger explodes into the open. He turns on the child. In the ensuing confrontation between father and daughter, Ibrahim tries to force young Zahra to divulge details about her mother's liaison:

> The blows fell on my face and head. I tried to think clearly as the words of the Lord of the Tram-car thundered and drowned out the nervous voice of my mother, afraid I might reveal all: "Tell the truth! Where did you used to go with your mother? Where did he used to take the two of you?"
>
> My mother cried out, "By God, you are mad, Ibrahim! Leave the child alone. Everything you hear is lies and slander! Leave the girl alone, Ibrahim!"
>
> He paid no attention to her, but continued to shower me with blows, his voice lashing at me, the words torn out from between his lips. I knew only dread of this god in his khaki suit, dread of his tram-car, dread of his strong body – that particular dread the strongest of all. I shook all over as I burst into a sobbing that couldn't drown out my mother's screams. He slapped her face and seized her hair. She ran into the kitchen, leaving me trapped in the room, like a wooden post, choking out an occasional sob. I heard my father shout, "You must be insane, Fatme! Shame on you! You must be out of your mind!" while she whimpered, "Leave me be. I wish to die."[40]

In the eyes of the "group", Ibrahim had failed in one of his primary roles. He had neglected to guard his wife's honour. As a result his own honour was in serious jeopardy.

The rigid code of sexual mores, which Fatme clandestinely broke, carries far more power than any concept of love or freedom or individual rights. No one can remain on close terms with an Arab if he attacks or besmirches his honour. For a male Westerner to associate with an Arab's wife is highly *risqué*. To embrace her or even to shake her hand can quickly be interpreted as the Westerner proclaiming that he knows that he could take the woman to bed if he so desired.

What the "group" primarily prizes in wives, therefore, is their support of their husbands. Often, in reality, this means that men dictate the limits of possible freedom of choice for females. Lois Beck and Nikki Keddie, in the introduction to their study of women in the Muslim world, describe the kind of parameters frequently functioning for the majority of those women:

In most cases, a girl's parents decide whether and for how long she goes to school; the parents of both parties decide on the marriage partner; . . . the mother-in-law and husband rule over much of the young wife's life, and the husband can . . . decide if the wife can work for wages, at what kind of job, and whether she can use any of her wages if she works. The husband, according to religious law, receives custody of the children (after a certain age) after divorce; women are thereby suddenly cut off from those by whom their role as females is defined, and are denied the continuing satisfactions of the maternal role. Most women are not allowed to remain unmarried, even after an early divorce, or to live alone. Women are threatened with repudiation or with a second wife being brought into the house if they do not bear sons. Many women find considerable satisfaction in traditional family life, but their legal and customary status is often precarious.[41]

In rather cruder terms, Fadwa expresses the stark difference, from her personal perspective, between male and female in contemporary Iraq:

Men are allowed to do so many things that women are deprived of. They don't have to worry about their appearance, while women have to wear tight, uncomfortable garments such as bras, corsets and high-heeled shoes. Men's hair is short and easy to take care of. They can choose who they want to marry and when to get married. If a woman dies, her husband wears a black tie for a few days and then gets married again as soon as possible, while a widow has to wear black clothes for years in mourning for her husband and her chances of remarriage are very slim. Men don't get pregnant and don't have periods. They're supported by society, God and the law.[42]

The distinction that Fadwa makes is one that reaches to the heart of many Muslim societies. In the Arabic language, for example, there is no literal equivalent to the English word "child". All nouns, in Arabic, are either masculine or feminine. There are therefore words for "boy", "girl", "son", "daughter", but none for "child", "infant", "toddler" and so on. In the consciousness of the Arabs, therefore, there are no children, only boys and girls. Hence there is no concept of child-rearing, but rather concepts of rearing boys and girls. Differences of practice appear immediately, as in the norms for breastfeeding. A girl is breastfed for one to two years, a boy for two to three years. By the time the male child is weaned, he has been used to asking (verbally) for his mother's breast and receiving it. Early on in a boy's life is impregnated the belief that a verbally stated wish will bring about its realisation. He has also learned that his mother, a female, is (in this respect at least) at his beck and call. He has yet to discover what God and the law say about his relationship with the female universe! Fadwa's complaint seems eminently reasonable. Issues of irritation and importance for contemporary women like her are summarised in Figure 5.

Figure 5
Issues for Muslim women

| reproduction and birth control |
| marriage: contracted by whom? and at what age? |
| polygamy |
| divorce |
| custody of children |
| inheritance |
| education |
| employment |

Many contemporary Muslim women see such issues as critical because they feel that they are unfairly hampered in fulfilling everyday requirements for living. Often they (the women) are expected to contribute to the economic well-being of their families in situations of low rates of male employment. Fatima Mernissi concluded from her interviewing of many women in her homeland (Morocco) that while the "pervasive male discourse" promotes a theory about a strong (male) sex and a weak (female) sex, Moroccan women actually see themselves as "a race of giants doing daily battle against the destructive monsters of unemployment, poverty and degrading jobs".[43] There is nothing weak, in her view, about Muslim women.

Even within traditional Arab societies, where the "pervasive male discourse" finds itself worked out in the dynamics of how males and females interrelate, women often manage to create a society of their own. In villages there can develop a high level of mutual female aid and solidarity against the menfolk. Love between women and even lesbian relationships are not so rare.[44] Women are not without power and influence:

> Within her home, a woman does not feel subordinate, oppressed, inferior or powerless compared to the men. She has her own tasks, which are hers alone. She watches over the smooth running of the household, and also all its inhabitants, including the men. She decides what domestic jobs need doing and how to do them. She can use the upkeep of the house as a weapon, by deliberately neglecting it for instance. She can take care that the food is of good quality or abundant, or she can do the opposite, all of which adds up to a considerable range of indirect pressures she can exercise, providing she is sufficiently secure and need not fear repudiation or the introduction of a second wife.[45]

Christine Eickelman spent 1979–80 in al-Hamra, an oasis of "inner" Oman. There, she recognised that, in the formal political system, women did not exist. Neither did they sit on tribal councils or legislative or consultative assemblies. Within the formal tribal genealogies and local histories they were not mentioned. And yet, she concluded, through their female networks they were able to gather information essential for decision-making, to scout, to advise, to strengthen or weaken alliances: "Their presence in politics is not so much covert as less visible *from an outsider's perspective*. Their participation is essential . . ."[46] Eickelman found that the officially segregated social worlds of men and women strongly depended on one another, a conclusion supported by other researchers.[47]

Fair or unfair?

We need to listen carefully to those apologists for Islam who claim that the faith as it should be lived does confer rights and dignity upon women. Hammudah Abdalati offers a section on the status of women in Islam in his chapter addressing outsider misperceptions of that faith. For him, "the status of woman in Islam constitutes no problem".[48] Another commentator suggests that over 1,400 years ago, Islam gave rights to women that the West has only recently permitted. Even leaders of the Western feminist movement, it is suggested, would be surprised to find in Islam a just fulfilment of their demands.[49] Appeal is made to the Qur'ân and to prophetic tradition (*sunna*) in order to support such claims: women can theoretically participate in government (Sura 60:12), in public life (Sura 9:71), war (Sura 3:195) and so on. We have already noticed Haifaa Jawad's strong case – against the norm – for a Qur'ânic view of equality of partnership between male and female. The esteem in which many historical female Muslims (supremely Fâtima, but others also, such as ᶜÂ'isha, Nafîsa, Shuhda, al-Khansa[50]) are held suggests that, within Islamic communities, women can be highly regarded. It is certainly not good enough to judge the seeming inequality between Muslim men and women from an uninformed, Western perspective. Andrea Rugh comments insightfully upon what she sees as a potentially successful role for women in Muslim societies. She discerns that Muslim Arab women can play the relationship game to their own advantage, from within its constraints:

> Women have an advantage, when family is central to a society, that has been overlooked by those focusing on authority patterns. They are the central figures in the central institution of the society . . .[51]

Moreover, it must be recognised that the roles of Arab men and women are bound to be significantly different from those of their Western counterparts simply because the meanings invested in the terms "male" and "female" differ in the two contexts. Those meanings, in each case, are tenaciously held by the majority of each respective society.

This is not to suggest that the roles of Arab men and women are by any means uniform and static. Different degrees of Westernisation, modernisation and urbanisation – plus the intrusion of the feminist movement into Arab societies – have led to changing perceptions of what it means to be male and female.[52] However, far more fundamentally entrenched in Middle Eastern society as a whole lies a traditional concept of male and female against which other, changing views are measured.[53] Mernissi rather naughtily brings out that traditional concept:

> "Can a woman be a leader of Muslims?" I asked my grocer, who, like most grocers in Morocco, is a true "barometer" of public opinion. "I take refuge in Allah!" he exclaimed, shocked, despite the friendly relations between

us. Aghast at the idea, he almost dropped the half-dozen eggs I had come to buy. "May God protect us from the catastrophes of the times!" mumbled a customer who was buying olives, as he made as if to spit.[54]

Beginning and bettering

Interestingly, for Westerners who are readers of the Bible, some of the concepts of personhood treasured by many contemporary Muslim societies are not so unfamiliar.

The Old Testament revelation was mediated through a Semitic culture in which male superiority and chauvinism were almost built into the structure of things. That male-oriented culture was available to God as a medium for communication and he was evidently content to use it.

In the early days of Israel in Palestine, the "nation" was not a nation in the sense that we would mean by that term today. She was, rather, a tribal league, a confederation of clans united to one another in the worship of Yahweh.[55] The people of Israel had emerged, battered, from years of discrimination in Egypt, under the leadership of Moses. His had then been the privilege, in the desert, of meeting face to face with the living God and learning how the confederation of tribes was to function as a free nation. The specially constructed Ark was to become the focus for the wanderings of the clans until it came to rest in Shiloh. There it would constitute a centre for worship and periodic renewal of the peoples' allegiance to Yahweh. The Sinaitic rules were to be the measure by which folk were to regulate their behaviour. At some stage in this period of Israel's history, Moses became the recipient and recorder of revelation concerning the origins of the tribes, the beginnings of humanity itself, and the creation of the whole world. During these years, the Pentateuch or Torah came to be penned.

The first five books of our Bible were consequently mediated through a culture already functioning on tribal lines. In the developing confederation of Israelite tribes, patriarchal prestige and authority were unquestioned. The uniting of the nomadic cattle-breeders in a sacred covenant during the wilderness interlude was made feasible by a perspective in which male clan leaders and heads of families spoke for all in their charge.[56] The dominant role of fathers especially, and men in general, was assumed and passed on as a norm.

In the transformation of these Israelite invaders towards nation-hood along the lines already realised in the peoples surrounding them, much of the ethos of the original tribal society remained intact. Nothing abnormal was seen in David, as king, taking to himself several women as wives. No one objected to his son Solomon's greater bent in this direction – at least, not until the wives concerned started to influence Solomon's allegiance to Yahweh! Tribal loyalties and patriarchal prestige continued to dominate national politics for many generations within Israel.

The God whom we meet in the Old Testament does not seem to concentrate any primary attack on this state of affairs. Indeed, it would appear that the norms of a patriarchal, patrilineal, patrilocal society were quite acceptable starting points for conveying Yahweh's revelation of himself to the whole human race. The Lord was happy to disclose his hand via kin groups which were based on descent through the male line and in which women went to live with their husbands' families when they married. Polygamists became founders of great tribes, chauvinists were conveyors of the divine will, and, as we have mentioned, a collector of women was king and wise preacher. The revelation from on high comes in such a context: via a fallible human culture. The revelation emerges as affirming of the culture concerned and willing to use its protagonists to declare that God is living in the midst of his people.

At the same time, in many of his words and acts throughout these formative years, the creator God showed himself dissatisfied with the fallible human culture concerned, purveyor of a worldview in which women (and others) tended to be strongly dehumanised.

The creation stories of Genesis describe the intention of the Lord as he made mankind. According to the panoramic picture of Genesis chapter one, the close-up description of chapter two and the summary given in chapter five, "Adam" (Genesis 5:2) is "man" as male and female.[57] "Adam" is the generic name for "humanity" as well as a personal name for Eve's husband. There are no capital letters in Hebrew so the context must determine the intended mean-ing. The interrelationship of "Adam" as male and female is, by intention, one of equality and mutuality. "Rib" language (as opposed to the symbolism of "head" or "foot") speaks of complementariness, neither superiority nor inferiority. Indeed, the Hebrew culture is strongly rebuked in the "leave and cleave" instructions given by God as his basic rule for marriage. According to Genesis, the male is supposed to leave his paternal home and cleave to his wife.[58] In actual reality, the woman left her home and moved into her husband's family house.

Throughout the Old Testament, many incidents are highlighted which give the sense of the Lord God trying to retrieve some sense of equality and dignity for the feminine part of his human creation. Widows, wives accused of adultery and non-inheriting daughters are all specifically catered for. Despised and forgotten women become channels of God's purposes on earth, forming part of the precious line to the Messiah. A Rahab, a Ruth and a Bathsheba show that prostitutes, foreigners and preyed-upon citizens can be caught up by a sovereign God into his redemptive purposes, a thought I want to return to in a moment. Even in the announcement of judgement upon a foreign nation (Edom), the Lord promises special care for surviving "fatherless children and widows" among the Edomites (Jeremiah 49:11). In an honour-conscious world, Deborah's leadership as a "judge" in Israel announces that the Lord has no problem in giving public, political honour to a woman (Judges 4:9). The angel of the Lord willingly appears to the sterile and childless – and in the text, unnamed – wife of Manoah, promising conception and the gift of a son (Judges 13:3). In subsequent disclosures the angel of the Lord contacts the man through the woman (verses 9–11). It is the woman who is asked to cooperate with the angel's requirements regarding diet, and it is the woman who gets the point of the revelation while her husband wrongly concludes that they are going to die because they have seen God. The unnamed wife soon becomes the one to name her promised son (verse 24)!

The New Testament opens with the recording of a genealogy and a dream. In his stylised description of the heritage of Jesus, Matthew offers a "record of the genealogy of Jesus Christ, the son of David, the son of Abraham" (Matthew 1:1). Thirty-nine times the phrase "So-and-so was the father of So-and-so" is offered. The link is given via the male line, accepting a patriarchal focus. The genealogy would thus be familiar ground for Matthew's Jewish readership. Matthew's genius, however, lies in what he then highlights against this standard genealogical procedure. It will not always be through the eldest son that the line continues: in God's grace, other sons may be preferred. That comes as a shock to the reader. More shocking is

Matthew's mention of women – five of them! And what women they were! Tamar, the widow of Judah's eldest son Er, was mistaken by her father-in-law for a prostitute and by him conceived the twins Perez and Zerah (Genesis 38). Rahab was a Canaanite prostitute who gave protection to Joshua's spies in the city of Jericho (Joshua 2). Ruth was a Moabite (the tribe that originated from Lot's incest with his daughter, Genesis 19:30–38) who became part of God's people through marriage to Boaz. The wife of Uriah (Bathsheba) committed adultery with King David while her Gentile husband, Uriah the Hittite, was fighting the king's war (2 Samuel 11–12). Mary gave birth to Jesus, conceived of the Holy Spirit while she was betrothed to Joseph.

Why mention women in a genealogy reflecting a patriarchal society? Why mention these women? Perhaps God is trying to say something significant here through Matthew. For each woman named, at least on the surface of things, their relationships with men are not culturally approved: one is a seducer (Tamar), one a prostitute (Rahab), one a possible seducer (Ruth – see Ruth 3:1–18), one an adulteress (Bathsheba) and one a pregnant betrothed virgin. Such people are included in the line to *Messiah*?

Looking under the surface, we get an inkling of why, in most cases, these women resort to scandalous actions in order to survive economically or politically or as a self-respecting individual. The women named by Matthew all live at the edges of the cultural norm, subject to the whims of men who may or may not care for them. Tamar struggles as an unprotected widow without a son, denied the right of levirate marriage by her father-in-law. Rahab is neither a virgin daughter nor a wife; she fends for herself and her family by selling her body to men. Ruth has no choice but to commit herself for protection, not to a male relative, but to another woman, her mother-in-law Naomi. Bathsheba, wife of Uriah, is accidentally caught up in an adulterous relationship with her king at that monarch's insistence. Mary finds herself pregnant, innocently, while betrothed to a "proper" man.

What's more, the women in Matthew's list each contrast with the males they are involved with in the sense that, though the women are culturally powerless, they, rather than the males, display the faith that carries forward what God wants to do. In societies in which women seem to count for little, in which men seem to determine the roles of male and female and assign to themselves the dominant part, the God of this genealogical record is saying: "I find women at the margins of such society very significant people. I find faith there. I find the lineage to Jesus Christ there." Against the backdrop of a recognisable Jewish genealogy, God is screaming: "I believe also in women!"

Sometimes some Christians have questioned whether there is a role for women in missions to Muslims because most Islamic societies are male-oriented. The first chapter of the New Testament contradicts that kind of questioning. To our sisters in Christ, God entrusts significant responsibility for bringing in his kingdom within Muslim cultures – maybe hidden, maybe at the margins – but certainly in the centre of his divine purposes. Sisters, go for it!

Beams and motes

Westerners who live amongst Middle Easterners behold very clearly the faults of male-oriented societies. I remember my blood boiling when I first saw a Turkish male beating a female relative in a field during harvesting. I wanted to stop the world and make everything right for the girl. Experience eventually helps one to hesitate: into what image would I change "everything" to make it all right for the female? Deep down, as my anger erupted, I held unspoken assumptions about equality, love, rights and freedom that came from my own cultural background. Perhaps some of those assumptions more closely approximated the biblical norm than did the Turkish lad's, but my own society was just as "failing" in other terms. At least the Turkish girl knew to which family she belonged; she lived with her own father and mother and siblings and would be protected for life by her older male relatives. I and my brother and sisters were all products of a broken-down Western culture. All four of us were adopted, rescued by our adoptive parents into a caring family from four disintegrated relationships. Who was I to judge?

In seeking to share the gospel with Arabs and other Middle Easterners, the norms of their society concerning male/female relationships must be accepted as the starting point, at least, for communication. For the majority of Muslim females, this will likely mean that they will hear the gospel as a result of their male protector's exposure to it. To go directly to women with the good news, even if feasible, would in most cases involve a circumventing of the authority of the controlling male in their lives. Sooner or later a major deterioration of the woman's position in the family would occur.[59] Charles Marsh describes a methodology in which he managed to share the gospel with Kabyle women in Algeria. He gained the respect of heads of families in different villages and as a result was invited to read from the Bible in their homes. The Muslim women, though ignored, were present and listening.[60]

Vivienne Stacey relates how a ministry of healing, entrusted to a national Christian couple in an Asian Muslim country, has been used by God to open up channels to some Muslim women there. The national pastor (Inayat) and his wife have learned to listen to the Lord in their praying for the womenfolk (and others) who come to them. Stacey notes an interesting pattern in this particular ministry:

> When Inayat prays for Muslims, they are seldom healed instantly. Time is needed for teaching. But after the first prayers they receive a touch from the Lord which convinces them that they will be healed, and so they come regularly, sometimes from considerable distance and at much expense. They tell others of the power of prayer in the name of Jesus the Messiah.[61]

In these instances involving Charles Marsh in Kabylia and Inayat in Pakistan, men and women were able to be together either in listening to the gospel or in ministering to others. Perhaps more usually, the interaction will proceed along the sexually segregated lines of male to male and female to female. In many Islamic cultures, as we have discovered, the men do not have the kind of relationship with their wives that allows them to sit and relax together. It is worth cautioning male missionaries to be very careful in assessing whether it is appropriate for them to converse with female Muslims. Equally, female advocates of the gospel need to come to terms with the reality that their female Muslim listeners require the understanding and encouragement of their male protectors if they are to make a lasting, positive response to the message they are hearing. Goodwin describes an incident in Afghanistan in which she confused gender roles to the embarrassment of her host and to her own hurt. The incident was not about sharing the gospel, but simply about asking after the health of a friend whom she had made. She approached a young male acquaintance in public while he was with some friends to inquire if his sister had recovered from her sickness:

He refused to acknowledge me, and the next time I saw him, he stormed at me that I had dared mention his sister, even used her name, in front of other men. He insisted my behaviour had shamed him.[62]

Goodwin writes as if she cannot, upon reflection, really believe that she had done such a terrible thing, or something so bad as to warrant that kind of violent outburst. The truth is that she had!

Sometimes the Holy Spirit miraculously intervenes to make possible what would otherwise be culturally unlikely:

In Kazakstan, twin 16 year old girls attended a showing of the Jesus film. Afterwards they discussed the content of the powerful story in that movie. Shortly after when their father fell gravely ill, they prayed for him in terms of the short prayer printed on a piece of Christian literature they had received. To their delight, their father improved. At school they met teachers who believed in Jesus. But still they were reluctant to commit. One night as the girls slept, one of them had a dream of angels coming to their window assuring her that Jesus really was who he said he was. When she awoke she shared her experience with her sister. Both invited Christ into their lives.

They started to pray for their parents. Shortly thereafter their mother had a dream in which she saw Jesus and heard him speak to her. When she awoke she realised that this was the one about whom her daughters had been speaking. Soon the whole family became followers of Jesus. This family began spreading the good news throughout their village. Others responded. Even relatives from Tajikistan accepted Jesus.[63]

Considerations of cultural difference are just as relevant to contemporary Christian witness amongst Muslims in the West. A few years ago, I was leading a seminar at a day conference in Liverpool Cathedral concerning the decade of evangelism. My subject was sharing the gospel with Muslims. A young woman came to speak to me at the end of the seminar. She couldn't understand why things had got so complicated for her. She had begun sharing her Christian testimony with a male Middle Easterner on a train in the United Kingdom. He had seemed touched and interested and they had stayed in contact. Gradually, she came to feel that he was more interested in her than in what she was sharing as a Christian. She was a married woman, a teacher and quite confused by what had developed. In reality, the message she had unintentionally conveyed to the Middle Easterner had been: I am a woman, married but alone in my witnessing, available for a relationship with you. Her intended message had been that of Christ's love for the man. The Middle Easterner had politely listened to her spoken message, assured by her approach to him that he could dismiss her words as merely the means to something more attractive. She gradually discovered that he had in mind a developing relationship which would eventuate in her sleeping with him. Oh, for him, the joys of a Western culture in which a lone woman can initiate a conversation with a man!

Sally Sutcliffe offers many examples of positive relating between Christian and Muslim women in Western contexts in her book *Aisha My Sister*. Throughout the text are conveyed possible, if challenging, suggestions for culturally sensitive witnessing:

> Friendship is deeply valued in Muslim culture; a female friend can be closer than a husband. Muslim women prefer personal friendships to one-off encounters and are very open to genuine offers of friendship. Our motive must be love, with no strings attached. If the only motivation is to win the person for Christ, this implies that if they do not convert the friendship is in vain. We will find that in making a genuine two-way friendship, we can share our faith naturally. This may mean sitting in our friend's home for many hours, weeks, months and years, accepting the hospitality offered and entering into a real friendship on eastern terms, not our goal-oriented western terms which demand results.[64]

Many Christian mission groups, with accumulated experience of working amongst Muslims, spend considerable energy orienting their male and female representatives to a cultural perspective which holds a very different view of human relationships from their own. Such orienting is absolutely necessary, not just to avoid unhealthy or compromising situations, but to ensure that Muslim cultures are really appreciated "from the inside" as it were.[65]

Difficult questions about contextualisation arise at this point. Should Western Christians imitate the norms of Muslim societies in ordering their own families when they go to live in Islamic contexts? I was very unhappy with one North American couple who came to me for pre-marriage counselling in Cairo. They were both fervent in their desire to share Christ with Muslim friends.

They had both lived with Muslim families and learned fluent Arabic. They wanted to marry and live in a poor Muslim community and be the means of introducing Christ to their neighbours and friends. So far, so good. However, their understanding of marriage was, to my mind, extremely over-contextualised. He as male would make all the decisions; she as female would simply obey. I felt that the over-contextualisation was an excuse for failing to face up to problems in their own North American family backgrounds. She was desperate to marry him at any cost. She reminded me of an innocent child, looking for a father. He was happy to have a wife along, but his own dysfunctional family background didn't augur well for anything but the most inappropriate form of relating, along extreme male chauvinist lines. My advice to them was not to marry and live immediately in a Middle Eastern culture, but to come to terms, first, with living as man and wife in their own North American culture. I felt that there could be no healthy crossing of the cultural divide for this potential couple until they had a firm base from which to cross, and to which they most likely would one day need to return.

One of the most helpful guidelines to contextualisation, especially with regard to male and female role models, is provided by Christine Mallouhi in her book *Miniskirts, Mothers and Muslims*. Mallouhi is an Australian, married to a Syrian, who has lived in the Middle East for most of her adult life. She draws on her own experience, both positive and negative, to illustrate ways in which spiritual (biblical) values can perhaps best be modelled by Christians living in Muslim contexts. To the Western reader's likely dismay, we discover that appearances are of paramount importance in a status-focused society. How does a male look and function? How does a female dress and behave in public? Why does Christian fellowship need to have precedence over Christian teaching? Mallouhi's insightful but disturbing exposé highlights the practical possibilities and pitfalls of demonstrating biblical values in ways understood by Muslims.[66]

For a mature non-Middle Eastern advocate of the gospel, whether married or single, the matter of contextualisation is a difficult issue to face. There may be a variety of responses, in terms of strategy, along the continuum from extreme accommodation to little accommodation. Whatever the response, it needs to arise out of an informed appreciation of the host culture's self-understanding as regards the theme of "male" and "female". Western missionaries need to know why the folk to whom they witness are very careful about the game of white teeth and red buttocks.

CHAPTER THREE

FAMILY AND INDIVIDUAL

He who marries the daughter of his father's brother is
like him who celebrates his feast with
a sheep from his own flock.

In Arab society, the *ahl* or extended family is the primary social unit. It constitutes the fundamental building block of society. And not just of Arab society! Ravone M'Baye makes the following claim about the significance of the institution of the family within Islamic societies generally:

> In Islam the family has played and still plays a key role; it is seen as the crux of interpersonal relations, as the hub where man's relationships with nature and God are fulfilled and tested. A whole system of kinship, filiation and relationship by marriage is laid down in the Qur'ân and the *sunna*; they also prescribe precise rules to deal with heritage and its transmission from generation to generation, and assign very precise rules to family members.[67]

The institution of the family, based on qur'ânic revelation and prophetic example, defines a kinship system, identifies how procreation may occur, and consolidates a cultural and spiritual norm for human interrelationship. "Extended family" is further extended by the possibilities of polygamy and fairly easy divorce. Hence, the need for clearly stated principles of relationship – who is "in" and who is "out", and how should the "in" people relate to one another?

It is the collection of related, extended families that by and large comprises the "group", referred to so frequently in Chapter 2. In the introduction to her life story as *Princess*, the unnamed Sultana sets the scene by describing the extended family or clan to which she belongs. King Abdul Aziz of the House of al-Sa^cud (died 1953)

The primary audience?

married more than 300 women, mostly for political reasons. More than 50 sons and 80 daughters derived from those marriages. Distinguished members amongst the offspring later intermarried and produced the princes who are prominent in the Kingdom today. At the beginning of the 1990s, according to Sultana, the "extended family" consisted of nearly 21,000 members! Of these, about 1,000 were princes or princesses (like Sultana herself) who were direct descendants of King Abdul Aziz.[68]

Most families are neither as illustrious nor as large as that deriving from the first king of Saudi Arabia, but the sense of "belonging" engendered within the wider group of relations is just as strongly felt. An individual finds his place in society within the extended family, not on his own terms. Often, the extended family lives together as a household. Such a household is typically composed of a nuclear family (parents and children) plus other close relatives, either married or unmarried.

Even in modern urban contexts, where self-reliant nuclear families tend necessarily to be the norm, the strength of the extended family ethos is often retained. That ethos manages to face challenges from a variety of sources, such as urbanisation itself, women going out to work, lifestyle choices deriving from birth control and so on. Perhaps this is partly because the extended family is tied to the ownership and inheritance of land and other property, details of the disposal of which are important elements of Islamic jurisprudence. It is also because members of the extended family are still held responsible for one another's conduct including the punishment of those who transgress society's norms.

"I am" because "we are"

The family is the focus of most activities, whether social, economic, religious, educational or political. The interests of the family almost always prevail over those of the individual. In the oasis of al-Hamra in contemporary Oman, for example, Eickelman confirms that "it is not individuals who form the basic political units, but the men and women who identify themselves as forming family clusters".[69] In India after partition, family identity affected networks in politics. Those from Arab descent (Syed, Shaikh), those from Persian descent (Mirza), those from Turco-Mongol descent (Mughal) and those from Pathan descent (Khan) comprised the *ashraf* or nobility in distinction from the *ajlaf* or commoners who were made up of Muslim families deriving from low caste Hindu converts.[70]

The extended family (*ahl*) is by definition a closed (if extendable) order. Everyone knows how and to whom he belongs. A person's full name identifies (his or her) father, grandfather and tribal origin. Genealogies function as definitions of association. Many Middle Eastern Muslims can recite the history of their family, tracing it back over generations, sometimes to relatives of Prophet Muḥammad himself. Arabs especially are proud of their heritage and are well able to cite the ins and outs of ancestors' squabbles, migrations, economic achievements and so on.

Within the *ahl*, the blood bond is very strong. A well-known saying expresses the strength of that tie: "Blood can never turn into water." Terms of endearment and respect affirm the importance of blood relationship. Indeed, until the birth of a child, two unrelated married persons hold stronger blood-bonds to their respective extended families than any tie to one another. Their marriage (under Islam) is a contract in which they retain their respective family names, property and complementary rights and obligations. After the birth of a child, however, bridegroom and bride become a unity in a much deeper sense. If their first child is a son (in some situations, if a daughter), the new parents are no longer called by their own names but are known as *Abû* (father) and *Umm* (mother) of So-and-so – the name of their eldest child.

The life of the *ahl* is marked by mutual interdependence. Individualism is low on the list of priorities for healthy existence. After all, "one hand alone cannot applaud". Visits within the group are made and repaid, taking much time and much expense. Moreover, they are often unannounced and "the full treatment" is expected in terms of hospitality. Money, food or clothes will be freely lent within the extended family circle. Cooking, sewing, childminding and many other activities will be unselfconsciously demanded and proffered. The extended family will get together to decide what one particular family within its number should or should not do. The extended family is expected to be present at all rites of passage. A mediator must be identifiable from within the *ahl* in cases of dispute.

Middle Eastern villages are traditionally divided along kinship lines and migrants to towns or cities will normally move to where family members have already established themselves.

Intermarriage contributes to family and "group" solidarity. In the Arab world, marriage is traditionally the joining of two families rather than of two individuals. In the Western world, a couple will go through successive phases of meeting, starting to like each other, friendship, dating, courting and engagement. Eventually, a wedding day may come should they both will it. The traditional vision of marriage in the Arab world is simply one stage: the official binding betrothal followed at any interval by the wedding day. After all, the two persons concerned are already known by each family group. Marriage, in this view, is mainly a matter of formalising a long-standing relationship between those parties. Such formalising occurs in a bargaining session between senior representatives of the families. The older generation thus continues to shape family life for the younger generation. In that shaping, the desires and values of men predominate over those of women. A gradual, developing relationship of increasing intimacy between the actual couple prior to marriage is hardly a consideration in the formalising process. In order to ensure the purity of the line, a fiancée must be a virgin. This partly explains why, in some Muslim cultures, girls have tended to be married off at a very young age. A girl's virginity is still viewed as a family possession of considerable importance today. That conviction has led to some specialised surgical operations in modern urban contexts, as Juliette Minces records:

> Young women of the bourgeoisie who have led a relatively free life during their years at university usually have their hymen replaced before marriage by accommodating surgeons whose fortunes are quickly made.[71]

Figure 6
The most common marriage preference amongst Arabs

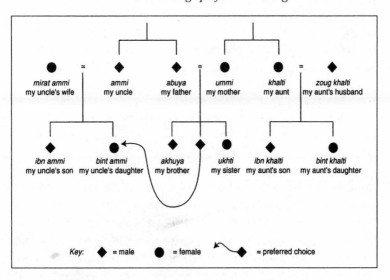

Arabic kinship terminology differentiates an individual's relationship with his paternal relatives from that with his maternal relatives. It also distinguishes his first cousins from those more distantly connected. The preferred norm for marriage is traditionally that of patrilineal, parallel cousins, as illustrated in Figure 6. The son marries his father's brother's daughter (his *bint ammu*).[72] In such cases, the bride price is often merely nominal, for the family links are guarantee enough that everyone will work towards making the marriage a success.

A girl would in most cases prefer marriage to her mother's sister's son. Such an arrangement would assure her of continuing association with her mother's (rather than her father's) extended family. In a world in which the wife is largely confined to the home, it becomes a matter of significance as to who would share that space with her and who would have unquestionable visiting rights to that dwelling. In such a case, the girl's mother would have continuing access to her daughter through her sister. In a study of the marriage preferences of working-class folk in Cairo, Andrea Rugh produced a table of priority (Figure 7).[73]

Figure 7
Preferred relative marriage in order of priority

Preferred order	For the man	For the woman
1	father's brother's daughter	mother's sister's son
2	father's sister's daughter	mother's brother's son
3	mother's brother's daughter	father's brother's son
4	mother's sister's daughter	father's sister's son

The descending orders of priority and their difference between male and female preference illustrate how males and females tend to see Arab society functioning. The men want to reinforce certain patrilineal ties and concentrate their lives in the homes of paternal relatives. The women want to reinforce ties with maternal relatives and increase the amount of time spent in maternally related households where they are familiar with those around them. Whatever the details of difference, the important point for our consideration is that all eight cases have to do with close relative marriage. In the Western world, such unions are illegal. Even when they were possible, they proved to be the exception rather than the rule. In the Middle East, those preferences are the norm.

Marriages along such lines tend naturally to cement the mutual interdependence of components of the extended family. Receiving help from relatives will not cause an Arab to lose face. To ask for help from the family is indeed a right, not an embarrassment. Kin help each other simply because they are kin. Equally, needy parents and grandparents expect to be respected and supported by their children and grandchildren so that they might age and die with dignity within the bosom of the family. As the oldest surviving members of the group, the honour and respect of the lineage is invested in them. Obedience towards parents is considered a sacred duty by all. Sura 17:23 declares:

> Thy Lord hath decreed
> That ye worship none but Him,
> And that ye be kind
> To parents. Whether one
> Or both of them attain
> Old age in thy life,
> Say not to them a word
> Of contempt, nor repel them,
> But address them
> In terms of honour.

Parents thus teach their children to be dutiful towards them, to support them if necessary and in general to be kind to them. The awe felt towards older members of the family, especially the father, is demonstrated in many ways. A 50-year-old man will put out his cigarette, rise to his feet and yield to his father on the latter's appearance.

The natural ties of extended families are enhanced through intermarriage. As a consequence, the generations are inextricably linked in a way unthinkable in the West. The son of a North American, for example, could attempt to assassinate the president of his country with no repercussions necessarily falling upon his father. The action of an

Arab's son, however, reflect strongly upon his father. Figure 8 helps us understand why this is so. Individuals are perceived primarily as members of the family cluster. Within that context, adult males and females carry responsibility for maintaining the family's good name. Improper conduct on the part of both men and women can destroy its reputation. Incidents bringing shame upon the group today may alter the reputation of a cluster for several generations to come.

Figure 8
The Middle Eastern family

In the Arab family, then, a person's identity in the *ahl* (extended family) is most important. It, supremely, says "who I am". The strongest links and associations in that *ahl* are invariably made with one's father's relatives or kin. As far as marriage is concerned, as we have seen, the most common union is that between parallel cousins on the male side. If no such possibility exists, a young man will seek as his bride a girl related to him through the family's male line. At marriage, a couple tends to move into the groom's parental household or else lives nearby in the same village or sector of the city. The father is an authoritarian figure revered by the entire household. What a son does or does not do consequently reflects very strongly on his father, the centrepiece of the extended family. Is a man going to be despised as the father of a murderer or a thief? Or is he going to be honoured as the father of a pillar of the community?

The labelling of relatives in Turkey further illustrates the importance of kin. Figure 9 shows how I, as a young Turkish male, would refer to various relatives.[74]

Relatives in Turkey are alluded to differently if they are older than myself, but not if they are younger. Vertical relationships dominate and age is appropriately acknowledged. In greeting an older relative, a Turk will kiss the back of the older person's hand and place it to his forehead. Turkish fathers or grandfathers are not "buddies" of their sons or grandsons. An older brother or sister each have a special term of reference. People are called by their kinship term, rather than their name, when addressed, especially if the individual being spoken to is older than the speaker. Males are also differentiated from females. Grandparents in both lineages are distinguished on the basis of gender. Children of my sister's children are only called by name, but offspring of my brother's children are called "grandchildren". The various terms reflect culturally significant groups of people rather than biological relationships. Age and maleness is emphasised. When a Westerner speaks about his "uncle", the term is nowhere near invested with the intensity of meaning that a Turk would understand.

Blood relationship defines quite clearly who are "insiders" and who "outsiders" in most Middle Eastern societies. Non-blood relatives may be given terms of endearment and treated as insiders but should a dispute ever arise, the boundaries will quickly be drawn along family lines.

The scenario most to be feared, consequently, is that of kinlessness – for whatever reason. A divorced older woman, a widow with no brothers or sons to support her, a Muslim who has been baptised a Christian – each face the potential trauma of discovering themselves stripped of kin. The original cry of desolation, issuing from

Cain's lips, expresses for all Middle Easterners the anguish of any such unprotected individual: "My punishment is more than I can bear . . ." (Genesis 4:13).

Figure 9
The labelling of relatives: Turkish style

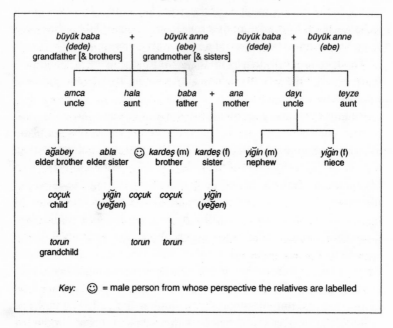

In traditional contexts where families were tied to land, and water-rights were often causes of dispute, tribal feuds were the stuff of life. Feuds arose because such societies tended to function according to the principle of "limited good". That principle affirms that there is only so much "good" – in this case, water – to go around. If one family seeks more of the limited good, then other families will have to suffer less of it. Fighting quickly develops.

Feuds still occur frequently, especially over land, livestock and women! Om Naeema describes the process that repeats itself endlessly amongst contemporary Egyptian villagers:

A young man might come asking to marry another's daughter, for example, and the parents will choose the richer of the two suitors. The poorer one will be vexed and say to himself, "If I had been richer or better, they would have chosen me." In his anger at being rejected, he might sneak into the field belonging to the girl's father and pull up the man's plants. He might poison the man's buffalo. Anything is possible. The fiancé of the bride would then intervene, now being a part of that family, and another feud will begin.[75]

The fact that the extended family is the basic building block of Arab societies lends both strength and weakness to such societies. In most Arab communities, political power and advancement is family oriented. It is not primarily a matter of academic excellence in a particular field that will guarantee a person a particular job in a government administration. It is rather a matter of knowing who could pull strings on his behalf. In his satirical novel *Respected Sir*, Naguib Mahfouz documents the disillusionment which gradually settles on Othman Bayyumi, archives clerk ("incoming mail") at the directorate of administration. The young, keenly motivated Othman passes his law degree with high honours by dint of working during his spare hours. However, he has no one within the directorate to lobby on his behalf. As a result, the short letter he writes to the director-general asking for a better job just circulates round the building without achieving any result:

> His note addressed to His Excellency would take its splendid course and proclaim to the world his superiority. It would first go to his immediate senior, Sa^cfan Basyuni, to authorise its submission to His Honour the Director of Administration, Hamza al-Suwayfi. That meant it would first be recorded in the Archives' register of outgoing mail and then recorded again in the department's register of incoming mail. This done, it would be taken to Hamza al-Suwayfi to approve its submission to His Excellency the Director-General. Thereupon it would be recorded in the department's register of outgoing mail and then in the register of incoming mail in the Director-General's office. Then His Excellency the Director-General would read it. He would take it in with his eyes, absorb it in his mind, and maybe it would move him. Then he would sign it and pass it to the Personnel Office for disposal. Whereupon it would be recorded in the register of outgoing mail at the office of the Director-General and then in the register of incoming mail in the Personnel Office. Thus action would be taken and a copy would be sent to Archives, where the letter was first issued, for retention in his service record. In this way the astronomical orbit would be completed and those who did not know would know.[76]

Mahfouz cunningly uses humour to criticise a system in which such a gifted young man fails to fulfil his potential simply because he "did not possess the magic of wealth, nor did he enjoy the privileges which belong to a great family".[77] Without family members or money to help him advance, Othman is doomed to remain at a lowly post despite his well-won degree in law.

The real-life drama of Nabil and Renata well illustrates the significance of the "who you know" requirement in many Muslim cultures. Nabil, a Syrian citizen, plans to wed Renata, a Polish woman, in Cracow. In order for them to marry legally, various permissions are needed from Damascus:

> The procedures to get the marriage approved took eighteen months. The Syrian authorities required a multitude of forms and papers. In order to ascertain whether Renata had any Jewish relations, she had to provide her ancestral genealogy for several generations back, and have it all translated into Arabic. These had to be sent to Damascus for approval, and then back to Warsaw. It was a bureaucratic nightmare! Finally Nabil took recourse to his father's old trick – using people with influence. He had a friend from high school days who lived in Damascus and who was friendly with one of the President's sons. Nabil begged him to do something, for he could see no way out of the bureaucratic maze. The friend kindly obliged and mentioned Nabil's case to the President's son, who phoned someone in the appropriate Ministry and, hey presto, everything was miraculously approved![78]

Many Muslim societies function in equivalent ways, especially where those societies are ruled by a single, large extended family. In recent years, the 1991 Gulf War brought to the notice of the Western world the power and prestige of the ruling al-Sabah family in Kuwait. Other Gulf states run on similar lines. Power-holding in the Baathist regimes of Syria and Iraq (until 2003) has been strongly limited to the extended families of their leaders.

The original splitting of Shîᶜa from Sunnî Muslims can probably best be understood in terms of family loyalties. Figure 10 shows some of the major clan-groups comprising the tribe from which Prophet Muḥammad descended.[79]

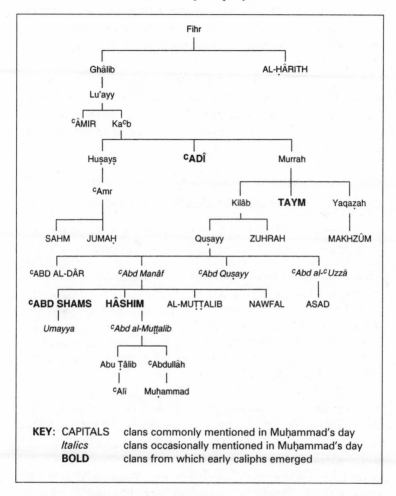

Figure 10
The clans of the quraysh

KEY: CAPITALS clans commonly mentioned in Muḥammad's day
Italics clans occasionally mentioned in Muḥammad's day
BOLD clans from which early caliphs emerged

Prophet Muḥammad himself left only a daughter, Fâṭima, as family heir. She married ᶜAlî, a cousin of her father. ᶜAlî was thus both son-in-law and cousin of Prophet Muḥammad. Leadership of the community after Muḥammad's death could either pass through Fâṭima and her husband (and their descendants) or through the more distantly related Companions of the Prophet. The Companions were men who, early on, converted to Islam and joined Muḥammad in his mission. Figure 11 shows the clan origins of those Companions who later became leaders of the Muslim community after AD 632.

The Sunnî, the majority, preferred the leadership to continue via the Companions and chose Abû Bakr as caliph after Muḥammad's death. The Shî^ca, a minority, preferred the succession to devolve via ^cAlî, cousin of Muḥammad and husband of Fâṭima. Three of Muḥammad's four immediate successors were murdered as a result of the ensuing argument. The die was cast and from early days on, the Islamic community became fragmented as a result of this primary feuding. Different theological convictions consolidated alternative human allegiances. To this day, many Sunnî and Shî^ca Muslims have strong reservations about one another.

Figure 11
Clan origins of the early caliphs

Name of Caliph	Tribal Origin	Mother's Tribe	Other Comments	Died AD
Muḥammad	Hâshim	Zuhrah		632
Abû Bakr	Taym	Taym		634
^cUmar	^cAdî	Makhzûm		664
^cUthmân	^cAbd Shams	^cAbd Shams		656
^cAlî	Hâshim	Hâshim		661
al-Ḥasan	Hâshim	Hâshim	resigned 661	669
Mu^câwiya	^cAbd Shams		cousin of ^cUthmân	680

The predominance of the collective – the "group" – over the individual has repercussions in all aspects of Arab life. Privacy is not valued and never sought. Often my family has had the experience of choosing a spot on a deserted Mediterranean beach and setting up a sunshade. The next Egyptians to come along invariably set up their spot right next to us instead of at some distance. The Britisher says, "I value private space, like the bedroom I grew up in." The Egyptian says, "I value close human contact, like the bedroom-cum-living-room-cum-dining-room I grew up in." A 32 year-old male Egyptian friend, who stayed with us while sitting his final exams at a university in Cairo, begged us not to stay out long of an evening as he was frightened of being by himself in the flat.

Life in general is community-oriented and as a result an individual's main aim becomes one of seeking to avoid the disapproval of his group. More positively, he seeks its praise and approbation. Conformity is the norm and the family group does for the Arab individual what peer pressure could never achieve amongst Westerners. The dual themes of honour and shame tend therefore to be strongly emphasised in cultures where the community is responsible for maintaining correct and honourable behaviour in its members. Honour and shame arise out of relationships with the surrounding people who are constantly watching. Jerome Neyrey focuses on this sense of public evaluation in his analysis of the concept of honour in the New Testament:

> Honor, then, has to do with public value and worth. Hence, "worthies" are they who wear white garments and walk in the company of the Lord (Rev. 3:4). He, who is himself truly "worthy" (Rev. 5:2, 9–10), acknowledges the worth of the others (see Luke 7:4 and Matt. 6:26). But honor exists only in the eyes of a public who expect certain things and evaluates individuals accordingly. It is, then, what is called a social construct, an idea created by humans which they fill with meaning.[80]

We shall look at this matter of honour and shame in detail in the next chapter.

Some relationships in society are guided by legal sanction. As we have seen, a husband, for example, is required to support his wife while she is expected to obey him. Other relationships are steered by social obligation. In societies where group identity and loyalty is valued, such obligations are strong. A friend is expected to pay condolences to a grieving friend. An elder son is expected to care for his widowed mother. This kind of social obligation is called a *wâgib* in Arabic. It takes the form of a service, a gift or an action which is initiated between two persons because it is believed to be owed by the one to the other. Another form of relationship obligation takes the shape of *marûf*, or offering of a favour. This is not a formally requested or expected initiative but one which begins and ends with the emotions. A *marûf* comes out of a close relationship with someone:

If a woman is totally dependent on her husband as I was in the early years of marriage, then she longs for sons. She prefers them to daughters because she feels they'll stand by her in time of need – they have the means to stand by her. My hopes were disappointed in the case of my eldest son and it is my youngest daughter who asks after me and insists on sending me E£5 from her paycheck every month. This is unusual because custom dictates that a daughter's allegiance will be to her husband's family when she marries.[81]

In this case, the son failed in his social obligation (*wâgib*) but the daughter made up for the lack by her generous, voluntary support (*marûf*) of her mother.

Mutual support, within strong family structures, is the supposed norm of most Muslim societies. The proper functioning of the family far outweighs the niceties of individual choice or desire for personal independence. Islamists, consequently, have a lot to say about family life for it constitutes the central bastion within Islam against all impure accretions. Sayyid Qutb, in his provocative book *Milestones*, for example, focuses on the constitution of a proper Muslim family in his chapter extolling the virtues of Islam as "the real civilisation":

If the family is the basis of the society, and the basis of the family is the division of labor between husband and wife, and the upbringing of children is the most important function of the family, then such a society is indeed civilized. In the Islamic system of life, this kind of a family provides the environment under which human values and morals develop and grow in the new generation; these values and morals cannot exist apart from the family unit. If, on the other hand, free sexual relationships and illegitimate children become the basis of a society, and if the relationship between man and woman is based on lust, passion and impulse, and the division of work is not based on family responsibility and natural gifts; if woman's role is merely to be attractive, sexy and flirtatious, and if woman is freed from her basic responsibility of bringing up children; and if, on her own or under social demand, she prefers to become a hostess or a stewardess in a hotel or ship or air company, thus spending her ability for material productivity rather than in the training of human beings, because material production is considered to be more important, more valuable and more honorable than the development of human character, then such a civilization is "backward" from the human point of view, or *jâhilî* in the Islamic terminology.[82]

Mending family life is a major aim of Islamists-in-power, as demonstrated most radically by the Taliban in Afghanistan during the late 1990s.

Echoes from Scripture?

The Semitic culture of Old Testament times had many parallels to today's Muslim cultures. Vertical relationships predominated then, so that decisions made by the head of a family held good for the whole of a family.

One wonders about the dynamics of Abram's moving out of Ur in the 19th century BC. We know that Abram was originally spoken to by God while in Ur and was required to leave on a journey of exploration (Acts 7:2). The Genesis account, however, has it that it was Abram's father, Terah, who took his son Abram, his grandson Lot and his daughter-in-law Sarai and left Ur in order to go to Canaan (Genesis 11:31). What really happened? Did Abram share his calling from the Lord with his father? Did his father own the vision and act on it, only to have second thoughts when he'd got the family as far as Haran? Certainly, Abram stayed in Haran until Terah died. Why? Could Abram neither persuade Terah to leave Haran nor depart himself against his father's wishes? After the death of Terah, the Lord nudged Abram again and this time the patriarch went willingly enough.

When the people of Israel finally entered Canaan under Joshua's military leadership, it seems that the Lord was still willing to work within the norms of a culture in which vertical relationships were so dominant. Achan's sin at Ai, east of Bethel, brought a temporary setback for the invading Israelites. Chapter 7 of the book of Joshua reveals the sad details of a man who set out to deceive the Lord and amass wealth for himself. That chapter also records that Achan's sons, daughter, oxen, donkeys, sheep and tent shared his mortal punishment. What the one man did, he did on behalf of his household. All parties understood that it was a family affair.

In such a society, it was reasonably enshrined in its law that the young should stand up in the presence of the aged (Leviticus 19:32). Certainly, also, it was easily understood that God's self-revelation should be expressed in terms of condescension. Although there is a powerful theme of God's covenant love running through the Old

Testament, for the most part the manner of human beings' relating to their Maker is not on familiar, but in respectful, terms. The great Moses quickly strips off his footwear in acknowledgement of human unworthiness before the Lord of the whole earth. Successive prophets fall face down in humility, "as if dead", when confronted by their Creator. Ensuing commitment and trust find expression in worship and obedience. The relationship between human beings and God-in-covenant is strongly vertical. The Lord of heaven and earth is not a person's "buddy".

I recall visiting a large auditorium in Heliopolis, Cairo, where a Coptic Orthodox priest preached every Thursday evening to a mixed audience of Egyptian Christians and Muslims. He was working his way through the book of Revelation, verse by verse. Men and women sat separately on the main floor while the balcony was reserved solely for women. Before the priest began to speak, an Egyptian layman came and chanted some of the prophecy of Isaiah. It was captivating and it stilled the audience, provoking them to turn from their own ways to the sovereign Lord, "the holy one of Israel" as Isaiah's catchphrase has it. Next, the repetition of verses by everyone present drove home the message conveyed in chant. In his subsequent preaching (one verse per evening!), Father Zechariah made liberal use of stories and illustrations. At the end of the evening, the sick and demonised were brought to the stage area for ministry. The miracles conveyed a tangible sense of the majesty and power of God, as well as his presence alongside needy humankind. In dealing with people outside the hours of such meetings, Father Zechariah concentrated on the heads of homes. In his public and private ministry, this gifted and humble priest demonstrated an ability to call Egyptians back to a true honouring of the one God before whom they submitted publicly, but whom they actually shut out of their daily living.[83]

When Peter and Stephen preached to Jewish audiences (as recorded by Luke in the early chapters of Acts), they emphasised the fact that God the Father had glorified his servant Jesus by raising him from the dead. The Father above authenticated the self-sacrifice of the Son by rescuing him from the grave and exalting him to heaven. At the same time the Jews were pronounced corporately responsible for doing the unthinkable to the Messiah – crucifying him! We should note that, to such audiences, Peter and Stephen did not preach a gospel emphasising God's love in incarnation and generosity in dying on our behalf. Rather, they preached a message about men showing disrespect to the God they should be honouring above all. Such men have crucified his Son and their only chance of forgiveness lies in the possibility that they acted in ignorance. Paul will later put forward his own ignorance as a mitigating factor in his awful persecution of Christians prior to his conversion. Stephen hardly allows the Sadducees even that possibility. According to him, they are guilty of the grossest form of disrespect, in the tradition of their forefathers. In contrast with such human dishonouring of the Messiah, God the Father has wonderfully honoured him. He has raised and exalted him! The apostles have themselves been commissioned by that risen Christ and the miracles abounding in Jerusalem are done in Christ's name, further honouring him! In the heady days of signs and wonders and conflict with the authorities, the apostles proclaim a message about honour and dishonour, about the shame of human denying of a vertical relationship between God and his people.

What about "me"?

Vertical relationships in a cohesive household structure can also be overwhelming. There are weaknesses, as well as strengths, in having one's individual identity bound so strongly to the community.

It is true of Arabs that they also want to be valued as individuals in their own right. Within clans, there is constant striving for headship as we shall discover in later chapters. Within families, sibling rivalry is the cause of many tensions:

> Individuals whose group identities and loyalties are clear-cut and well known, and who are sociable and ceremonious, are also wary, cantankerous, volatile, and seemingly withholding of themselves from others.[84]

One Arab author philosophises about his sense of loneliness and lostness arising from the absence of a compelling sense of love within his experience of family:

> Who among us Arabs can claim that he was acknowledged, loved, wanted and accepted by the family or atmosphere in which he grew up?

None, I am sure. Can anyone be loved who is no more than a useful object, produced to continue the family line, or for the troublesome old age of parents, or for the male chauvinist glory of the father who proves what a real man he is by the number of his offspring?[85]

The strong, extended family structure in many Muslim cultures sadly allows the possibility of sexual abuse of girls (especially) by males who are allowed access. Some fathers, uncles and brothers take false advantage of their privilege of access and authority in this way. Zahra, of Hanan al-Shaykh's novel, is a victim in just such a situation. The wrongful familiarity of an uncle towards her when she moves to Africa and stays in his apartment brings flashbacks of a cousin's earlier abuse of her when she had stayed one time with her aunt and grandfather:

Later, as I was sleeping on the floor next to my grandfather, in a darkness so intense as to be completely saturated with darkness, it seemed as if a cold hand furtively moved in my panties. I woke and jumped up in a fright, and the hand suddenly disappeared. But the fear and the coldness had gripped me and shaken me. Even in that total darkness that could absorb no more darkness, I thought, for an instant, I saw the glint of [her cousin] Kasem's spectacles. Then there was nothing. It was an uneasy night, an unreal night. I stayed awake till dawn. I did not relax my head on the pillow until a faint light began to fill the room.[86]

Strong political leaders, such as Saddam Hussein, have been ruthless with family members who posed potential threats to their continuing in authority. Kith and kin may have helped get them to power and may have contributed towards keeping them in power, but the ties of family have been quickly abandoned by the power-holders as soon as any hint of criticism or opposition was perceived.

A heady individualism seems to burst out of the constraints of family ties whenever a person feels that he or she has the strength to successfully defy the weight of tradition. Such strength may derive from political power (as with Saddam Hussein) or spiritual authority (as with a "saint" or a "wise woman"). Within the norms of a society in which the group mentality counts for so much, some individuals seek to alter the assigned view of themselves by "becoming" someone different. We shall return to this observation in Chapter 8.

Family breakdown

In every society, human beings being what they are, families and family structures break down. Muslim cultures are no exception. Times of change bring great strain to traditional ways of behaving. War, migration, wealth creation, urbanisation, education, television and health care all contribute to the broadening of horizons and the fragmenting of customary habits. It is to be expected that visiting Westerners are most likely to meet Muslims whose assumptions about reality have at least been challenged by alternative perspectives. Included amongst them will be secularised, Westernised acquaintances who live apart from their families and adopt customs strongly at odds with the mores of their forefathers. Others among them will seem simply overwhelmed by the superficial consumerism, moral laxity and heady individualism that so often arrives on the back of imported Western technological expertise and the tourist industry.

Internal, personal shortcomings also effect family breakdown. The pain of seeking to abide by societal custom is brought out in the story of Naeema, as told by her mother. Naeema is the only daughter of an Egyptian fisherman and his wife. Naeema is engaged to her parallel cousin on her mother's side (mother's sister's son). The in-laws continually delay the marriage, obviously having hoped initially to gain financially from the relationship. No treasure trove is forthcoming from the poorer fisherman's family. In the end, the in-laws settle on a more lucrative possibility and forsake the traditional family relationship. Naeema's mother can only express her frustration by resorting to magic. The object of her incantations is her estranged sister's son:

> After abandoning Naeema, my sister married her son off to someone else, and I cast a spell on him, hoping that he would find no peace and that his life and that of his family would be a series of misfortunes.[87]

In this situation, lucre, if not water, proved thicker than blood, and the traditionally minded family suffers from the breakdown of customary mores.

One is reminded of the extended-family-gone-wrong that belonged to the man closest, reputedly, to the Lord God's own heart.

The history of King David's household reads like a modern soap opera. Life in the palace begins to fall apart when David's son Amnon rapes his sister Tamar. Another son, Absalom, conceals his non-forgiveness of Amnon for months before murdering him at a banquet. As a consequence, David's relationship with Absalom deteriorates so much that the two are permanently estranged. Eventually, Absalom seeks revenge for his father's rejection of him by wooing away support from King David at the very gates of Jerusalem. His strategy works and he very nearly wins the kingdom. He certainly beds ten of his father's young wives in public (2 Samuel 15:16, 21–22), shaming the old king in a manner only recoverable by the ultimate form of punishment. The irascible son must be killed. That final solution is eventually reached, but sadly it also frustrates David's strong longing for reconciliation with Absalom. A further dispute about the succession to the throne bursts into flame before King David dies, involving two other sons. This extended family is truly dysfunctional, full of sibling rivalry, violence and disrespect for the aged.

Extended family and Christian mission

For most Muslims, to be truly free as an individual normally means to belong to a community:

> The concept of freedom in Islam implies a conscious rejection of a purely liberal and individualistic philosophy of "doing one's own thing" as the meaning of life, or as the goal of society. The goal of freedom is human creativity. Freedom is defined as belonging to the community and participating with the people in cultural creation.[88]

Individualism, in the sense that it is valued in the West, is inconceivable as a force for good within the majority of Muslim communities. It strikes me that when Christian mission attracts individual Muslims, it is likely to be people who are not fitting well into their own communities who are being won. Of course, each individual is precious and to be welcomed with discernment into the family of the church. I know, however, from my experience as a pastor on an estate in Merseyside and in inner-city London (in the "free" West!) that I could not build a church around certain, very "individual" characters who form part of the community of the faithful. The needy misfits of Western society who require the succour and support of the church are naturally to be embraced and encouraged. But the assumption cannot be made that whoever is converted is necessarily a candidate for leadership.

In the development of Christian communities in situations where the members were formerly Muslim, we need to consider carefully the implications of leadership choices. Could it be that it would be better to expect strong-minded, older, male figures to form the local leadership rather than women, single migrant males, students, returnees from overseas or non-nationals? Leaders of the appropriate kind may not appear (especially in public) to be very humble. Their style may not be very egalitarian (especially at first); they may even appear to be very chauvinistic. If it is anywhere near "normal" for the society, one will get the feeling that group identity is being put before individual "rights". Any evangelistic appeal to convert will be made to heads of families. The message will likely be expressed in strongly vertical terms. Themes of loyalty/disloyalty, generosity/selfishness, honour/dishonour will be emphasised. Church discipline may seem very authoritarian. Throughout the structure, "family" concerns will be paramount. Believers will think and act plurally.

Around the Muslim world today there are many examples of such groups, growing amidst pain, founded around heads of families who are able, within their cultural contexts, to help build a new family – the family of the church.[89]

In the New Testament, as the church grew rapidly amongst Jewish communities, it is twice recorded that the number of men who converted or who comprised the community of "brothers" was 3,000 or 5,000 (Acts 2:41; 4:4). Luke's intention is not to suggest that there were no female nor young members included. He is not being deliberately provocative or male-oriented. It is simply that in such a society, decisions were group decisions, expressed through the senior male.

The gospel is quite at home in a culture which functions on a tribal or family basis. It can infiltrate the structures of such a society as well as it can appeal to members of a culture strongly committed to individualism.

Jean-Marie Gaudeul relates the remarkable story of a Sudanese clan who came to Christian faith via an encounter of the clan leader with a venerable old man in a vision-experience. The clan had moved in 1960 to Wad Medani, a little over a hundred miles south-east of Khartoum. Shortly after their migration, the leader of the clan was approached by an older man with a long grey beard. The bearded gentleman warned him to embrace the true religion and then identified that religion as Christianity. A subsequent encounter with the same figure galvanised the clan leader into summoning the family heads and weighing with them the implications of his vision-experiences. The result of the deliberations-in-council was a decision to approach a local Roman Catholic priest. This official somewhat nervously gave the seekers a Bible and some Christian literature. When the leaders of the clan returned, having absorbed the books, and asked for baptism, processes were set in motion that eventuated in baptism and the attempted integration of the clan within the local Catholic community.[90] The clan chief and family heads acted quite normally as decision-makers on behalf of the whole community in this conversion experience.

Similarly elsewhere:

> In Chad, deep in the bush, a team of students and a missionary preached in a mostly Muslim village. As they sang a hymn of invitation, "Today is the Day of Grace," one villager shouted out "Yes, today is the day! We have prayed that this message would reach us. God has heard us. Now is the time for our decision." Without hesitation, 56 Muslims came forward to commit themselves to Christ, including the village chief and his three wives.[91]

Chad, of course, offers possibilities for evangelism very different from those pertaining to many Muslim countries throughout the contemporary world. Nevertheless, the accessibility of the gospel to a Sahelian culture in which family is of primary importance is surely welcome news to those who seek to share Christ with Muslims in other cultures, similarly oriented. Attention to the important details of family structure and loyalty will perhaps help the experience of evangelists in Chad in 1993 to be repeated around the Muslim world. Christian missionaries need to learn why a father's brother's daughter is the number one bride!

CHAPTER FOUR

HONOUR AND SHAME

He who has no sense of shame does as he pleases.

Loyalty to family and kin is fundamental to Middle Eastern societies. In cultures in which bonds between persons count for so much, it is not primarily law which channels and corrects human behaviour. Rather, it is the connected concepts of honour and shame.

Grounds for pride

The well-known anthropologist Julian Pitt-Rivers summarises the powerful concept of "honour":

> Honour . . . provides a nexus between the ideals of a society and their reproduction in the individual through his aspiration to personify them. As such, it implies not merely an habitual preference for a given mode of conduct, but the entitlement to a certain treatment in return.[92]

Society (the "group") says that a good reputation – defined in a certain manner – is required. The individual aims to obtain or maintain such a reputation. A person with a good reputation can be sure of enjoying society's approbation.

Honour (*sharaf*) refers to uprightness of character, integrity, glory even. It evolves from and announces the stainlessness of one's way of living. Honour may be derived from a variety of sources. It might come from one's lineage. An Afghan friend described to me how three major family groupings in his country carry prestige: the Sayyids (deriving from Prophet Muḥammad), the Khawajas (deriv-

85

ing from Caliph Abû-Bakr) and the Hazrats (deriving from Caliph ᶜUmar). It is joked among his people that "he who has no family has no backbone".

Piety brings honour. A person may be blind, or lacking many social graces, but if he has learnt the Qur'ân by heart, he is honoured as a *ḥâfiẓ*. A lovely tale is repeated among the Nubians of Dahmit in Upper Egypt about a local saint named Hazim Zild Mahmoud. This man was a humble Nubian shepherd. As far as formal education was concerned, he was a simpleton. He knew only two words in Arabic, those meaning "stick" and "goat". Therefore, as the story goes, whenever he wanted to recite the formal prayers of Islam, he would say, "My goat and stick. Please God, make my prayer longer." One day a scholar from al-Azhar University in Cairo came to the village to bring some formal religious education to the primitive people. Included among the students was the native saint. After several months, the Azharite felt that he had accomplished what he set out to achieve. With a big fanfare, he left the village by boat, setting off down the Nile. The local saint, Hazim, was left on the bank where he turned to say his prayers. A cloud of forgetfulness descended on his brain and out came the old familiar words, "My goat and stick. Please God, make my prayer longer." In frustration Hazim shouted after the departing Azharite, but the scholar couldn't hear him. In the end the saint walked over the water, caught up with the departing boat and asked the Azharite for assistance in remembering the lost phrases. The Azharite turned in amazement to Hazim and said, "Don't worry about the formal prayers, the *baraka* you have is plenty! Pray how you like!" The simple saint's personal piety so overwhelmed the northern scholar that he could not but honour the charismatic southerner![93]

Hard work, wealth, success, generosity – all bring honour. And honour commands politeness and respect. The father of a Lebanese friend of mine grew the nails of his little fingers about three quarters of an inch long. He was declaring his status as that of a person above involvement in manual labour, a point of honour in his society. I also remember my frustration and anger when the company I worked for in Beirut moved offices. The two other foreigners and I rolled up our sleeves and helped in the hard work of hauling books, filing cabinets and furniture. We "got our hands dirty". The Lebanese who func-tioned at an equivalent level to ourselves in the company dressed as chic as normal and lifted not a finger to help. We got mad at them and they at us. In reality, we all got the kudos we were aiming for. We foreigners made it a matter of pride that we had mucked in and helped. Our Lebanese colleagues made it a matter of honour that they weren't seen to be involved in any menial tasks!

Heard with respect

Age brings honour. Children frequently hear such sayings as, "He who is one day older than you is wiser by one year." In societies in which vertical relationships dominate, children are brought up to respect the wisdom of grandparents, uncles and aunts as well as parents. Any member of the older generation may participate in the disciplining of a child. The child's learned role is to show exaggerated respect. Within many cultures of the world, having a hoary head brings honour!

In traditional Bedouin society the tented area reflects the honour of its inhabitants. It is a space only entered by invitation, except in special circumstances. A tribesman who has committed a crime might seek temporary refuge from his enemies in such a tent complex. The honour of the lineage protects him until the dispute is settled. Generosity and hospitality, attitudes for which the Bedouin are justly renowned, still lie close to the hearts of most Arabs. It is a point of honour to be hospitable.

The Old Testament character of Job wonderfully illustrates what is meant by an "honourable" man. Job is richly blessed. He has many sons, many herds and many possessions. He is highly regarded in his community and is able to sustain others with his gifts and his wisdom. In a culture in which honour is such a valued characteristic, it would be hard to express more strongly the conundrum that the book of Job elucidates. Here is a truly honourable man, a man, indeed, honoured by God himself: how can it possibly be that he suffers?

We have already noted that relationships between the sexes are governed by what the "group" prizes. Here we need to note that concepts of honour strongly inform the preferences of the group with regard to male/female relationships. It has to be admitted that there seems to operate a considerable double standard with regard to sexual behaviour. There is a rigorous compulsion upon women to retain their premarital virginity and later to refrain from any extra-marital sexual relationships. They are to keep their ^{c}ird (female honour) free from contamination at all costs. Similar restrictions do not apply to men, considerable numbers of whom (at some stage of their life) visit prostitutes in the towns and cities with comparative freedom. It constitutes no degradation of a man's honour if he plays with a prostitute, for she is nothing anyway. The Arabic word for "virgin" (^{c}adhrâ') is a feminine noun always used to refer to women. There is no masculine equivalent. A phrase has to be utilised to express the fact that a male has had no sexual experience before marriage. Perhaps the double standard diminishes in intensity when it is understood that honour requires the protection (not restriction) of females because they are a precious commodity. In their purity is invested the honour of all the lineage.

The Semitic culture of Old Testament times reflects the tensions of a society operating along equivalent lines. At one stage a wronged woman, Tamar, made use of the accepted male access to prostitutes to claim the justice owing to her by her father-in-law, Judah. Old Judah, founder of one of the tribes of Israel, had a problem. His eldest son had married Tamar and had died, leaving her childless. He consequently married his second son, Onan, to her as custom required but the relationship didn't work out. Onan was punished by the Lord for refusing to allow Tamar to have children by him. The penalty was death! Judah was fearful of marrying his third son to the woman in case he also ended up as a corpse. So he prevaricated. Eventually Tamar's patience wore out. She decided to trap Judah into acknowledging that he had not dealt properly with her. She dressed as a prostitute and sat by a road used by Judah. Soon he walked by, was attracted to the girl by the roadside and made an approach. A little later he was sleeping unwittingly with Tamar, thinking he was merely playing with a harlot. Ironically, as a result of their intercourse, Tamar conceived twins. When Judah later heard that his widowed daughter-in-law was pregnant he was furious. She had dishonoured his family's reputation and he wanted to burn her to death. She, however, had proof that Judah himself was the father of the boys in her womb. The tribal leader had to admit that his failure to preserve the honour of the family (in refusing to marry his third son to her) had caused the situation in which she had had to behave like a woman with no honour (Genesis 38).

As I have intimated, premarital virginity in girls has not so much to do with sex *per se*, but is a sign of the successful seclusion of females by their male relatives. In the women's proper seclusion lies the men's (hence, the tribe's) honour and prestige. In her novel *The Innocence of the Devil*, Nawal El-Saadawi expresses through the memory of Narguiss what such an emphasis often means for a female:

Honour.

Her father's voice rang out as he pronounced the word. He opened his mouth as wide as he could to let it out, as though he were yawning. He rolled it with his tongue pronouncing the two syllables separately. They seemed to fly out from his mouth together with drops of saliva. The ears of the women sitting in the shelter of the river bank picked them up as they echoed sharply. Their bodies shrunk into their *gallabeyas* at the sound. They held their knees and thighs closely together, leaving no space. They muttered words from the Koran to chase away devils and evil spirits. Honour meant chastity, and chastity was more valued than land. The men inherited it in a line from father to son. No one would dare as much as to touch someone else's honour, be he a spirit, or a genie with powers above those of ordinary men. The stigma of dishonour, of losing one's honour, could only be washed off by blood. And blood alone was the mark of an intact honour [hymen] on the wedding night. The *daya* [midwife] would be there with her finger tapering into a long sharp tip at the nail which she plunged into the fine membrane. Blood poured out on to the white towel which was held high to flutter above people's heads. The women let out a chorus of shrill *you yous* and the drums beat. The breasts of the men and the husbands could now swell and their noses rise as high as the ceiling above. For honour meant the honour of the male, even if the proof of it was in the body of the female.[94]

When it comes to a traditional wedding, in many Muslim societies there is no hesitation about celebrating a girl's sexuality in very open ways. The bride's defloration is almost public, and certainly the groom can be assisted by a midwife or close female relative if he is unable to consummate the marriage himself. Evelyn Early records the recollections of Zakiyya as that Egyptian woman thinks back to her wedding night:

> "After my wedding, we consummated the marriage in the same room in which we now sleep. I was scared and tried to find a window so I could jump out! Ahmad was patient and just laughed. My father-in-law kept pounding on the door to see what had happened. Finally my mother-in-law and my aunt came in and held me and Ahmad used his finger with a piece of gauze which was bloodied. My father displayed it when people brought money, and then my family took it and washed it. My sister-in-law was de-virginized by a midwife."[95]

The showing of a blood-spotted cloth feels distasteful to Western onlookers for whom sexuality is a private matter. For Middle Easterners, the coloured bed linen doesn't convey thoughts of intercourse but of honour and pride.

In a fascinating study of the Iqar'iyen, a Berber-speaking community of sedentary farmers living on the eastern Rif (Morocco), Raymond Jamous summarises his analysis of their preoccupation with honour in terms of aggressive and submissive behaviour. Amongst the Iqar'iyen, honour seems to derive from the exercise of authority over domains that are conceived of as forbidden (*ḥarâm*), such as land and women. Kin groups watch over land, and individual males take care of their women. Honour can be increased or obtained by invading the forbidden domains of others in "exchanges of violence". Exchanges of violence take different forms such as contests of oratory, conspicuous spending of wealth, theft of property, physical injury and actual killing. By such exchanges, a group or an individual can challenge or counter-challenge an opponent. Through the ongoing process, honour is continuously being won, lost and regained. In order that exchanges of violence be restricted from running completely out of control and ending in unrestrained feuding, mediators with access to *baraka* (grace or blessing from God) are on hand and are sought out by the Iqar'iyen. The mediators are local saints and they dispense an honour which derives from God; its price is obedience to the saint concerned. Jamous' analysis highlights the fact that the domain of the forbidden is central both to the conduct of honour (protecting of land and women) and to the conduct of submission towards saintly *baraka* (deriving from lineage via women and land).[96]

The theme of honour and its gain, retention and loss, forms a strong component of most Middle Eastern cultures. For men, it is a matter of publicly proving oneself a man. This is achieved through behaviour that exemplifies socially constructed masculine ideals. For women, it is a question of living in such a way that epitomises culturally agreed-upon feminine ideals (see Figure 12).[97]

Figure 12
Honour for men and women

Honour for Men		
⇧	⇐ Honour for Women	
⇧	⇧	
assertiveness	sexual purity prior to marriage	
⇧	⇧	
success in competing with men of equal rank	complete fidelity to one's husband after marriage	
⇧		
control and protection of women of one's family		

Walking the tightrope

It emerges, therefore, that a major goal in many Middle Easterners' lives is to accumulate honour and avoid its erosion. Social control, for such people, is essentially exercised by the dynamics of shaming, for it is through shame that honour is quickly eroded. Such a form of

"Facing" the world

social control depends on everyone knowing everything about anyone. This is quite easily achieved in a community-oriented society. "Gossip" becomes the public expression of the shaming mechanism. Saving face – preventing gossip – is all-important within such a culture. A single-shame experience threatens to expose and damage the whole self, or family.

Rarely, in the relating of Christian missionaries to Muslims, and especially to believers from a Muslim background, is the seriousness of saving face understood. Western Christians, for example, consider dishonesty a serious sin. I smacked my daughters once for doing the bad deed, whatever it might have been, and once more "for lying to me about it". At all costs, honesty must be adhered to. That same presupposition about the primacy of honesty dictates how I relate to brothers and sisters from a non-Western background. What happens if the Muslim, or the believer from a Muslim background, gives the Westerner like myself an answer which he thinks the Westerner wants to hear, even though that answer isn't strictly truthful? In his view, he has "lied" in order to preserve the Westerner's honour and to save his own face. To question the Middle Easterner, even in private, is to question his integrity. It is to announce that he has got his priorities wrong. It is to communicate that it is more important (more Christian?) to walk all over relationships for the sake of some impersonal ideal concerning honesty. It is to shame him. Of course, lying is not approved of in Muslim cultures any more than it is in Western cultures. There are subtle ways, however, of letting the other person understand that you know what is really the case. Those subtle ways maintain the human relationship:

> "Face" [*wajh*] is the outward appearance of honor, the "front" of honor which a man will strive to preserve even if in actuality he has committed a dishonorable act . . . One is considered justified, for instance, in resorting to prevarication in order to save one's face. If it comes to saving somebody else's "face", lying becomes a duty.[98]

Duane Elmer illustrates the "subtle way" of handling misdemeanours in a face-saving culture. He describes a situation in a hospital in Nigeria where an employee is known to be stealing. Senior Western and Nigerian staff consult in order to find a strategy for dealing with the thief. The Westerners opt for directly confronting the individual with the fact that he is known to be stealing. The Nigerian hospital administrator, however, proposes another approach – he wants to tell a story. Agreement is reached, the hospital staff members are brought together and the administrator tells his story of two villages. The tale begins with one person in one village stealing from his neighbours. Soon every person in that village distrusts all his neighbours. Folk in the second village monitor the growing disintegration within the first village and one day seize the opportunity to attack it. The first village is captured and its people are enslaved. End of story! In the hospital, the stealing stopped. The thief had received the message that he had been discovered yet there had been no losing of face. Moreover, all the staff of the hospital had learned a valuable lesson.[99]

Lying and cheating in much of the Middle Eastern world are not primarily moral matters but ways of safeguarding honour and status, ways of avoiding shame. A differentiation is made between what is presented to the outside world and what is true "on the inside", as it were. One's public face is different from one's inner self.[100] The Shî[c]a concept of dissimulation (*taqîya*) is a case in point. This allowance whereby true Shî[c]a Muslims may act as if they are not true Shî[c]a Muslims was actively promoted by Imam Khomeini during the Shah's reign. It was only at the appropriate moment that the dissimulation was laid aside and the true colours of Iran's clerics and people shown to the light of day.[101] Temporary marriage is another concept (seemingly hypocritical with regard to fidelity) which is intermittently promoted by Shî[c]a Muslims. A man away from home may take a "wife" for the duration of his absence in order to stop him from flirting with other men's wives or behaving in equivalent dishonourable ways. In Moghadam's view, the practice of temporary marriage in Iran underlines her contention that female sexuality is essentially seen as a tradeable object. She angrily suggests that "the two categories of permanent and temporary marriage can be viewed as sale and lease options for the consumption of female sexuality".[102] Leased sexuality notwithstanding, a major component of the practice is the avoidance of shame ensuing from likely (male) misconduct. That concern for shame avoidance eclipses any recognition that temporary marriage might be construed as straining at a gnat and swallowing a camel as far as sexual purity is concerned.

Often, in Middle Eastern cultures, a person will offer to accomplish something in order to save face, knowing that he cannot deliver the goods because he doesn't have the connections to achieve the promised end. The ensuing delays, postponements and renewals of promise are a bluff, providing time for a human connection to emerge which might save the day. A Westerner caught up in such dynamics quickly concludes that the person stringing him along is being dishonest. In reality the Middle Easterner is avoiding shame by making the promise today and not worrying about the consequences tomorrow. Not worrying about the consequences in the future is less of an evil than the possibility of losing face should he not make the promise now.

Another common dynamic in Arab contexts is the expressing of generosity by one person towards another whilst the very person making the expansive gestures is actually plotting against the other. Two-facedness is a normal part of Arab diplomacy. This has been demonstrated recently in the exposure of the funding by Saudia Arabia, the United Arab Emirates and Kuwait – all strong allies of the USA – of many Islamist movements, some of which have been implicated in recent terrorist attacks against American military and civilian personnel in different parts of the world. Similarly, Saudi Arabia has pursued a policy of open support for the Middle East preace process while massively funding HAMAS, the Palestinian militant branch of the Muslim Brotherhood which is adamantly opposed to the existence of Israel. In these delicate (and other, equivalent) situations, everyone except the foreigner knows what "games" are going on. High at stake in those games – higher certainly than any superficial reading of right and wrong – is the matter of honour and shame.

In the story *The Haj* by Leon Uris, the patriarchal father of the main Palestinian family in the book finally dies when he is told about an incident in his family's life that had been kept hidden from him for years. Earlier, during a civil disturbance and consequent act of punishment by the authorities, Iraqi soldiers had run amok in the quarter of Jaffa where the family lived. The father, Haj Ibrahim, was absent at the time and sadly, his womenfolk had been horrifically raped. Towards the end of the book, Haj Ibrahim murders his daughter after she defiantly refuses to marry a relative of his choosing, announcing that she is a virgin no longer but has willingly slept with men. Haj Ibrahim's son, who had witnessed the scene in Jaffa when he was a young lad, hates his father for killing his beloved sister. He seeks to avenge her death by telling his father about what had happened those many years before:

"Oh yes, yes. I am going to kill you Father, but I'll do it my own way. I don't need your dagger. I'm just going to talk. I'm going to talk you to death. So open your ears, Father, and listen very carefully." He stared at me. I began. "In Jaffa, I witnessed both of your wives and Fatima being raped by Iraqi soldiers!"[103]

The old man cannot believe it, but his son insists it is true and crudely describes the scene in detail. The shock of Haj Ibrahim's immense loss of honour gives the old man a heart attack and he dies – of shame.

The holy cities of Mecca and Medina are out of bounds to non-Muslims. Why? Because they are places, supremely, where the integrity of Muslim peoples must not be compromised by the intrusion of non-believers. Even the more general geography of Arab territory has to be kept intact from any incursion that would bruise Arab pride. The United States of America learned, during the 1991 Gulf War, how critical it was to keep Israeli warplanes from overflying Arab territories despite the Jews' desire to avenge the Iraqi SCUD attacks on their country. With Arab already fighting Arab, it couldn't possibly be allowed to look as if some Arabs were actually cooperating with the Israelis.

Letting the side down

Shame is a social phenomenon. It is equivalent to disgrace or humiliation. It operates as a form of control on behaviour. "What people say" or "What people might say" is a strong constraint on actions. As such, "shame" carries two possible connotations. Sometimes it refers in a positive way to women's honour – a woman will refuse to act in a certain way "for the shame of it". Sometimes it signifies a diminution or loss of social standing – shame has taken hold of an individual or family, a tribe or nation.

The use of oaths in such profusion in many Middle Eastern societies illustrates the lengths to which people go in order to avoid being shamed. Their frequent use betrays both the universal distrust and untruthfulness which abounds and the attempt to cover it up. Preserving appearances is very important. As one proverb declares: "Eat for yourself and dress for others."

Shame comes from being a "bad" person. One may lose esteem

through cowardice, having no money, being menial, remaining unmarried, letting down one's family or religion.

As suggested, sexuality is a great cornerstone of honour and the likeliest cause of shame. Women have consequently to avoid at all costs any sense of impropriety. A famous incident in the life of the Prophet serves as a warning to all Muslim women. It concerned the Prophet's wife ᶜÂ'isha. The incident is recounted in several collections of *hadîth*. In this version, ᶜÂ'isha tells the story from her perspective:

Narrated Aisha: Whenever Allah's Apostle intended to go on a journey, he used to draw lots amongst his wives, and Allah's Apostle used to take with him the one on whom the lot fell. He drew lots amongst us during one of the Ghazwat [battles] which he fought. The lot fell on me and so I proceeded with Allah's Apostle after Allah's order of veiling (the women) had been revealed. I was carried (on the back of a camel) in my howdah [carriage] and carried down while still in it (when we came to a halt). So we went on till Allah's Apostle had finished from that Ghazwa [battle] of his and returned. When we approached the city of Medina, he announced at night that it was time for departure. So when they announced the news of departure, I got up and went away from the army camps, and after finishing from the call of nature, I came back to my riding animal. I touched my chest to find that my necklace which was made of Zifar beads (i.e. Yemenite beads partly black and partly white) was missing. So I returned to look for my necklace and my search for it detained me. (In the meanwhile) the people who used to carry me on my camel, came and took my howdah and put it on the back of my camel on which I used to ride, as they considered that I was in it. In those days women were light in weight for they did not get fat, and flesh did not cover their bodies in abundance as they used to eat only a little food. Those people therefore, disregarded the lightness of the howdah while lifting and carrying it; and at that time I was still a young girl. They made the camel rise and all of them left (along with it). I found my necklace after the army had gone. Then I came to their camping place to find no call maker of them, nor one who would respond to the call. So I intended to go to the place where I used to stay, thinking that they would miss me and come back to me (in my search). While I was sitting in my resting place, I was overwhelmed by sleep and slept. Safwan bin Al-Mu'attal As-Sulami Adh-Dhakwani was behind the army. When he reached my place in the morning, he saw the figure of a sleeping person and he recognised me on seeing me as he had seen me before the order of compulsory veiling (was prescribed). So I woke up when he recited Istirja' (i.e. "Truly to Allah we belong and truly to Him we shall return" [2:156]) as soon as he recognized me. I veiled my face with my head cover at once, and by Allah, we did not speak a single word, and I did not hear him saying any word besides his Istirja'. He dismounted from his camel and made it kneel down, putting his leg on its front legs and then I got up and rode on it. Then he set out leading the camel that was carrying me till we overtook the army in the extreme heat of midday while they were at a halt (taking a rest). (Because of the event) some people brought destruction upon themselves and the one who spread the Ifk (i.e. slander) more, was Abdullah bin Ubai Ibn Salul.[104]

The slander involved the fact that a wife of the Prophet had spent time alone with a young soldier. A rumour quickly circulated that she and he had made love. Prophet Muḥammad was extremely upset and ordered ᶜÂ'isha to remain in her parents' house until he could determine whether the accusations were accurate or not. ᶜÂ'isha was extremely upset to think that her husband could conceive of her behaving in an improper manner. After a month, a revelation came to Muḥammad (Sura 24:23) which exonerated ᶜÂ'isha and determined penalties for the sin of slander.

In the Old Testament, sexual overtones are often utilised in passages dealing with shaming. Those overtones sometimes come by way of euphemism. In Isaiah 7:20 the Lord threatens to use the Assyrian emperor as a "hired razor" to shave the head, beard and "hair of your legs" of the rebellious people of Israel. The Assyrians were famous for their use of shaming as an element in psychological warfare; they frequently paraded bound captives naked through their streets. The shaving of the "hair of your legs" is consequently treated by some commentators as a euphemism for the removal of genital hair. Quite blatant is the incident where David sends a delegation to King Hanun of the Ammonites to convey his condolences over Hanun's father's death (2 Samuel 10). Hanun's courtiers smell a plot and persuade their inexperienced young king to shave away half the beards and half the trousers of David's men. The latter are sent home, "greatly humiliated", with bare bottoms. Shame and sex are often interrelated.

The nasty incident between Jacob's family and the Shechemites (recorded in Genesis 34) well illustrates the fact that, in that kind of society, men's honour is made vulnerable through the sexual behaviour of their women. In other words, sex constitutes a political or "honour" matter. Did Shechem actually rape Dinah or did his treating her "like a prostitute" (verse 31) rather mean that he persuaded her to consent to his overtures? Certainly the text emphasises the positive emotions he held towards Dinah: "His heart was drawn to Dinah daughter of Jacob, and he loved the girl and spoke tenderly to her" (verse 3). Certainly, also, the young man wished to marry her. I'm not trying to diminish the violation aspect of a powerful male having his way with a visiting maiden. But I am questioning whether the shame lies simply in the act of violation or whether it is really focused in the Jacobite perception of an outsider, a foreigner, violating the boundaries of the kinship unit. By this latter interpretation, Shechem had shamed the sons of Jacob in his seducing of their sister by announcing in effect that they were unable to protect the prestige and honour of their tribe. Perhaps that explains more appropriately the brothers' violent and all-embracing reaction. Every male in Shechem's city is killed, every donkey, flock, herd, child, woman carried off – to make what point? Simply: "You must not make love to our sister" or more comprehensibly: "We will avenge any hint that our position as honourable males is being undermined"?

Naguib Mahfouz describes the lives of ordinary Egyptians in his book *The Beginning and the End*. One character is Bahia, engaged to be married to Hassanein. Despite her being engaged, Bahia is ultra-cautious about accepting any of the amorous advances of her fiancé:

> With a perplexed smile on his face, he listened to her. His eyes were devouring her plump body with pleasure. She was wearing a decent, almost prudish dress which revealed her arms, the lower part of her legs, her delicate white neck, and the outlines of her soft, plump body. His eyes remained fixed on the round, minutely latticed parts of her dress above the chest, designed by the dressmaker to fit her blossoming bosom that seemed almost on the point of bursting out. As he imagined that he was softly stroking her breasts with his fingers, his body shook with a quiver of desire. He imagined that he was squeezing them, but their stiffness resisted him. Thirsty with desire, he swallowed. But he knew she would neither respond to him nor allow him to come too close to her body, and that she would persist in her adamant attitude of refusal. He had hoped that with the passage of time he would reach her, but he finally realized the futility of his hope.[105]

Bahia knew that her life depended upon her staying pure beyond all suspicion if she was ever going to proceed to marriage with Hassanein.

In real-life Egypt in the 1980s, other girls died because males' honour had been undermined:

> A Bedouin strangled and then electrocuted his 16-year-old daughter because she had been raped and brought him disgrace, police said.[106]
>
> A young wife . . . left her husband's house . . . because of their continual quarrelling. Her family searched for her but with no success till two of her brother's friends chanced to see her in Saida Zeinab. The brother hurried to the place where he found his sister in the company of two young men . . . The brother planned his revenge and after a while phoned his sister and told her that he had forgiven her and she could return to her father's house. In his father's house the brother killed his sister . . . [He] gave himself up to the police and told the investigator that the killing wiped out the shame which his sister had brought on him and his family.[107]

Similar incidents occurred in Pakistan in the 1990s. The Human Rights Commission of Pakistan estimates that in 1999 alone "more than 1000 women were killed by their husbands or other male relatives for allegedly committing adultery or other acts considered to impinge on family honour".[108]

In April 2000, Serb police and militia entered a remote Kosovar Albanian Muslim village. There they raped ten women villagers. Human rights investigators later discovered that the women were terrified that they would be blamed for what happened with the consequence that they would be expelled from their husbands' families and separated from their children. An investigative report of the Organisation for Security and Cooperation in Europe reveals that many "a 'good' woman would rather kill herself than continue to live after having been raped".[109]

Sana al-Khayyat quotes in translation unpublished verses by an Iraqi poetess expressing a female perspective on the kind of honour crimes highlighted in the previous paragraphs:

> Dawn will come and the girls will ask about her,
> Where is she? And the monster will answer:
> "We killed her."

A mark of shame was on our forehead and we washed it off.
Her black tale will be told by neighbours,
And will be told in the quarter even by the palm trees,
Even the wooden doors will not forget her,
It will be whispered even by the stones.
Washing off the shame . . . Washing off the shame.
O neighbours, O village girls,
Bread we shall knead with our tears.

We'll shear our plaits and skin our hands,
To keep their clothes white and pure,
No smile, no joy, no turn as the knife so waiting
For us in the hand of father or brother
And tomorrow, who knows which desert
Swallows us, to wash off shame.[110]

A powerful theme

In the honour/shame syndrome lies a strong motivation for making a
success of a marriage. Personal human relationships, in Arab
cultures, mostly begin with family honour and, hopefully, move on
to mutual love. One is reminded of the story of Abraham's provision
of a wife for his son Isaac. The girl has to come from his own
extended family and that will require a long journey back to
Babylonia for his trusted servant Eliezer. The faithful servant is led
by the Lord to the very girl who would be most appropriate for Isaac
to marry. She is the daughter of Abraham's brother's son (see Figure
13). Eventually, Eliezer conveys the second cousin back to the
Negev and Isaac marries Rebekah. The Genesis account states: "So
she became his wife, and he loved her" (Genesis 24:67). This
arranged marriage began with honour and progressed to love.

In Arab cultures, arranged marriages offer the potential of strong
support for the new husband and wife. Amongst other considerations,
a couple will be encouraged to live in a harmonious relationship with
each other partly because a divorce would bring unbearable shame on
the whole extended family:

Hasib and Fairouz were very keen to get their sons married to suitable
girls as soon as possible. It was the custom for parents to arrange the
marriages of their children. Fairouz spent over a year looking for the

right girl for Anwar, carefully checking out families and their back-grounds. She wanted the perfect match – a good-looking, well-educated girl from a religious and wealthy Sunni family with a good reputation and easy to get on with as prospective relations. The women of the family would spend many hours discussing different girls, describing them in detail and comparing their virtues. Everyone in the extended family was involved in these discussion.

Finally Fairouz found the perfect match. The Muslim custom is to repeat a special prayer twice, just before falling asleep, asking God for guidance. Any memorable dreams that night are then assumed to be God's answer to the petition. Pleasant dreams meant "yes"; but night-mares indicated a definite "no".

Grandmother, father, mother, uncles and aunts – all performed this ritual on the same night. The next morning they would report back. On this occasion everyone reported pleasant dreams – one had dreamt she was swimming in beautifully clear water, the other that he was walking high up in the mountains with a wonderful view all around him, the grass green, the sun shining – all were positive, and so they took it as confir-mation from God and set about planning the marriage arrangements.

The couple was married just after Anwar graduated from university. They experienced quite a bit of marital trouble during their first year, as they had not known each other at all before their wedding. Then the extended family would get involved, to mediate, until they were more used to living together.[111]

Figure 13
Isaac and Rebekah

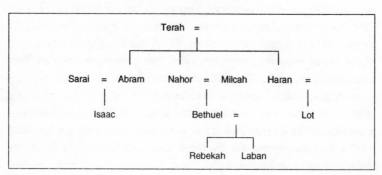

Without family support, marriages can become very lonely affairs. A friend told me of a situation in a North African country in which an associate of his – a doctor from Egypt – wanted to marry an

Egyptian woman who was a nurse in the hospital where they both worked. After an elaborate engagement, the head of the young doctor's family back in Egypt objected to the planned union because the woman was an orphan, without any family. Moreover, as a nurse, she was seen to be involved in a profession with exceedingly low kudos. The honour of the doctor's family was at stake. The family threatened to exclude the doctor if he went ahead with the marriage. The couple decided to proceed with their wedding and sadly all communication with the young man's family was terminated. No serious attempt at reconciliation was made.

The honour/shame syndrome has important consequences for other aspects of human interrelation, besides marriage. In the West, public interaction is ordered on a written, contractual basis. In a culture where human relationships predominate, oral contracts are deemed preferable. Written contracts imply distrust, constituting an insult to a person's honour.

Similarly with processes of education. Oral methods and oral views of cultural transmission are deemed more valid than impersonal, inductive ones. A "literate" person is likely to be someone who has committed more things to memory. He holds in trust the heritage of the group. Such a person is considered more learned and is held in greater esteem than someone with a broader or deeper, more methodical power of thought, but who has committed less knowledge to memory.

The Arab–Israeli conflict cannot be understood apart from the intense shame the Arabs suffered in the overwhelming defeats they sustained in the 1948, 1956 and 1967 wars. A redemption of Arab honour on the battlefield was desperately needed, and sought. The Arab "victory" of 1973 made it possible for peace in the Middle East to become part of the Arab agenda. Now, at last, they could sit across a negotiating table from Israelis as men of honour and integrity. The aftermath of the Iraq war of 2003 cannot be appreciated without reference to the themes of honour and shame. For sure, the majority of Iraqis were happy for the regime of Saddam Hussein to be brought to a close. But equally, the majority of liberated Iraqis had no desire for Americans or British to rule them, organise them or tell them how to form a government. Deep resentment among Iraqis and most Arabs, probably among the majority of Muslims, is felt for the fact that an American, "Christian" White House planned and executed a regime change in Iraq outside the aegis of the United Nations, came to the Middle East with tanks and bombs to effect that change, and then outstayed its muted welcome by far too long.

Inequality through performance is prized by Westerners. We don't mind promoting some people to high office and assigning others to menial tasks, but we do it on the basis of individual ability. In fact we make differentiation along the lines of personal achievement one of the major goals of our educational and economic systems. Inequality through honour or shame is despised by Westerners. "Equal opportunities" is one of our slogans. We don't appoint people to lectureships in our universities because they happen to be upright relatives of the Chancellor or President. For Arabs generally, the shoe is on the other foot. Honour and human connection are greater promoters of advancement than individual achievement. In international incidents like World War II, therefore, the Arab is not so much swayed by arguments of right and wrong. Rather, he will wait until he perceives who might win a contest and thereby gain honour. He will then want to join that team.

Many Muslims who become followers of Jesus suffer the anger of their family, even expulsion from it. The main reason for such suffering is not because the family hates Jesus but because it senses unbearable shame in having a member deny his or her cultural and religious heritage. The whole family will be seen as "letting the side down" in an unbelievably major way:

> My son,
> do not abandon the commandments of God to follow the devil's wiles. It is I who warn you: do not leave in my heart a wound whose pain I shall feel as long as I live. Have I not worry enough in caring for your little brothers? Do not let my heart suffer and burn with pain. Do not be the cause which makes me bow my head before God. What pains I have already suffered for the sake of yourself and your brothers! And you pay me back by an offence, worse, a shame, which will attach to me and to the whole family for ever.[112]

In terms of honour and shame a Syrian father writes in such a manner to his son in 1966, having just heard that the youth has become a Christian while studying abroad.

In the Old Testament, the word "honour" and its derivatives occur

115 times, and 73 times in the New Testament. The name of Jabez stands out in a careful reading of the genealogical lists: he is eulogised for being "more honourable than his brothers" (1 Chronicles 4:9). Our Western eyes quickly skip over this accolade. The culture of which we are a part would possibly commemorate a man for academic, political, sporting or media achievement, hardly for being honourable. In Semitic cultures, however, honour is carefully celebrated.

As a consequence, "sinning" tends to be perceived, according to the evidence of the Bible, as the violating of honour. Such a perception is not just a facet of popular culture but is part of the authoritative teaching of the revealed text. In the case of Amnon's physical assault on his sister, a sense of shame pervades her being, although she has done no wrong. She pleads with him not to rape her, predicting the sure result in terms of a shattering of her honour: "What about me? Where could I get rid of my disgrace?" (2 Samuel 13:13) Job's confused complaint revolves around the fact that God has stripped him of his honour (Job 19:9) and yet the upright man is unaware of any disloyalty on his part.

The ultimate test of Jesus' loyalty to his Father is couched precisely in terms of the violation of honour. Is he willing to suffer unjust shame? The Son submits to arrest in the garden of Gethsemane. Hours later, at Calvary, he "endured the cross, despising the shame . . ." (Hebrews 12:2). Not long after Jesus' resurrection and ascension, his apostles are twice arrested for preaching in his name in the centre of Jerusalem. Although they are saved from death by the judicious Gamaliel, they are all beaten severely and banned yet again from preaching. The apostles leave the Sanhedrin rejoicing "because they had been counted worthy of suffering disgrace for the Name" (Acts 5:41).

One of the loveliest parables in the New Testament is often lost on Western Christians who have learned to see it only in terms of "the prodigal son". Jesus' own introduction should at least warn us that as much attention should be paid to the two other main characters in the story: "There was a man who had two sons" (Luke 15:11). The story is about disloyalty, the breakdown of commitment to kith and kin. The younger son wants his father dead so that he can receive his inheritance straight away. The older son abandons his expected role of reconciler and mediator between violated father and disloyal younger brother. The story is full of shame – easily perceived perhaps in the prodigal's abandonment of personal integrity, so that in the end he is worse off than the despised, unclean pigs. The older son is disloyal also, though more subtly so. He does not play his required role in the family when relationships begin to disintegrate. At the end, his abandonment of commitment to his father's joy and love display the step he has himself taken, away from the family. He speaks coldly of "slaving" for his father. "You never : . ." is on his lips. "This son of yours . . ." is how he thinks of his brother now. As the parable concludes, the hearer is left with a terrible thought: is this second prodigal son about to slap his pleading father, turn on his heel and march away from the distraught parent? His words and actions have been unthinkable, shameful.

Supremely in this story, as told by Jesus, shame is featured in the father's willing embrace of it. He accepts the younger son's rejection of him and lets him go. He accepts the humiliation of having to plead with his elder son for the latter to join him in his celebrating. In the little words of verse 20, the incredible (for a Semitic culture) is disclosed. The father "ran to his son" – down the street, through the village, showing his undergarments! The old man runs to reach, accept and protect the lad who should by rights be disinherited and sent packing. In the Middle East, old men never run! They never have done! This old man embraces the shame and takes the initiative with his younger son, just as a little later he will embrace more shame and go cap in hand to his elder son.[113] Jesus is hinting that such is the larger story of God and humankind. God is full of honour and integrity, yet dishonoured and shamed by his earthly children. Heaven's answer is to come in the Son to be dishonoured, to embrace the shame, to be beaten to death.

Keys for communicating?

The Arab Muslim lives in a group-oriented context where vertical relationships are predominant. The cultural theme most valued is honour. Shame is to be avoided at all costs. Daily living becomes a question, largely, of navigating successfully through the uncharted water that lies between honour and shame. One cannot express too strongly the significance and influence in many Muslim cultures of the honour/shame syndrome.

Figure 14

Huber's illustration of shame sanctions in Hebrew biblical culture

Shame as . . .	Seen in . . .
an element in psychological warfare	the cruelty of the Assyrians; they put a hook in the nose of Manasseh king of Judah and parade him shackled; other captives they are known to have displayed naked in order to humiliate them (2 Chronicles 33:11)
a sanction on behaviour in the judicial system	flogging being limited to 40 lashes lest "your brother be degraded in your eyes" (Deuteronomy 25:3)
grounds for appeal by the psalmist justifying entitlement to divine help	the psalmist's cry, "Do not let me be put to shame, nor let my enemies triumph over me" (Psalm 25:2)
potentially attributable to God himself in order to point out incongruities and elicit blessing	the psalmist's reminder, "Remember how fools mock you [Lord] all day long" (Psalm 74:22)

Western cultures, being deeply committed to individualism, tend to cohere around concepts of law and guilt, rather than loyalty and shame. Westerners must abide within the law. They are not overly concerned with saving one another's face. A strictly law-based, guilt-oriented expression of the gospel may be appropriate within Western cultures, but it doesn't make the most sense for cultures that operate by different convictions.[114] Once again, the Bible offers deep insight into cultures functioning on an honour/shame basis.

L.B. Huber wrote her doctoral thesis on the biblical experience of shame/shaming. She illustrates four ways in which the culture of ancient Israelite society lent itself to shame sanctioning (see Figure 14).[115]

Among the prophetic writings, the book of Jeremiah graphically expresses what sin means, in terms of shame. Half the chapters in the prophecy contain the word itself. Others use words like "dishonour", "disgrace", "blush", "derision", "hiss" or phrases implying shame like "lift up your skirts". Johanna Stiebert has the following to say about the strong sexual metaphors in Jeremiah's prophecy:

Effusive and (notable in Jeremiah) bestial sexual activity is a vehicle for condemning apostasy and is linked to foreign practices. It appears to be aimed at effecting revulsion and restraint in the form of proper shame.[116]

The point of shame in Jeremiah's prophecy is that the Old Testament people of God have abandoned their loyalty to Yahweh, the God of their forefathers. They are engaging in every type of open sin including idolatry and yet they are denying that anything is really wrong because they are still offering sacrifices at the temple (Jeremiah 7:4). Jeremiah declares that Israel has become shameless:

> You have the brazen look of a prostitute;
>   you refuse to blush with shame.
> Have you not just called to me:
>   "My Father, my friend from my youth,
> Will you always be angry?
>   Will your wrath continue forever?"
> This is how you talk,
>   but you do all the evil you can.
>
> (Jeremiah 3:3–5)

Jeremiah uses shame discourses like this to draw attention to the people's misconduct; it has led to a fracture in their relationship with the Lord. The prophet wants to inculcate a sense of shame that is strong enough to cause the people to redress the situation. For sure, in their misdeeds, the people are breaking the law; they are guilty of lawlessness. But the thing that hurts the Lord most is that, in their lawlessness, they are expressing their prior rejection of him. They "sin" by refusing to really relate to him as Father or Friend. They spit in his face and dishonour him before all the nations. What's more, they are not ashamed of themselves! Exile becomes God's only option. The people have to be evicted from the land because the pollution they have brought upon themselves as a result of idolatry has rendered the land itself infertile.

One clear expression of repentance comes out in the book. It is that of "Ephraim", and it occurs after the judgement of God has begun to fall on the inhabitants of Jerusalem. Some of the leaders of the people are already in exile and God detects the inklings of sorrow amongst them:

After I strayed,
    I repented;
after I came to understand,
    I beat my breast.
I was ashamed and humiliated
    because I bore the disgrace of my youth.

(Jeremiah 31:19)

Repentance is expressed in terms of the recognition of shame and disgrace. The people are waking up to what has really happened in their relationship to God. That is why, in this chapter, the grounds are laid for a new relationship in a new covenant. "I will be their God, and they will be my people" (verse 33) is how the Lord expresses it. The recovery is promised in terms of a renewal of kinship.

Barth Campbell, in his study of honour and shame in the first letter of Peter, makes the broad claim, "The pivotal value in first-century Mediterranean society is honor"[117] and he goes on to describe aspects of "ascribed honour" and "acquired honour" much as we have exegeted them in this chapter with regard to contemporary Muslim cultures. Concerning the letter written by Peter to bring comfort to a Christian community in conflict with pagan outsiders, Campbell asserts:

> The honor-shame terminology is abundant in the letter. Remarkable is the fact that, whenever an explicit reference to insider-outsider conflict in 1 Peter occurs, there is a corresponding reference to the honor to be granted the believers.[118]

Peter's intention, according to Campbell, is to encourage in his readers an honourable response in the honour/shame contest. Suffering, for a Christian, can be honourable (1 Peter 4:16).[119]

In his intriguing study on honour and shame in the Gospel of Matthew, Neyrey maintains that from chapter 2 to chapter 22 Jesus is presented as a most honourable and most honoured person:

> Everyone in Galilee, Tyre, Sidon, Syria, the Decapolis, Judea beyond the Jordan, and Jerusalem has heard about Jesus. Furthermore, he enjoyed a very positive evaluation, as crowds constantly flocked to him

and even served as a buffer between him and his envious enemies. Jesus may not enjoy a good reputation at Nazareth (13:57), but he does everywhere else.[120]

In sharing the gospel with Arabs and other Muslims who operate within honour/shame concepts, it will surely help if we learn to read our own faith from within those constructs.[121] There is plenty of assistance for us in the Bible, as we have begun to see.[122]

Phil Parshall comments that repentance and tears come quickly to people who function on an honour/shame basis when they know that they have been apprehended in an act that embarrasses them.[123] Can we convey to our Muslim friends that their disloyalty to God is known and is shameful? With regard to their answerability to the Lord of heaven and earth, have they become people who do as they please because they have lost a sense of shame? The mechanical, outward ritual acts may be in place, but are they concerned about God's honour?

One Western missionary describes a situation in which a young Christian from a Muslim background was being mercilessly punished for the shame he had brought on his family by turning to Christ. A revelation was needed in order for the family to realise that the greater shame was theirs, in resisting God's work in the young man's life:

His father was impossible. He would not respond to any of our explanations, or even to our returning good for evil. Seeing that the pressure was getting too much for the boy and that he might soon go back to Islam, I asked God to send his father a vision.

God answered. That night a white shining figure appeared to the father and said, "You have beaten your son and he did not recant. You had him bound in chains and he did not recant. If you touch your son again, you are going to die. He is showing you the way of salvation. Listen to him!"

The next day the father became a Christian![124]

A legitimate apologetic for the difficult issue of Jesus' crucifixion could conceivably be expressed in terms of God's honour. Lordship and submission are scriptural concerns (John 5:22–26; Philippians 2:9–11) and explain why Jesus acted as he did, why the cross was a means of bringing glory to God, not a contradiction of it. In Hebrews

12:2, Jesus is depicted as despising the shame of the cross. Perhaps his obedience to his Father, despite the cross, is a biblical example of positive shame, or shame "transfigured". Jesus is linked in Hebrews 12 with the exemplars of faith in chapter 11 who shared a disregard for "certain cultural norms of the honorable and shameful".[125] The crux of what was going on in Jesus' dying is vividly expressed in terms of honour and shame in the Hebrews passage. Neyrey sees both Jesus' birth and death presented, via narrative, in a way which highlights the matter of honour. "The actions of God at Jesus' birth are both grants of honor and defence of that honor," he claims.[126] The same divine patronage is at work at the occasion of Jesus' dying (see Figure 15).

Figure 15
Neyrey's highlighting of the divine defence of Jesus' honour
in Matthew's birth and death narratives

Infancy narrative	Passion narrative
Jesus as king of the Jews (2:2)	Jesus as king of the Jews (27:11, 29, 37)
Jesus as Son of God (2:15)	Jesus as Son of God (27:40, 43, 54)
negative reaction: all Jerusalem was troubled, along with the chief priests and scribes (2:3–4)	negative reaction: chief priests (26:65) and all Jerusalem (27:25) reject Jesus
God's providential care of Jesus: rescue from death (2:13–14, 20) and defence of Jesus' role and status	God's providential care of Jesus: rescue from death (28:6), vindication of Jesus' role and status (27:51–54) and ascription of maximum honour (28:18)
prodigies at Jesus' birth (2:2, 7–9); dreams on Jesus' behalf (2:13, 19)	prodigies at Jesus' death (27:51–54); dreams on Jesus' behalf (27:19)

According to Neyrey, then, the "honour" issue is integral to our understanding of what was at stake in both the birth and death of Jesus Christ. With biblical justification, it seems to me, it is as fair to emphasise the vertical relationship between Jesus and his Father as it is valid to emphasise the horizontal relationship between Jesus and humankind. Western Christianity applauds the latter emphasis, concentrating on incarnation and the personal self-giving of Christ so that whoever believes in him might be born again (John 3:16). Perhaps it is time to stop expecting the Muslim to see the love of God in the cross of Christ. It might be easier for him to glimpse there something of Christ's loyalty to his Father, something of the Father's glory in watching his Son obey him to the end, vindicating "family" honour and engendering providential acts that defend the Son's honour and true status.

There is a potent picture in the Old Testament of "rescue by honouring" in the climax to the calamity over the loss of the Ark of God. The Ark has been captured by the Philistines and removed to Ashdod. When it is set beside Dagon in Dagon's temple, bad things happen to Dagon in the middle of the night! Dagon ends up on his face before the Ark, head and hands broken and scattered on the temple floor. At the same time, terrible plague spreads throughout Ashdod. When the captured Ark is sent off to other cities, plague breaks out there also. After several major cities have suffered, the Philistines give up and decide to send the Ark back to its place among the people of Israel. But not without compensation, not without appeasement! The Philistine priests and diviners work out that a guilt offering should accompany the returning Ark. Their conclusion is that "five gold tumours and five gold rats, according to the number of the Philistine rulers" should constitute that guilt offering, hopefully making everything all right with Israel's God. The aim of the offering? " . . . to pay honour to Israel's god" (1 Samuel 6:5). Atonement is expressed in terms of the appeasing of honour. It is a lovely, frightening picture of what is at stake when God's honour is compromised by human sin. It looks forward to another act of atonement – this time on behalf of the whole of humanity – when Christ will become the sacrifice that appeases the honour of a wronged Creator.

Everrt Huffard suggests that a "Christology of honor" is as scriptural as any (Western) emphasis on the love of God being declared in Christ.[127] Of course such love is shown, but is it not significant that the synoptic gospels make little reference to it and Luke doesn't even mention *agapê* (God's special love for humanity) in his recounting of the missionary sermons of Acts? A concern for God's glory, honour, blamelessness and unmerited generosity seems rather to be documented – themes which make profound sense in the kind of cultural settings we are considering in this book.

In the difficult discipleship situation cited earlier (admittedly from a West African Muslim context), the authoritative vision from heaven convinced the human father that he should no longer oppose his son's conversion to Christ. The vision-word from God was strong enough to nullify the traditional theological reservations which Muslims have about the crucifixion. Such present-tense experiences of God's holiness are perhaps the best attestation to the possibility that in the original crucifixion event itself, a holy God was also strongly in charge maintaining his honour.[128]

CHAPTER FIVE

HOSPITALITY AND VIOLENCE

Feed the mouth and the eye will be bashful.

Middle Easterners observe many conventions of behaviour. There are certain phrases to be uttered or actions to be taken at the occurrence of almost any given event. Such conventions are learned from childhood. The weight of parental and religious authority ensures the passing on of appropriate behaviour from generation to generation.

"Our home is your home"

High on the list of conventions to which serious attention has to be paid is that which deals with hosting/visiting.

The Qur'ân encourages the sharing of hospitality:

> It is no fault . . . that ye
> Should eat in your own houses,
> Or those of your fathers,
> Or your mothers, or your brothers,
> Or your sisters, or your father's brothers
> Or your father's sisters,
> Or your mother's brothers,
> Or your mother's sisters,
> Or in houses of which
> The keys are in your possession,
> Or in the house of a sincere
> Friend of yours . . .
>
> (Sura 24:61)

In the *ḥadîth* literature, stress is laid on the need to accept an invitation to a feast. A person coming home from a journey should emulate Prophet Muḥammad in entertaining his friends at meals.

Time for coffee?

Social functions in which people eat together are recommended: "Gather at your meals, you will be blessed therein."[129]

Arabs and other Middle Easterners are famous for their generous hospitableness. Visits between relatives are frequent. Often they are made unannounced, at any time of day. They can last a considerable length of time. They might even be made at a place of work, not just at someone's home.

In the working out of community life, some visits are obligatory. The celebrations at the various rites of passage call for visiting/hosting, but so also do occasions such as the return of a person from a trip or the arrival of new neighbours, or the knowledge that someone has been taken ill. The serving of food and drink is central to such visiting/hosting. Eating together, or "sharing salt", honours visitors and hosts alike.[130] Only at the time of death might hospitality be restricted to the austere soberness of black coffee. A refusal to receive visitors is unthinkable, while to fail to make an obligatory visit threatens the fabric of life in an extended family.

The importance of hosting/visiting lies not just in the requirement that it occur, but in the manner in which it is carried out. How does a person receive guests? Is it with generous joy or grudging accommodation? A person will be judged on the basis of his hosting "face". How many miscommunications have unwittingly occurred between Westerners and Middle Easterners over the practical realities of this cultural theme? Westerners, as we shall see, have a highly developed sense of personal time and private space. We don't like those no-go areas invaded. "Private" and "personal" are nonentities for most Middle Easterners. For them, there's nothing quite like a visit to get the batteries recharged!

From the initial moment of greeting, to the order of seating and the words used to punctuate the visit, an elaborate game of "host and guest" is frequently played out. In that game, extravagant customs are expressions of habit rather than of ostentation. The atmosphere is usually relaxed and informal despite the fact that quite detailed points of etiquette constantly punctuate the encounter. God is invoked or praised continuously as the initial phrases of welcome proceed to the asking after one another's health. Wives are never asked about directly, but under the euphemism of "your home". During the visit, the guest is never allowed to be left alone. Conversation is continual. The host carefully avoids acting as if he has other business to attend to. Smiles, jokes, set phrases are all paraded to make the guest feel welcomed and special. No hosting/visiting can come to a conclusion without food or drink being offered and accepted. At the final end of a visit (and there are appropriate ways of extricating oneself from someone else's hospitality), ceremonious thanks and blessings are exchanged. God again features strongly in the reciprocated well-wishing.

In Arab homes, guests are always anticipated. A whole room is often set apart for accommodating any visitors who may appear. Poor people will put themselves in debt to family, friends or a local shop in order to feed a guest with food that celebrates by its quality the honour of the visitor. The same is true in other Muslim cultures:

> Travelling through Afghanistan, Tom's jeep broke down. It was late at night, and he stopped in a small village. There were no hotels or inns, so he knocked on the first door he found, wondering what would happen . . . Using sign language, he managed to communicate that he needed somewhere to sleep. The owner gave Tom a floor space and some blankets. It was pitch dark, and Tom was quickly asleep. Some time later, the owner woke him with a bowl of soup in his hands. It smelt wonderful, and the warmth and spice ensured that Tom slept like a log for the rest of the night.
>
> In the morning, people came to welcome Tom to the village. One who had been educated in England explained how honoured Tom's host had felt because Tom had chosen his home. But he was sorry that he had no food in the house. He had killed his pet dog to provide soup for Tom . . .[131]

It is significant that in Genesis 18, the meal which Abraham prepared for his otherworldly visitors is described in greater detail than the conversation which ensued between the patriarch and the Lord! No pet dog this time, but probably pet calf. Note Abraham's typical understatement: "Let me get you something to eat" (verse 5); literally in the Hebrew: "And let me bring you a bite of bread"! The morsel of bread turns out to be a banquet of fresh cakes, curds and milk and the best veal ("a tender yearling"). Also typical is the hosting posture, Abraham "standing" (verse 8), shaded a little from the heat by a tree, but standing nonetheless: far enough away not to be intrusive, close enough to be attentive to the guests' needs – not sharing the meal but serving the honoured visitors. It's not surprising that few Westerners believe in angels! Hospitality is not one of our greatest traits – especially during rest-time, private time. Abraham's expansive hospitality becomes the archetype of "entertaining angels unawares". At the time of the event itself, Abraham's generosity led the Lord to share with his human host his intended action in Sodom.

Jesus, according to John's account of his life, began his public ministry by going to a meal, the famous wedding feast in Cana (John 2:1–11). The same Gospel recounts his last night with his disciples – again sharing a meal, a "last supper" (John 13–17). The risen Christ is soon discovered, on the beach in the early dawn, preparing breakfast for his friends (John 21:9–13). "Again and again", in the words of Glaser and Raja, "Jesus showed his love for people by sharing salt with them. He was their friend."[132]

In traditional rural areas, an entire village feels judged by its ability to host strangers and visitors. Jesus' parable about prayer (Luke 11:5–8) makes its point from the unstated but known assumptions about village hospitality. A person receives a guest in the middle of the night and it is incumbent upon him to feed that visitor, to give him "bread". However, the host concerned has no food in the house. So what does he do? He goes to his friendly neighbour in the village and asks for help. No matter that the time is midnight! No matter that the door is locked and the household sleeping! The villager knows that his neighbour will get up and give him the bread he needs, if not because of their friendship, then because of something else. English translations of Luke's words at this point in the parable tend to say " . . . because of the man's persistence" or some equivalent phrase. That is not, however, the sense of the original. There, the Greek word means "shamelessness". The neighbour is bound to get up and lend assistance because of the shamelessness of the person requesting help. The man's reputation as a host, and consequently the village's reputation with regard to hospitality, must be kept alive. Jesus' point is not about importunity but about reputation. Prayer is not about our going on and on at a sleepy old God who only grumpily gets up and answers our requests because of our continual nagging! Prayer is about our calling on God whenever the need arises in the sure conviction that whatever is required will gladly be provided. Our heavenly "Neighbour" will not allow the reputation of his kingdom for grace and generosity to be compromised. Jesus began the parable with the words, "Suppose one of you had a friend . . ." None of the disciples had a friend in their home village who would not provide the needed loaves of bread – it would be unthinkable in a culture in which hosting/visiting was such an important theme.

For disciples on the road, involved in itinerant evangelism, Jesus tells them deliberately to look for a "worthy" person in each town or village. They are to make that person's home their home for the duration of their visit (Matthew 10:11). Under the aegis of an honourable person who freely hosts the strangers, the disciples find a champion for their message. Their activities are thus considerably legitimised in the eyes of the other inhabitants.

A reputation for being hospitable is important to an Arab. Many times we ate in the homes of Egyptian friends, only to be told at the end of a sumptuous meal: "You haven't eaten anything yet!" The only way to convince such hosts that one is well satisfied is by leaving food on the plate.

Through the medium of hosting/visiting, other important messages are conveyed. In his novel *Palace Walk*, Naguib Mahfouz tells the story of an Egyptian family during the period when opposition is growing to British Protectorate rule. Al-Sayyid Ahmad Abd al-Jawad is the head of a family living in Palace Walk Road. The man hypocritically rules his family with a rod of iron while personally enjoying a double life of pleasure and womanising outside the home. At one point a next-door-neighbour dies and Al-Sayyid Ahmad gradually sets his mind on the deceased man's widow as a potential victim for his charms. One day the lady visits Al-Sayyid Ahmad at the shop he owns and the liaison, mutually desired it appears, takes off:

> Al-Sayyid Ahmad was bent over his ledgers when he heard a pair of high-heeled shoes tapping across the threshold of the store. He naturally raised his eyes with interest and saw a woman whose hefty body was enveloped in a wrap. A white forehead and eyes decorated with kohl could be seen above her veil. He smiled to welcome a person for whom he had been waiting a long time, for he had immediately recognised Maryam's mother, or the widow of the late Mr. Ridwan, as she had recently become known. Jamil al-Hamzawi was busy with some customers, and so the proprietor invited her to sit near his desk. The woman strutted toward him. As she sat down on the small chair her flesh flowed over the sides. She wished him a good morning.
>
> Although her greeting and his welcome followed the customary pattern repeated whenever a woman customer worth honoring came into the store, the atmosphere in the corner near the desk was charged with electricity that was anything but innocent. Among its manifestations were the modest lowering of her eyelids, visible on either side of the

bridge connecting her veil to her scarf, and the glance of his eyes, which were lying in wait above his huge nose. The electricity was hidden and silent but needed only a touch to make it shine, glow, and burst into flame.[133]

By means of the standard formalities of greeting and counter-greeting, hosting and visiting, hints of other matters are projected. An illicit relationship begins to blossom. Mahfouz describes with humour and pathos how the ordinary events of everyday Egyptian life can be invested with hidden meaning.

In a culture in which the etiquette of hosting/visiting is so important, another Egyptian might have been more circumspect in what he allowed to be publicly broadcast. It was the pictures of Jimmy Carter hugging President Sadat's wife Jihan, at the time of the Camp David accords, that really set the Egyptian Islamists' teeth on edge. Quite blatantly, the Egyptian first lady was crossing the boundaries of proper behaviour, communicating to all the world that she was a loose woman. What shame her husband, the leader of the nation, brought upon his people and upon their religion! In his visiting, President Sadat did not act in a customary manner, setting a proper example. For this and other "failures", the Egyptian leader would soon pay with his life.

What messages do Western Christian witnesses convey, perhaps quite unwittingly, in the way that this important theme of hosting/visiting is ignored? Do we refuse hospitality or offer it grudgingly? Do we go out of our way to visit so that the Arab can play the role he most enjoys – that of host? Are we people who briefly stop by to pass on a message or obtain some information and refuse the proffered food and drink? Do we give the impression that other important matters are claiming our time even as we are entertaining guests? "Our home is your home" is the phrase on Arabs' lips many times every day. "An Englishman's home is his castle" is what we're reared with. The two ways of thinking about "home" are radically different. No wonder Westerners find it difficult to understand some of Jesus' stories which hinge around assumptions closer to the Arab's ideals in hosting/visiting!

"There is no fingernail without blood beneath it"

In tension with the motif of generosity exists an altogether different theme. Besides the leaning towards hospitableness, relationships in many Muslim cultures are marked by considerable violence.

In communities deriving from a tribal base, severe force is a common element of societal challenge and control. The only way to change the status quo is to test it. However, there is no point testing the powers that be unless there is a good chance of overthrowing them. Conspiracy marks the preparation for such a challenge. Bloodletting is a frequent accompaniment to its execution. Violence is proof of serious intention and plays a prominent part in communal decision-making, even if it is only a violence of word, as in the use of oaths.

In traditional Arab settings, fighting arose most frequently over concerns about land, water, grazing or women! The proverb concerning fingernail and blood, quoted above, gives due warning to an aggressor who is threatening to kill another person that inevitable avenging by the victim's family needs to be reckoned with before it's too late.

Feuds, then, are one expression of violence in Middle Eastern communities. Yashar Kemal's first novel, translated into English as *Memed, My Hawk*, revolves around a love story and a feud. It is set amongst the peasantry of the cotton-growing plains of the Chukurova, Kemal's own childhood home. Ince Memed, the chief character of the novel, is the only son of a poor widow. He is brought up in servitude to the rich Abdi Agha, lord of five villages in the Taurus highlands of Anatolia. After being thrashed by Abdi Agha, Memed plans to elope with Hatché, his sweetheart, who has been unwillingly engaged to the Agha's nephew. As soon as the Agha discovers that Hatché has fled to the hills with her lover, he beats Memed's mother to death in front of her close friend, Mother Hürü. Memed's personal hopes are dashed when the Agha subsequently overtakes the fleeing couple. Memed resists strongly, wounding the Agha, killing the nephew and escaping in the darkness. Hatché, however, is captured and imprisoned, to await hanging on the trumped-up charge of killing her fiancé. Memed, still only a young man, becomes a brigand in the mountains. His two ambitions are to rescue his beloved and to settle accounts with the powerful, vindictive Agha. Up in the mountains, living the life of a bandit, Memed soon expresses qualities similar to those he despises in the Agha. He grows to have no compunction about stealing and killing. Indeed, the imperative to hate is necessary if ever he is to achieve his life's ambition of revenge.

The book draws to its conclusion with Memed's ambition finding fulfilment. The Agha gradually loses power and face in the villages because of the opposition inspired by the mountain bandits, including Memed. No longer will the simple folk serve him as they did before. The government forces, meanwhile, cannot entrap and capture Memed. The young lad lives with his rescued wife and son in the mountains, ruling the roost. Now "the whole world is afraid" of the "man" who has broken the backs of the Aghas. Eventually the police catch up with the bandits. They surround them and in a shootout Hatché is killed. An amnesty comes into effect after a while. Many brigands descend from the mountains to make their peace with the authorities. But not Memed, even though house and fields have been reserved for him in his native village. He takes advantage of the amnesty to ride into town and seek out Abdi Agha's house. There he shoots the lord in his bed. Then, swiftly, Memed rushes to his native village to report his action:

> At sunrise he galloped into the village and drew rein in the middle of the square. The horse was grimy with sweat, its sides heaving like bellows, its neck and rump covered in foam. Memed was perspiring too, the sweat streaming off his back. His face and his hair were all wet.
>
> The shadows stretched out endlessly towards the west. The sweating horse was bathed in light, shining all over.
>
> The villagers saw him there in the square, like a rock, upright on his horse. Slowly all the people gathered round him, forming a big circle. There was not a sound. Their eyes were fixed on him, hundreds of eyes. They kept obstinately silent.
>
> The upright, rock-like rider in their midst stirred a little. The horse took a couple of steps and halted again. The rider raised his head. His eyes swept over the crowd. Mother Hürü, pale, dried-up, bloodless, her eyes wide open and fixed on him, stood waiting for some word, some sign from him.
>
> The horse stirred again as Memed rode towards Mother Hürü, then stopped. "Mother Hürü," he said. "It's done. Now you have no more claims on me!"

He turned his horse towards Alidagh, galloped through the village like a black cloud and was gone, lost to sight.[134]

Revenge is finally taken! It proves to be both sweet and bitter. The reader is left satisfied that the Agha has met a deserved fate but saddened at the cost of revenge to Memed, Hatché and the village community.

Often, succession to leadership is sorted out by violent means. The murders which marked the battles for leadership in the early decades of Islam after the death of the Prophet have already been referred to. Those turbulent years were full of violence.[135] In more recent times, violence has punctuated the way in which many political leaders have arisen and been replaced in Muslim countries since independence from colonial rule.

The case of Iraq illustrates the point. In the late 1950s, Abdul Karim Qassem formed a conspiracy with other army officers. In July 1958 the group overthrew the monarchy, murdering King Faisal who was 23 years old. Several women of the royal family, the prime minister and members of his family were amongst the others killed in the revolution. A three-man Sovereignty Council was set up with Qassem as premier. Qassem swiftly shifted sponsorship of the nation from Britain to the Soviet Union. In 1961 the Kurds rebelled, demanding self-rule. Qassem sent Iraqi troops against them. An internal dispute arose with one of Qassem's closest fellow conspirators and in 1963 that officer (Abdul Salam Arif) and a colleague (Ahmad Hasan al-Bakr) mounted a coup in which Qassem was shot. Later that year Abdul Salam Arif led a military revolt against his erstwhile colleague al-Bakr, and took control of the government. Arif continued as leader with his pro-communist agenda until 1966 when he was killed in a helicopter crash. His brother, Abdul Rahman Arif, succeeded him as president. In 1968, al-Bakr overthrew Abdul Rahman Arif and set up a Baathist-controlled military government. Saddam Hussein came to prominence in 1963 acting as vice-president to Ahmad Hasan al-Bakr. Saddam Hussein had worked with al-Bakr in using force to bring the Baath party to power in Baghdad. The 1960s were filled with fighting between Communists and Baathists until the latter eliminated their opponents. In 1979 Saddam Hussein jettisoned his allegiance to al-Bakr and ousted him from power, executing 22 of the former president's chief advisors in the process. Saddam Hussein managed to stay in power from the late 1970s to 2003 by carefully surrounding himself with family and clan relations, especially people from his home town of Takrit. During his period of rule, the country knew devastating internal and external violence. The suppression of the Kurds in Iraq, the eight-year war with Iran and most recently the invasion of Kuwait and ensuing Gulf War ravaged the economy and infrastructure of the nation. The bullying apparatus of his Baathist regime held in check any possibility of an uprising occurring from within the country. The aftermath of the Gulf War of 1991 was a defining moment for ordinary Iraqis. The victorious military coalition, led by the United States of America, encouraged the rebellion of Iraqi Shi^{c}as in the south of the country but failed completely to support them in their rebellion. The subsequent punishment of the Shi^{c}a peoples by Saddam Hussein extinguished any expression of resistance in the subjugated southerners. It took an outside force to topple Saddam Hussein and that has posed its own problems for Iraqis. For sure, they are pleased about the banishment of the bloody dictator, but just as surely they feel compromised that a Western, "Christian" force has been the sorter-out of an internal, Arab Muslim affair. The violence endemic to politics in Iraq is mirrored, in varying degrees of magnitude, within Turkey, Algeria, Libya, Egypt, Syria and Iran.

The *intifada* of the Palestinians constitutes a recent example of the politics of violence in which Arabs tend to find themselves caught up. From the Palestinian point of view, prominence is given in their media to the destruction wrought by the Israelis in their occupation of Palestinian areas – destruction and death that need answering. Flattened buildings, battered youths, dead children and wounded women are constantly and graphically displayed via the media to the international community. Julie Peteet comments:

> To the Palestinians, the battered body, with its bruises and broken limbs, is the symbolic embodiment of a twentieth-century history of subordination and powerlessness – of "what we have to endure" – but also of their determination to resist and to struggle for national independence.[136]

Honour comes from unmasking the sufferings in front of outsiders and being seen to continue resisting. Perhaps a similar mindset motivates the survivors of Usama bin Ladin's *al-Qaida* organisation.

Defeat at the hands of American bombs and helicopter gunships in Afghanistan can be transformed into the victory of survival, evasion, regrouping and striking back. Better still if the ensuing suicidal violence can be perpetrated by Muslims who are nationals of the countries currently embarked on their "war on terror"! The politics of violence finds an accommodating bedfellow in fundamentalist Islam.

Holy firepower

The world has become used to hearing calls to *jihâd* (holy war).[137] *Jihâd* usually aims aggression against outsiders, against those perceived as lying outside the in-group. Appeal to the religious duty of *jihâd* has been made in all kinds of belligerent settings. Perhaps the most sad have been those situations in which Muslim has declared holy war on Muslim. Iran, in its attempt to export its Islamic revolution to the Sunnî nations of the Gulf, and Iraq, in its hostilities against Kuwait and Saudi Arabia, each made use of the *jihâd* justification. The more extreme Islamists of Egypt declared holy war on the "apostate" Sadat in the 1970s and early 1980s. The organisation to which the president's assassins belonged was called the Jihad Organisation. Its ideologue was a young Egyptian named Muhammad Abd al-Salam Faraj. The rationale for the group's militancy was set out in a pamphlet which Faraj wrote. The title of his work was *The Neglected Duty*, and the duty that was neglected was, of course, *jihâd*.[138] Faraj strove successfully to stimulate his fellow Islamists to armed rebellion against Sadat's idolatrous rule.

Actions perceived as amounting to "apostasy" often provoke Muslims to severe violence. Although some references in the Qur'ân suggest that punishment for apostasy is best left to God in the hereafter, most Muslims base their convictions on another Qur'ânic verse which speaks of punishment in this life:

> The punishment of those
> Who wage war against God
> And His apostle, and strive
> With might and main
> For mischief through the land
> Is: execution, or crucifixion,
> Or the cutting off of hands
> And feet from opposite sides,
> Or exile from the land:
> That is their disgrace
> In this world, and
> A heavy punishment is theirs
> In the Hereafter.
>
> (Sura 5:36)

Al-Bukhârî, compiler of one of the two major lists of Traditions (*hadîth*) recognised by Sunnî Muslims, quotes this verse of the Qur'ân at the beginning of his section dealing with apostasy. He goes on to record Traditions in which Prophet Muhammad punished apostasy with execution.[139] In today's Muslim world, death stalks those who dare step outside the received faith of kith and kin. The handling of apostasy, as legalised in Iran or Pakistan or as permitted in Egypt or Morocco, is in most cases considerably violent.[140] Compulsion in religion is allowed to have a heyday when what seems to be at stake is an undermining of group honour.

In the emotionalism of many Middle Easterners, and especially in the Arab's uninhibited anger or exaggeration, an element of violence can be discerned. Shaming or belittling is one of the major factors of social control operating in most Muslim communities. Gamal al-Ghitani makes use of this stratagem in his novel *The Events of Zaafarani Alley*. In a section entitled "The Second Quarrel" he describes an all-too-believable sequence of female (Busayna) be-littling female (Umm Yusif) within the closed-in life of a poor, Egyptian, urban community. The Alley is witness to a crescendo of verbal abuse:

It happened on the same day at one in the afternoon after Oweis had finished telling the Alley part two of the Tekerli story. . . . The quarrel proceeded as follows:

She [Busayna] called out loudly to Umm Suhair who lived across the street from Umm Yusif. Umm Suhair loudly answered in the name of God and hoping that everything will be all right. Busayna declared that no good will come to this forsaken Zaafarani so long as the hearts were ungrateful and as women who were more like scorpions than people nested there. Umm Suhair realized that this was the prelude for a quar-rel. A number of women looked out of their windows. Khadija, the Sa'idi woman, ran to her window joyously repeating "A quarrel! A quarrel!" Busayna noticed that the two windows of Umm Yusif were still closed – a fact that made her cut short the usual prelude leading into every quar-rel she fought. She declared that that harlot of a woman, whose tongue was fit to be a strap of leather on which razors could be sharpened, that wife of the train stoker . . .

At that point Umm Suhair made a gesture, Sitt Umm Nabila shook her head, Zannuba, the divorcee, clapped her hands and shouted "Wow! . . . Wow!" And still Umm Yusif did not open her window . . . Busayna shouted that some women who were never satisfied by their husbands . . . were losing their minds now, and she pointed her arm in the direction of Umm Yusif's house. She clapped repeating: Wife of the stoker! Wife of the stoker! Oh women of the Alley! Oh Alley of women! She wanted them to be her witness against the wife of the stoker who exposed her bare breast when she looked out of the window, who didn't wear any underwear and who badmouthed her even though last year she had lent her five pounds Egyptian when she turned to her in tears begging her to save Tahun . . . Tahun the stoker! Tahun, the stoker, because part of his inventory was lost and he was given the choice: pay or go to jail. Then she regretted later on because good people told her that Tahun al-Mathun al-Matahni al-Matahin had stolen part of that inventory and sold it in the junk yards of Wikalit-il Balah . . . Still, Umm Yusif did not respond. Khadija, the Sa'idi woman, was certain that if she did, a really big quarrel that would help her cope with her loneliness would ensue; Umm Yusif, after all, had a talent for heaping abuse that was not to be sneezed at. So it seemed there was some mysterious reason making her take this. Umm Suhair was certain that there was something that Busayna was holding back. Busayna was now stretching her body on the balcony, waving her shoe, declaring that she was going to beat Umm Yusif on her most sensitive parts.[141]

Violence frequently comes to be associated with authority: in the family, within a peer group or in tribal rivalries. As it is socially acceptable for men to show irritable, angry behaviour, the atmosphere in many homes can be highly charged, fraught and quarrelsome. Orthodox interpretations of Islamic law, moreover, sanction the corporal punishment of a wife by her husband:

> Allah has said in the Holy Qur'an (Sura 4:34) "that if it appears that your wives do not obey you, first advise them. If they do not listen, give up sleeping and sitting with them. If even now they do not obey or listen, then beat them (lightly). If they begin to obey thereafter then do not try to find excuses to harass them".[142]

Such interpretations of Islamic law tend to colour expected and accepted norms within Muslim homes. Sometimes, domestic violence can continue unchallenged because (with religious authentication) that is the way things are. Arabs, and other Middle Easterners, often seem to require a scapegoat for the off-loading of their own anger. Aggressive feelings tend not to be turned inward, but are directed towards others. People easily burst into quarrels or threats, though such outbursts usually remain verbal and subside easily. It is more talk than act.

Yashar Kemal, in his story about Fisher Selim, describes the city of Istanbul from a bird's eye perspective:

> And in Istanbul city, people were killing, gouging each other's eyes out, robbing banks, running, choking under pelting rain, choking with the ghastly corrosion, the sewers, the refuse heaps, falling on the garbage like screeching rapacious seagulls, crazed, a ravenous, despairing horde assailing the city. Half-naked tramps, itinerant vendors, small-time

black-marketeers, murderers, rapists . . . And deluxe motor cars, elegant shops, painted bejewelled women, no longer human, smelling of mould . . . One single car selling for three million, an apartment for seven million . . . The rent alone sixty thousand lira . . . Gardens planted with flowers imported from far-off Japan, tended by gardeners also trained in Japan, villas, luxurious yachts, gambling dens . . . Black-marketeers selling smuggled cigarettes, whisky, electronic machines, spending money like water, shedding blood like water too . . . And the starving . . . Driven to suicide by hunger . . . Three hundred thousand prostitutes. The destitute, the homosexuals . . . And the police, present at every corner, in every brothel, extorting bribes, killing like any other network of thugs, letting murderers off scot-free and laying the blame on their victims, swinging their truncheons and shooting in blind frenzy not at the killers and racketeers, but at the slain, the underdogs . . . All intermingled, the jewels, the furs, the hunger, the dirt, the sewers, the night-clubs, the haggling, the trafficking in human flesh . . . Corrupt, the Golden Horn, ever since bygone Byzantium, the people, the carrion, the factories, the filth, the nakedness . . . Corrupt, Beyoglu, Galata, the merchants, the Genoese tower, the buying and selling, the glittering Ottoman gold coins . . . Corrupt, a medieval city always and for ever, until the day it wastes away and goes to ruin . . . And; wallowing in mud, the squatters, fleeing the country in droves from hunger and want . . . Zeytinburnu, the pocket-sized dwellings of clapboard, sheet metal, old packing cases . . . Scanty light, a trickle of water from a fountain . . . Gultepe, Fikirtepe, Kustepe, all the hills ringing Istanbul, crowded with ramshackle hovels, rape and abuse, jealousy, bloodshed . . . Corrupt, the proud domes and minarets, the tall apartment buildings, insolent, sick-ening, extravagant, chaotic . . . All that is beautiful and good and human destroyed long ago . . . The few remaining trees chopped down. Corrupt, perishing in a noisome stench of decay, a swiftly disintegrating aged city, Istanbul. Its heart crawling with millions and millions of maggots, the water, the earth, the people rotting away, the very stones and steel putre-fying, a garbage heap, a body ripe for devastating plagues and pestilences . . .[143]

Kemal's paragraph in *The Sea-Crossed Fisherman* graphically depicts life as he perceives it in Istanbul in the 1970s and 1980s. Violence is its primary hallmark.

Other contemporaries bear the marks of Middle Eastern violence. In his reflections on years of captivity in cruel circumstances, Brian Keenan wrestles with the question of why it should be that his captors could do what they did to fellow human beings. He notes that many of his guards had a fixation about sex. Sexual potency and physical prowess seemed closely linked in their psyche. Rambo films were the stuff of life. Strong prisoners they admired and secretly feared. Behind the fixations and fears Keenan perceived a particular concept of God:

> Allah, the god of retribution and judgement, dominated their minds. How can a man love the thing he fears? When fear commands the mind then the heart is imprisoned. In time I came to understand the greater and more profound prison that held our captors. For years we were chained to a wall or radiator, but they were chained to their guns; futile symbols of power, not power itself. This was something these men could never know: real power embraces; it cannot destroy.[144]

The strongly motivating force of *ḥasad* or envy expresses a violence of mind and emotion. Fear of the evil eye is a major constraint on behaviour for many Muslim peoples. Unlike its positive counterpart, *baraka* (blessing), the damaging effect of the evil eye can be communicated with just a glance. No physical contact is necessary. Attia Hosain recalls childhood memories of a beggar who used to frequent her family home in Pakistan:

> Once again every Thursday Kamli Shah, the holy beggar, would cry out his harsh-voiced prayers that changed to threats if he were kept waiting. "Mohammed Mian! Daughters of Mohammed Mian! Children of his sons, Kamli Shah is here. Do not forget him. Then Allah will remember you. Bhagwan will remember you!"
>
> Cross-legged in the middle of the road, within the gates, he sat, bare-bodied with matted hair and beard and staring eyes. And fear of their mad concentration, their possible power, made it impossible to send him away empty-handed. Even now his voice singing over the walls of the zenana brought back shivers of childhood's terror.[145]

A newly-wed Canadian lass came to see me one day in Cairo. She was very tearful and couldn't understand what had gone wrong. She had married a fellow Canadian and travelled to Cairo to set up home with him for the duration of his contract in Egypt. In the apartment building where they lived, she had made good friends with the young

Egyptian couple who shared the same floor as herself and her husband. The Egyptian wife had just had a baby and the Canadian bride had visited their flat to congratulate them. She had fawned over the baby with such phrases as "Oh what a lovely baby!" The young Egyptian father had got very upset and thrown her out of the apartment. The Canadian lass had no idea why. It was my task to explain to her how her well-intentioned actions were perceived by those for whom the violence of envy is a daily dread. The Egyptian couple feared that she, a newly married, as yet childless, woman might inadvertently have struck the vulnerable infant with her "eye" of envy or jealousy. They were frightened that their baby might suffer through the naked phrases of praise and exclamation. My Canadian friend would have to learn how to neutralise any unintended jealousy with special words which make it all right for praise to be given: "*Mâ shâ'a 'llâh* (What God has made!), your baby is beautiful!"

Violence – a biblical theme

The Bible is no stranger to violence. It includes the theme as a prominent motif throughout its pages.

In the early chapters of the Pentateuch, for example, violence surfaces in the actions and reactions of the patriarchs. The founders of the tribes of Israel have a sister named Dinah. She is daughter to Jacob and Leah. We have already considered what the interaction between the princely Shechem and the pretty Dinah (Genesis 34) might have been about for the couple themselves. Perhaps she was violated against her will; perhaps she was seduced by the young nobleman. Perhaps she was convinced that he genuinely loved her. Whatever the truth about the details of Dinah and Shechem's relationship, there is no doubt about the attitude of Dinah's brothers to the affair. While the lovesick prince installs Dinah in his house and persuades his father Hamor to make arrangements with Jacob so that she can become his wife, the brothers of Dinah work out their response.

The Bible tells us that when Jacob and his sons first hear what has happened between Dinah and Shechem, they burn with grief and fury. Anger rises because Shechem has shamed them all – he has done a disgraceful thing "against Israel", reads the text, not "against Dinah". The only appropriate answer that they can come up with is that of revenge. In a carefully constructed plot, the brothers conspire to avenge their honour. They insist that Shechem and all the males living under Hamor's auspices be circumcised. Only then can the Israelites allow intermarriage. The stratagem works and while Hamor and his masculine citizens are incapacitated after being circumcised, two of Jacob's sons kill every male they can find. They retrieve Dinah from Shechem's house and loot the city. Jacob protests to the two vengeance-takers that they have now made him a stench to the other inhabitants of the land. His sons shrug their shoulders and suggest that they had no choice in the matter: "Should he have treated our sister like a prostitute?" (verse 31).

A far more drastic conflict, emanating from a similar concern for avenging honour, developed years later after the people of Israel had settled in Canaan. A total of 65,000 soldiers died in a battle over a Levite's concubine. Benjamites in Gibeah had abused the etiquette of hosting/visiting. When the Levite had stayed the night in a lodging in Gibeah, men from the area had raped and indecently assaulted the visitor's concubine until she died on their hands at dawn. The Levite had appealed for justice to the other tribes of Israel, who responded by amassing an overwhelming force. The commanders of the combined troops invited the Benjamites to hand over to them the guilty perpetrators so that they could be executed and Israel could be purged of evil. The Benjamites' refusal led to a bloodbath in which tens of thousands lost their lives. It was violence with a vengeance![146]

In some senses, the God of the Old Testament comes across as violent, though always in a sense which is perfectly ethical. I would want to challenge any simplistic contrast in which the God of the Old Testament is a God of judgement and the God of the New Testament is a God of love. He is consistent throughout. In these paragraphs, however, my aim is to show that there is a chord in God himself which coincides with one of the major themes of Arab culture. Just as there is an incredible, divine hospitality, so there is a divine "violence".

In Yahweh's anger with Moses for losing his temper, in the judgement upon Eli's faithless household, in the rejection of Saul, in the abandonment of the northern kingdom of Israel and later the southern kingdom of Judah, and in the many prophecies against the nations of the world, violent language is used and violent events occur. But it is not violence for violence's sake. It is the ultimate consistency where human beings will not admit their disloyalty and return to a covenant relationship with the God who has created them. The people of Israel had a choice from the beginning: blessing or cursing. Either they could live in a close family relationship to the God who loved them because he loved them (Deuteronomy 7:7) or they could endure the hell of stepping outside his family.

Mark, the Gospel-writer, uses violent language to describe God's breaking in on the earthly scene to rescue lost humankind. A favourite word of the evangelist is *schizo*; it means "to split asunder". When Mark begins his Gospel with an account of the baptism of Jesus, he describes in effect a breakout from heaven!

> At that time Jesus came from Nazareth in Galilee and was baptised by John in the Jordan. As Jesus was coming up out of the water, he saw heaven being torn open (*schizomenous*) and the Spirit descending on him like a dove.
>
> (Mark 1:9,10)

The account then moves at a fast pace, describing the effects on earth of that breakout. In chapter after chapter, Jesus takes the initiative against sickness, lunacy, demonisation, death, the elements, Pharisaic opposition and so on. The only reversal comes with Judas' betrayal of Jesus in Gethsemane. After that event, Mark writes no single word about Jesus' attitudes or reactions. From then until after the resurrection, Jesus "does" nothing: in fact he is the object of 56 verbs!

Mark uses his special word again at an important hinge in his account. As Jesus dies on the cross, the curtain of the temple is torn (*eschisthê*) in two from top to bottom. Mark notes the miraculous occurrence inside the Jews' holy building and goes on in the very next verse to describe the reaction of the Roman centurion at the foot of the cross to the manner of Jesus' dying. In the death of Jesus, Mark proclaims, God rips open the veil between himself and his people, and also widens the family to include the Gentile, as well as the Jewish, world.

As Mark signs off at the end of his account, we are left with the pace quickening once again. The breakout from heaven continues on earth via the apostles:

Then the disciples went out and preached everywhere, and the Lord worked with them and confirmed his word by the signs that accompanied it.

(Mark 16:20)

At various times, Jesus interprets his own ministry in quite violent terms. When some onlookers claim that he is driving out demons by the authority of Beelzebub, prince of demons, Jesus warns them that such a possibility is logically impossible. A family divided against itself could never stand. No! He drives out demons by the finger of God and that is proof enough that the kingdom of God is come (Luke 11:20). The spiritual dynamic that marked Jesus' ministry denoted warfare against the enemies of God's kingdom:

From the days of John the Baptist until now, the kingdom of heaven has been forcefully advancing, and forceful men lay hold of it.

(Matthew 11:12)

Outbreaks amongst Muslims

Some of the exciting advances of the gospel among Muslims today derive from singular "outbreaks from heaven". One example comes from a Middle Eastern nation in 1992 when God poured his Spirit upon scattered rural communities:

They said it happened spontaneously, and not just in one village, not even in villages close to each other, but in places hundreds of kilometers apart. What happened?

Suddenly the numbers of people attending the churches began to grow. And while they were gathered to worship, the Spirit of God would descend upon the people, and their worship would take on a whole new dimension. They worshipped until late into the night. They started to pray for one another. People were being healed. Muslims were coming to see what was happening. Muslims were being saved. And they came back the next night, wanting more. And the next night, and the next . . .

It is clear that God is doing something here. This kind of spontaneous revival is the only way it could have happened. A small revival in one church might easily have been squelched by forces of the enemy. But this was God's tactic. You cannot contain something that is erupting all over the country.[147]

Another example concerns an individual living as part of a very poor Muslim community in the capital of that same country:

> H. and T. moved into a new house about eight months ago and formed a close friendship with Mrs H. It did not take long to discover that she was demon possessed as the result of a curse put on her by her aunt years ago when she refused to marry her cousin. The demons had tormented her for twelve years. She has burn marks on her body. Sometimes she was her normal self and other times she had supernatural strength and spoke in different voices when she was controlled by the demons.
>
> Her family had done everything they knew to help her to get free. This curse was against her getting pregnant and against any children surviving. A child born to her died at two days old.
>
> H. and T. prayed for her in the name of Jesus and sought the help of a national believer who is experienced in deliverance ministry. Praise God she was set free. She believed in Jesus and was delivered from the power of the demons. Right after this she conceived and the pregnancy is proceeding well.[148]

The threat of supernatural violence has sometimes been enough to afford protection to Muslims who have become followers of Jesus. Subject to the law of apostasy and often placed in great danger, some believers from a Muslim background have discovered the Captain of the hosts of heaven working on their behalf:

> In a Middle Eastern country a Sheikh became a Christian. He and his family were in grave danger as three other Sheikhs planned to kill him. They each heard the Lord telling them: "Be warned, do not touch my servant." They were awe-struck, knowing that God had spoken to them and warned them; needless to say they abandoned their plans.[149]

The violence of spiritual warfare is a reality which must be properly prepared for by those seeking to share the gospel with Muslims. Prayer, with fasting, is a priority not to be displaced by other concerns for strategies and techniques. One friend of mine who went to work overseas in a Muslim community wrote home in the midst of what seemed like a deliberate attack upon her life and ministry. She herself was suffering from a concoction of serious diseases, while a young mullah with whom she was sharing the gospel was killed on the order of his father. The aim of her plea by letter was to put in place a prayer-team of hundreds of Christian people who would seriously intercede for her and the emerging church (of people from a Muslim background), all day, every day. As a result of that determination and the consistent praying done by her partners, God has used the lady concerned in a unique ministry amongst leaders of the indigenous Muslim communities. She became the local interpreter of "acts of violence" – dreams, miracles, divine coincidences, fires, floods, healings and so on – which rained down from heaven upon Muslim leaders. Her task was to explain what God was saying to them through the violence. In the earthly repercussions from serious spiritual warfare, the people concerned gradually discovered that the Lord wanted to be the most gracious Host they had ever met.

CHAPTER SIX

TIME AND SPACE

Haste is of the devil.

Suppose you are out shopping in a town in England and you need to check the time. You might glance up at a clock tower, or seek out the double-faced clock in the post office window. Banks, building societies and jewellers have all kinds of mechanical and electronic gadgets that will tell you exactly how early or late you are for your next appointment. In almost every shop there is bound to be a clock visible somewhere.

Driven by the clock?

The world of the Middle Easterner, by contrast, hardly features the clock at all. Such instruments rarely adorn shops or streets, nor even banks and post offices, in his towns. For the Middle Easterner, time is far more likely to be measured by purposeful divisions of the day.

In traditional, agricultural contexts this has meant getting up at sunrise and bedding down at sunset. In many spheres of occupation, people are paid by the job rather than by the hour or day. Time is conceived of in qualitative and personal terms rather than in quantitative and abstract terms. Which events in the day are "life" and which are background noise? Which persons require time expended on them and which groups can be offered less time?

Middle Easterners do not feel pressurised by the passage of time. At airports, train stations and coach stops, families arrive when they arrive and are quite prepared to wait hours, all night even, for their turn to travel. Equally, a person may attend an appointment considerably "late" with no thought of apologising. Precision, punctuality and haste are concepts connotating lack of self-esteem. In fact, only minions, slaves and servants are expected to perform tasks at the

"Timeless" street scene?

"time appointed". It is people with no dignity who are dominated by others' demands for action at a certain time. Such domination is refused by those with self-respect.

A few major "groups" demand an extended time commitment

from an individual. Those groups include the family, small face-to-face communities and little industrial establishments. In all such settings, the personal ties of the people to the head of the family or the boss of the workplace are strong. Work is not defined in terms of time allowed, but in terms of task to be fulfilled. It is difficult for other more impersonal and widely embracing institutions of political or economic life to compete with these smaller, close-knit communities. In some ways, this factor has been a major contributor to the failure of socialist programs in various countries of the Middle East. There cannot easily be developed a commitment to a political ideal or an impersonal bureaucracy when there are other more immediate, traditional ties competing for loyalty.

Middle Easterners do not see time as most Westerners see it – primarily lineal with an emphasis on the future. The idea that it might somehow be "saved" is laughable. The notion of progress is for the most part squeezed out by other more important concerns. In Arabic, to say "tomorrow" simply means to acknowledge some vague moment in the future. To restrict that perception to the next 24 hours specifically requires a repeated word: "tomorrow tomorrow".

In the Middle East, time is neither accumulated nor budgeted. Interruptions are enjoyed. They are not a "waste" of time, but the treasured highlights which time must serve. Westerners who go shopping or visiting government offices to try and pursue visas or tax return forms find themselves caught in a vortex of greetings, movement, give-and-take, jokes, tea-drinking, absenteeism and so on. There is no queue! There is no (Western) sense of order! First come is not necessarily first served! If the Westerner has all day at his disposal to enjoy traipsing endlessly round smoke-filled rooms, obtaining numerous stamps and signatures, he might reflect at the end of the experience on the number of human contacts he has made. The Western, impersonal, hole-in-the-wall mentality is miles removed from the hurly-burly of repartee, innuendo, jokes, story-telling, complaining and intrigue that is the primary occupation of most Middle Eastern civil servants.

Bureaucracy multiplies and becomes endless because every person in the system has his own honour. You don't just rush into an office and put a form in front of someone and expect them to sign it. You learn the appropriate approach to each person. I recall spending a day retrieving an item from customs at Cairo international airport.

I employed a facilitator to help me. We filled the day going from office to office accumulating signatures. As we entered each office, obeisance was done and an approach was made: " . . . in the name of Prophet Muḥammad" if the official were a Muslim, " . . . in the name of Jesus Christ" if the official were a Christian. Each person, if he could be found, had to be honoured, and such honouring "takes" time.

Middle Eastern societies work on the basis of who you know rather than what you know. This has to be the case where relatives and clans are supposed to look out for one another. Mutual favours build up banks of opportunity to be exploited at appropriate moments. Operating on the basis of who you know obviously takes a lot more time than working on the basis of what you know.

Ghassan Kanafani's story *Men in the Sun* hinges around a tragedy arising from this nexus of time-consuming give-and-take. A driver of a tanker attempts to smuggle three workmates across the sweltering desert into the Gulf states in order for them to gain jobs. As they approach a border post he slides them into the huge, empty metal tanker-drum and closes the lid. He roars up to the customs house and jumps down from the cab with papers that need to be signed:

> Abul Khaizuran hurried up the steps and made for the third room on the right. Immediately he opened the door and went in he felt, from the glances directed at him by the officials, that something was going to happen. But he didn't pause, pushing his papers in front of the fat official sitting in the centre of the room.
>
> "Aha! Abu Khaizurana!" shouted the official, as he slid the papers to one side with deliberate carelessness, and crossed his arms on the metal desk. "Where have you been all this time?"
>
> Abul Khaizuran panted: "In Basra."
>
> "Haj Rida asked after you more than six times."
>
> "The lorry had broken down."
>
> The three officials exchanged glances and then burst out laughing again. Abul Khaizuran said tensely, shuffling from one foot to another: "Now, Abu Baqir, I've no time for jokes. Please . . ."
>
> Stretching out his hand he moved the papers closer in front of the official, but again Abu Baqir pushed them away to the edge of the desk, folded his arms and smiled wickedly.
>
> "Haj Rida asked about you six times."
>
> "I told you, the lorry was not working. And Haj Rida and I can come

to an understanding when we meet. Please sign the papers. I'm in a hurry."

He slid the papers closer again, but once more Abu Baqir pushed them away.

"Your lorry wasn't working?"

"Yes. Please! I'm in a hurry."

The three officials looked at one another and quietly gave a knowing laugh. The desk of one of them was completely bare except for a small glass of tea; the other had stopped working to follow what was happening.

The fat man called Abu Baqir said, belching:

"Now, be sensible, Abu Khaizurana. Why do you hurry your journey in terrible weather like this? The room here's cool, and I'll order you a glass of tea. So enjoy the comfort."

Abul Khaizuran picked up the papers, took the pen lying in front of Abu Baqir and went round the table to stand beside him. He pushed the pen towards him, nudging his shoulder with his arm.

"I'll spend an hour sitting with you when I come back, but now let me leave, for Baqir's sake and Baqir's mother's sake. Here!"

Abu Baqir, however, did not move his hand but continued to stare stupidly at the driver, on the point of bursting out laughing again.

"Ah, you devil, Abu Khaizurana! Why don't you remember that you are in a hurry when you are in Basra? Eh?"[150]

The customs officer continues to delay Abul Khaizuran with jokes and innuendoes about how he spends his time in Basra between trips. The border officials know that the driver has, for some reason, been castrated when he was younger and they tease him about a female belly-dancer at a club he frequents when in Basra. When they have enjoyed their joking to the full they eventually sign the papers and send Abul Khaizuran on his way. Further down the road, the driver anxiously pulls up and opens the lid of the tanker. The three stowaways have long since suffocated in the choking heat of the lorry. Time ran out for them.

Kanafani's story is actually a parable about the Palestinian issue. The impotence and helplessness of each of the four "travellers" is highlighted. Their desire for personal material wealth rather than the liberation of their homeland is mocked. The corruption of the Arab regimes, allowing the Palestinians to suffocate in the airless world of refugee camps, is exposed. The story has tremendous force, for the scene of delay and banter is all too real!

The Middle Easterner is strongly preoccupied with the past. There is an almost innate tendency to retrospection. Human happiness and achievement lie behind him. Folklore is commonly concerned with ancient history. The Qur'ân is the greatest focus, in

Catching up with the past

history, of the Arab's claim to fame. He looks back to the glories it celebrates. Next to the Qur'ân, prophetic tradition (*sunna*) is accorded great authority. The aim of Muslims is to walk in the ways of their forefathers:

Narrated Abdullah: The best talk (speech) is Allah's Book (Qur'ân), and the best way is the way of Muḥammad, and the worst matters are the heresies (those new things which are introduced into the religion); and whatever you have been promised will surely come to pass, and you cannot escape (it).[151]

The penultimate book of al-Bukhârî's collection of *hadîth* deals with "Holding Fast to the Qur'ân and the Tradition".[152] Muslims, and especially Arabs, look back to the days of Prophet Muḥammad and the early spectacular growth of Islam. That golden age is romanticised and made perfect. It provides a vision with which no current government can compete. When the Islamists of contemporary times march along the streets of Assiut or Amman or Aleppo chanting "Back to the Qur'ân! Back to the *sunna*! Back to the rule of Muḥammad!" their shouts strike a responsive chord in many listeners' hearts. For Arabs, copying the past is a positive aim. "Innovation" is a bad word. Arabs will rather patiently wait for old times to renew themselves. There is a genuine suspicion about new ways. They are oriented towards the past, in complete contrast with Westerners who are oriented towards the future.

In concepts of personal development, a similar glance backwards is to be discerned. This time, the look is back to a person's infancy. Many Arabs believe that the quality of a mother's milk, and the manner in which it is offered to a child, will affect the way the child's character develops. That initial launch into life cannot be replayed. The past is strongly determinative of the present.

Most Arabs deliberately raise their children in the same way that they themselves were brought up. The advice of a Dr. Spock, via a contemporary book, would be unthinkable. The traditional way is the only valid course to follow. The most important feature in such traditional upbringing is the requirement that the individual subordinate himself to his family, to the "group". The major burden of education lies with the child's parents and other adults at home. Schools emphasise obedience and memorisation, again lending weight to the importance of conformity to ideals handed down from the past.

The communication of ideas takes considerable time. Public speeches in the best of Western contexts are rarely brief and brilliant. In Arab and other Middle Eastern contexts they are interminable. Conciseness of argument and quickly-made points are not in view. The aim is not to convince but to impress. In debate, an Arab is as concerned with the emotional impact of what he is saying as with the reasonableness of his argument. That is why it is very important to congratulate an Arab speaker on the sagacity of his thought and the sharpness of his wit in putting his thoughts across. Winning an argument of logic is only half the game. The other half is the effect of the performance. An elaborate introduction is made; digressions are embarked upon so frequently that in the end the speaker often loses himself in details. He is absorbed in the rhetoric involved, as are his listeners. Speech is filled with similes. The emotional side of the presentation often conceals the central point, but the audience is won over by what it has been made to feel.[153] Hasan al-Banna, Egyptian founder of the Muslim Brotherhood, was renowned as an orator. Judge al-Hudaybi, who later succeeded Banna as director of the Brotherhood, describes the effect on him of listening to al-Banna:

> How many speeches have I heard, hoping each time that they could speedily end . . . This time, I feared that Hasan al-Banna would end his speech . . . One hundred minutes passed, and he collected the hearts of the Muslims in the palms of his hands . . . and shook them as he willed . . . The speech ended, and he returned to his listeners their hearts . . . except for mine, which remained in his hand.[154]

A Westerner considers rhetoric and linguistic polish a loss of time while vagueness of thought fills him with unease. An Arab is hurt by lack of appreciation of his eloquence. Moreover, he may misinterpret the directness of Western approaches to discussion as bluntness, with its implications of rudeness and non-appreciation of the person with whom one is conversing.

In a world in which the extended family is of such primary importance, concepts of time and space help to reinforce the significance attached to those fundamental relationships. Visiting takes time, but it must be done, and done joyously, for it cements ties between people. Behind Charles Marsh's advice to Christians who would witness to Muslims lies an understanding of a concept of time different from that of Westerners:

> Take every opportunity of being friendly with Muslim neighbours, shopkeepers, or others. Show them that you love them in practical ways. Do not try to preach at them. Be a good listener . . . Invite the Muslim

to have coffee with you in your home, and always accept an invitation to have coffee with him, especially in his home.[155]

In disputes, each person has his honour. The role of mediator is a role often played by Arabs and other Middle Easterners. National questions and private disagreements are settled by artfully managed

What price an orange?

negotiation. Careful attention is paid to the essentials of saving face. Such intricate diplomacy isn't done in a flash. It takes time.

Bargaining is the delight of almost every Middle Easterner, whether he is selling or buying. It is the game of economic life:

The merchant sits in his shop reading a book or chatting with his neighbour in the next booth. The customer appears and asks the price of a pair

of slippers. Merchant and customer may argue over this for as much as
a half an hour. Friends and by-passers may even join in the sport. The
customer pretends to go away, the merchant to put back his goods.
Finally the customer buys the slippers, usually at a reasonable price.[156]

Of course, as far as the Middle Easterners are themselves concerned,
the final price is pretty much known beforehand. So why the elaborate game? The pitting of wits, the banter, the insults, the oaths, the
mock despair and eventual resignation to a "hard bargain" – all
constitute the spice of life for people who are inveterate talkers. This
is not "wasting time"! This is life being lived to the full!

The educational system in most Muslim societies revolves around
rote learning, even up to degree level and beyond. This is partly
because the students are honouring their lecturers by learning their
texts by heart. They are also celebrating previous scholarship. There
are no short cuts to rote learning. Whole texts are digested to be
regurgitated in exams. The Westerner sees such a form of education
as a waste of time. In Muslim societies, it reinforces values which
have to do with according honour to older people and acknowledging the significance of the past.

Every day, supposedly, religious piety punctuates the conduct of
Muslims with five sessions of prayer:

> Thus as the Night breaks and removes its veil from the face of the Dawn,
> the muezzin, calling to Allah, stands up pervading the horizon with his
> call, engaging the ears of Time, inviting the attention of the heedless,
> awakening the somnolent to rise up and welcome the fresh Morning
> from Allah.[157]

Fridays are important for the communal midday gathering at the
mosque. Fasts and feasts come round regularly and in the keeping of
them the Muslim finds meaning. Where does time go during the long
hours of Ramaḍân? Day becomes night and night becomes day. Not
a lot gets done, but religious and social relationships are reinforced,
renewed and reinvigorated. Such benefits far outweigh concerns for
efficiency, time-saving and the achievement of economic goals.

In many parts of the Muslim world, "time" is considerably under
threat from the inroads made by unbridled consumerism. The attendance to the past is increasingly being undermined by the demands

of the present. "What you need now" is shouted at people from bill-boards and television advertisements to the detriment of what those people have historically been. Words – influential, seductive, need-generating words – gradually overtake traditional thought patterns. Orhan Pamuk gives expression to such a marginalisation of time-taking and past-orientation in his novel *The New Life*. This metaphysical thriller, served up as a road novel, became the fastest-selling title in Turkish history on initial publication. It evidently struck a chord with Turks. The clever story evokes a people teeter-ing between being Eastern and Western:

> When God blew his soul into the creation, Adam's eye beheld it. We then saw matter in its true guise, yes, just like children might, but not in the unreflecting mirror that we see now. We were such joyful children back then, naming what we saw and seeing what we named! Back then, time was time, hazard was hazard, and life was life. It was a state of true happi-ness, but Satan was displeased by our happiness; and he who is Satan conceived of the Great Conspiracy. One of the pawns of the Great Conspirator was a man named Gutenberg, known to be a printer and emulated by many, who reproduced words in a manner that outstripped the production of the industrious hand, the patient finger, the fastidious pen; and words, words, words broke loose like a strand of beads and scattered far and yonder. Like hungry and frenzied cockroaches, words invaded the wrapping on bars of soap, on cartons of eggs, on our doors and out in the street. So words and matter, which had formerly been inseparable, now turned against each other. And when asked by moonlight what is time, life, grief, fate, pain, we were confused like a student who stays up all night before an exam learning his lessons by rote, although we had once known the answers in our hearts. Time, said a fool, is a noise. Accident, said another, is fate. Life, a third said, is a book. We were confused, as you see, waiting for the angel to whisper the right answer in our ears.[158]

"Before" and "after"?

Perhaps one could differentiate Western from Middle Eastern culture in terms of the former being a "reality" culture and the latter a "value" culture. For Westerners, facts are important primary indices of reality. For Middle Easterners, "facts" are more negotiable commodities.

One day I was in a discussion with a Muslim about Jesus. He was trying to tell me that Jesus was a Muslim! Less than a year previously I had graduated from Oxford University with an honours degree in modern history. I was attempting to explain to my Muslim friend that Jesus was born in AD 0 and Prophet Muḥammad in AD 570. Hence it was impossible that Jesus could have been a follower of the faith that Muḥammad introduced. He suggested we went to see an imam. I agreed and, with the imam participating in the discussion, the three of us quickly acknowledged that Jesus lived 600 years before Muḥammad. I thought my point was proved until the imam went on to concur with my friend that Jesus was a Muslim. For me, the historical framework was the most pressing – indeed, it was absolute. For the Muslims, the value framework was more important.

Actually, I knew a little of what they were talking about. I'd had my fair share of discussions about issues in the Bible which tend to be a problem for Westerners. Was Abraham a Christian? a Jew? a "believer"? If a person can only come to know God the Father through Jesus Christ, how did David and Isaiah get to know God when they had not heard of Jesus Christ? At what point did the disciples of Jesus become Christians? Difficult questions arise for Westerners, not really because the answers to these "posers" are difficult (we all accept that these characters had a saving relationship with God) but because the structure of thought in the Bible is different from our own. The biblical framework is not primarily based on a linear view of time in which historical facts are subject to their coding in a space/time continuum. The biblical world, like those of many contemporary Muslims, is one in which value is far more significant than surface reality.

In the Old Testament, time is described in both a quantitative and a qualitative sense. The quantitative approach, in which days, months and years convey the relevance of what is happening, features strongly in three main areas. The royal annals belonging to the period of the divided kingdom of Israel/Judah are given chronologically. The reconstruction of Israel's primal history is given chronologically through the years of Abraham, Isaac and Jacob. The apocalyptic material of some of the prophets, like Daniel, is couched in numbered days and years. For the most part, however, the Old Testament endorses a qualitative approach to time. Revelation is conveyed, not so much by a sequence of events, as by what happens when God impinges on humankind at any given moment. How to get across what is going on now between God and his world, God and his people – that becomes the major focus of revelation. With such an end as the major focus of communication, other methods than a purely historical approach are validly employed. Poetry and balance are the prime means used to describe the sequence of initial creation in Genesis 1. Panorama and melodrama convey the rise and fall and lostness of those created in God's image in the following two chapters of Genesis. Major, "successful" kings of Israel might be glossed over in the sacred chronicles while minor ones become focal points for exploring what God is trying to get across to his people during their reigns. Silence speaks louder than words in the gap between the end of the Old Testament and the start of the New. Even the Hebrew word for "day", the most fundamental of all the terms used in regard to time, conveys different shades of meaning, from moments to entire aeons. In compound formulaic use, it gets across a sense, outside of chronology, of urgency (as in the "day of the Lord") or despair (as in "those days" in Israel when, with no judges, everyone did as they saw fit) and so on.[159]

In ancient Israel, history came to be perceived differently from the nations around – nations like Egypt, the Hittites and the peoples of Mesopotamia. Whilst the surrounding populations honoured lots of gods owning different aspects of time, displacing one another or promoting their own particular groups or interests, the Israelite conviction was that one God was Lord of history. Although, prior to the exile, the people of Israel did not consistently behave as if this conviction was absolutely true, that is the tenor of normative Old Testament revelation: one God is Lord of all time. Time therefore has a goal and a meaning, and the purpose of revelation is to shed light on that goal and meaning. Chronology is only significant insofar as it gives opportunity for revelatory events. The qualitative approach to time "gave historical event its revelatory significance, keeping Hebrew man continually alert to the possibility of the creatively new in his relationship to God and his fellow men".[160] The theological import of this is that in the Old Testament, revelation about the past or revelation concerning the future serve a "paranetic concern" – they are intended to motivate the present. They promote value or relationship or creativity – something to do with how present-day humanity at any one moment in time interacts with its

Creator. Enoch and Abraham, Isaiah and Naaman are all men who know God. The recognition of that reality is far more important than any problem with the fact that chronologically they existed prior to Jesus' crucifixion, or even (for some of them) outside the people of Israel.

In the New Testament, time is similarly treated. We have already noted the "violent" outbreak from heaven to earth conveyed by Mark in his "biography" of Jesus Christ. In that account, the striking thing is that we never find out how much chronological time the story takes:

> We do not know how old Jesus was, how long his public ministry lasted, or how many years he spent teaching and working miracles before his journey to Jerusalem. Except in the case of the passion narrative, the narrator suppresses these specific time clues about the story and the narrative duration.[161]

Chronology is present, but it is neither the only nor the most important measurement of "time". Brenda Schildgen identifies other significant measurements in this Gospel. They include "narrative time" where Mark cites texts from the Old Testament; the chronology gives way to inserts from the Law, the Writings, the Prophets and Psalms. Such inserts are important for his "biography" because traditions of the past were sacred, and the remembering of them gave power or authentication to words or actions in the present. Memory rather than intuition thus served as power or authority – rather similar to many current Muslim cultures and completely different from contemporary, linear, future-oriented Western culture. Another measurement of time used by Mark is "suspended time" where parables are recounted or one story is enmeshed within another story – in the suspension of chronology, more of the divine nature of Jesus of Nazareth gets exposed. "Mythic time" and "ritual time" are two other measurements of time that Schildgen identifies within Mark's Gospel.

When Jesus Christ, in his outbreak from heaven to earth, first speaks in Mark's Gospel, what does he say? "The time has arrived" (Mark 1:15; the Greek word that is used here is *kairos*). We don't know how old Jesus is; we don't know what year this is; but we do know that the most important measurement of time is now being referred to. As Schildgen deftly puts it: "The first words spoken by Jesus in the Gospel of Mark signal the start and the end of the Gospel in time."[162] Yes, it's the beginning of the story of the outbreak. But it's also the end of considering life in a simply chronological way. Chronology has been changed for ever by this *kairos* or crisis moment. Now, eternity is in view. Jesus' "time" is the eschatological moment, the turning point for all history – "crisis time". From Jesus' first words in this Gospel, crisis time is central to understanding all the actions, actors and their relationships in Mark's "biography". And that's why his Gospel continues to engage the reader of every age. It is not just conveying "history" that happened back then. It is getting across a suspension of that kind of perspective and saying to the present-day reader as much as to Jesus' hearers-in-the-flesh: crisis time is here; eternity is here; how are you going to respond to this breakout from heaven?

Old and New Testaments are strongly imbued, it would seem, with a sense that crisis time or revelation time is more important than linear, chronological time. "Value", if you like, is seen as more significant than surface "real time" events, just as it is in many contemporary Muslim cultures. Jesus Christ, nevertheless, has a challenge to make to a worldview in which value could come to be over-enthusiastically enthroned at the expense of the real. He quizzed his contemporaries about the matter of filial obedience in the words of a parable (Matthew 21:28–31). Which son is better: the one who, when asked by his father to do something, replies that he will and then doesn't do it; or the son who replies that he will not and then does it? Middle Easterners tend to feel that the son who answered that he would do the requested task is the better son, because he showed appropriate respect for his father in the way he replied. Such respect consists in conforming to an ideal in word rather than in actually obeying the father's request. Such a denial of reality for the sake of an ideal value is unacceptable, according to Jesus. In his view, it is the son who does the deed, whatever his immediate words, who most closely conforms to the ideal of filial obedience. This is a "hard saying" for many Muslim cultures for it goes against the grain of their sense of appropriate behaviour.

Similarly, it is sometimes very hard to get a straight answer from a Middle Easterner about when something is going to happen (future tense). He doesn't want to be pinned down. Time is not that easily controlled. Too many other factors take precedence. The future cannot be confidently predicted by mere human beings. My wife and I gradually came to learn that the Arabic phrase *in shâ'a 'llâh* ("if God wills") could mean "definitely yes", "definitely no" or any shade of response in between those two extremes.

"Stretch your legs according to the size of your blanket"

Unlike the other motifs-in-tension examined in successive chapters of this book, the themes of "time" and "space" tend to reinforce one another. They are not seriously in tension at all. They do, however, illustrate a difference in perspective from general Western assumptions concerning the time/space continuum. So I have chosen to consider them side by side.

Like time, space is conceived of in organic and personal terms by Middle Easterners. Community is strongly emphasised in the faith of Islam and that sense of togetherness finds reflection in the use of space, in both rural and urban settings. The format of a village speaks of who its inhabitants are. Its physical form makes a very public statement of hierarchy and social domination.[163] Which homes have tiled roofs? Whose houses lie near the village fountain? Which residences sit on the main street? Which parts of the village are areas of male or female domain? Who are the landowners, who the tenants, and who the day labourers? Even in towns and cities, the physical geography of a building or an area speaks of the paramount concerns for a sense of hierarchy, a separation of gender roles and the submersion of the individual in the goals of the group. Indeed, the fundamental Islamic concern for community, social harmony and formalised human interaction has made it, at least potentially, an urban religion with a distinct civil character.

The bazaar and the mosque are two very important physical locations in a town. It is within them that most human transactions take place that are not strictly family activities. Roy Mottahedeh describes the bazaar and the mosque as "the two lungs of public life" in Iran. Not only prices, but men's reputations are continually adjusted within the world of the bazaar as information is shared through the networks of kin and friends. Mottahedeh documents the role of bazaar and mosque as focuses of opposition to regimes and unpopular government policies in Iran during this century.[164]

Certainly, both "lungs" played significant roles in the run-up to the 1979 Islamic revolution which ousted the Shah and brought home Khomeini.

A place to pray, to learn . . .

The *medina* of a city, and especially the central bazaar or *sûq*, is a world in itself. In its labyrinthine confines, manufacturing as well as selling takes place. Similar occupations occupy neighbouring sites. Cloth merchants have their retail outlets set side by side. Coppersmiths share the same noisy atmosphere. The internal layout of the bazaar ensures that goldsmiths trade alongside goldsmiths, money-changers alongside money-changers, leather dealers alongside leather dealers. The interests of "the group" are paramount in the internal spacing of the bazaar. A check is kept on pricing and the acquisition of wealth. The main aim of the bazaar is not to facilitate

Medina's exit

competition and economic growth but to ensure equality of benefit and social interaction.[165] Equality of benefit in a market? How?

In many Muslim societies, especially at the level of bazaar and *medina*, the concept of "limited good" functions as a leveller. In Western societies where economic possibilities are held to be open, the entrepreneur or the imaginative salesman can chase as much wealth as he wants. The possibilities are endless. By contrast, the concept of limited good suggests that there is only so much good in the world to go round.[166] As a consequence, if one manufacturer or tradesman takes more of that limited good, others will have to make do with less. There is a constant tension between the need to cooperate to obtain one's group's ends and the desire to consolidate gains for oneself at the expense of others within the group. The physical layout of the bazaar enables this tension to function.

Muslim communities make a strong demarcation between public and private space. Public life takes place in the streets of the service and commercial sectors while private life looks inwards to courtyards and rooms within walls. Residential districts tend, therefore, to be shielded off from the main streams of public life:

> The houses, often closely knit together, or built wall to wall in the case of courtyard structures, form inward-oriented autonomous units which are protected against visual intrusion from the street or from neighbouring buildings.[167]

In the confines of a home, "space" is again used in a way that reflects social norms. A household is divided into separate quarters where male and female members may feel at home. Male spaces, especially during the day, need to cater for the possibility of entertaining non-family male guests. Female spaces need to be retained as private at all times. As Stefano Bianca neatly summarises, homes need to afford public, male space – what he calls the *selamlik* factor – and private, female space – what he refers to as the *haramlik* factor.[168] Often, in crowded towns and cities, the small amount of overall space available does not allow separate areas of a dwelling to cater for different needs. Rather, versatile space becomes the norm. There tends not to be a dedicated dining room, living room or bedroom but the one space becomes each of those "rooms" in turn. Furniture, then, rather than architectural space serves to distinguish activity. The bed becomes the chair or the table and vice versa. Indeed, for some lower and middle class families, furniture is seen as a banking device to be sold when money is needed. It is not sacred to certain spaces. Home is more about family and family interaction than about space and artefacts. People, not things, nor primarily place, make "home". Versatile space thus has both a social and an aesthetic significance. It successfully supports the priority of the family in Islamic culture, making it possible to offer accommodation and hospitality to all members and relations of an extended family. It also determines the kind of moveable, multi-function furniture needed to accommodate both family guests and make possible the changing of one room of the dwelling into public space during the day.

Space conveys shades of relationship. Who can be seen in what space? Women especially have to be very careful concerning how they appear according to whether the space they stand in is public or protected. Mernissi, commenting on "spatial territories" in Morocco, distinguishes between the "public universe of the 'umma" and the "domestic universe of sexuality".[169] The former, in which women's inclusion is ambiguous, is regulated by equality, reciprocity, unity and so on. The latter, which in essence constitutes the women's world, is regulated in her view by inequality, lack of reciprocity, disunity and so on.

Equally, it has to be said, men may not intrude into space reserved for females. Evelyn Early recalls how "the fact that the home is the woman's castle was dramatized for me one morning when a husband returned home unexpectedly from work to find his wife and her friends cooking. He paused to knock, not daring to enter without alerting the women within".[170] Patricia Jeffery analysed the public and protected worlds of a Sûfî shrine in Delhi in the 1970s. She wrote up her findings in a book called *Frogs in a Well*. Amongst many interesting incidents, she reports one particular outburst of anger from the secluded women in the community that managed the shrine. They were incensed because the government had sent an adult male to follow up its anti-malaria campaign. Such officials were required to check that houses did not contain stagnant water, a potential breeding ground for mosquitoes:

> They used to be considerate to us, and take into account that we *pirzade* [descendants of the saint buried at the shrine] women live in *purdah* [seclusion, literally "curtain"]. For several years they used to send quite young boys to each house to spray with DDT. That was good for us. But last year, they sent an adult man – and of course we couldn't let him come in as none of our men were at home. That is very cruel of the government. Do they want us all to catch malaria?[171]

An Arab mostly finds significance as a social being. Self-esteem, for him, tends to be engendered within the context of a group rather than as an individual. Therefore there is little care for concepts of private space. Moreover, he has grown up knowing that his actions are seen by other members of the household. Similarly, household activities are seen and heard by next-door neighbours. Private space is, by and large, a foreign concept. British and other Western people, by contrast, are very conscious of their personal space. They don't like it being invaded.

One of the first uncomfortable realisations that a Westerner undergoes as he gets to know Arabs is that the Arab chooses to converse head on, at a small distance and in a loud voice. The Arab is very put off by the Westerner's constant attempt to shift to a less personal stance, 45 degrees to one another, so that the two parties cannot smell each other's breath. The Arab often seeks physical contact with the person with whom he is conversing. Men hold arms or hands. The Westerner of course abhors any physical contact in public with a person of the same sex. The "diplomats' dance" ensues in any long conversations across the culture divide. The Westerner seeks to move out of a spatial relationship which, to him, conveys incredible intimacy while the Arab advances to make the contact that reassures him that he is a person being taken seriously by another human being. The two pirouette around the cocktail lounge, each seeking to be comfortable, in spatial terms, with the level of interaction going on.

In any developing friendship with an Arab, the question of Palestine/Israel comes up. Most Arabs are well versed in details of early 20th-century diplomacy (such as the MacMahon correspondence) about which Westerners seemingly know little.[172] The Arabs' sense of betrayal by Britain and France especially, but also by the United Nations, is based upon twists and turns in international diplomacy that is hard for Westerners to comprehend from a perspective other than their own. After all, those twists and turns were largely underwritten by the then imperial powers, each with their own agenda for the Middle East. Even today, when there appears to be encouraging movement towards the reality of self-rule for Palestinians in Israel, the major question of the status of Jerusalem hangs over all negotiations like the sword of Damocles. The kind of feelings evoked by Halim Barakat in his novel *Days of Dust* must be understood by Westerners if they are to relate at all to Arabs over the issue of space at the heart of the Middle East:

> From a high spot in Amman, Ramzy Safady gazed down at the River Jordan. His heartbeats were getting faster, or slowing down perhaps – he did not know which. The land beyond the river was now out of bounds to him. He could not cross the Jordan. Previously he had not been able to visit Haifa or Jaffa or Acre or Safad or Nazareth or Ramla or Lydda; but now he could no longer visit Jerusalem or Ramallah or Bethlehem or Hebron or Nablus or Jenin or Qalqilya or Tulkarm. What was happening to his country? He felt that it was like a child with a disfigured face. He felt like shutting his eyes tight.
>
> Together with his friends, he went to the Hussein Bridge. Everyone was silent and grim. They approached the crumpled bridge cautiously. A large Israeli flag was fluttering on the other side.
>
> Ramzy leaned on an iron support of the collapsed bridge. He stared at the trees across the river, and at the Israeli flag and the Israeli soldiers carrying machine guns. Tears were streaming down his face; he did not want anyone to see him like this.
>
> He could not cross the bridge. Some of his friends in the West, and especially in America, were amazed that he would not recognize the status quo. But to recognize the status quo meant to accept his exile. And they had no idea what it meant to be in exile.[173]

Colin Chapman's book *Whose Promised Land?* constitutes a helpful and balanced investigation of the conflict between Israel and the Palestinians. After surveying the historical, religious, moral and contemporary complexities wrapped up in the continuing crisis at the heart of the Middle East, Chapman issues to all the following challenge:

> Whenever Jews, Christians or Muslims use their scriptures to claim the land for themselves, they need to hear again this simple sentence buried away in the book of Leviticus where God insists that ultimately *the land belongs to him*: "the land is mine and you are but aliens and tenants" (Leviticus 25:23). If God gave it to one group of people for a particular period of time, they were to see it as a *gift*, and not as something that they owned *by right*. The gift was a means to a greater end, not an end in itself.[174]

Without some such theological vision, it seems to me, there can be no lasting way back from occupation and *intifada*, from crushing military overkill and terrorist suicide-bombing. The present-day issue of space at the heart of the Middle East has to be faced up to by Western Christians if they wish to relate positively to Muslims in today's increasingly interlaced world.

"Space", for many Muslims, is not limited to the empirical world in which all human beings exist. Rather, it includes the spirit world, a real but intangible universe, part of the greater reality in which the "here and now" is set. That spirit world is a vital phenomenon, very much affecting what happens in a person's life. Different trans-empirical beings inhabit different spaces within it. It is interesting to note that places where there is little human interaction to be antici-pated are often seen as areas belonging to evil spirits. Deserts, toilets and cemeteries are especially perceived as subject to such contam-ination.

Tayeb Salih's well-loved story *The Wedding of Zein* celebrates the life of a young village eccentric. Zein is crazed, constantly in trou-ble with people and perpetually "slain by love" for different girls of the village. The villagers laugh at him, scold him, protect and tease him. They are also in awe of him, wondering at the successive "mir-acles" which occur in their community during the year of Zein's betrothal. Zein's idiosyncratic nature and peculiar looks are explained in terms of a digression into spirit-space by his mother when she was carrying the young lad home earlier in his life:

> He had grown up with only two teeth in his mouth, one in his upper jaw and one in the lower. His mother, though, says that his mouth was once filled with pearly white teeth, but that when he was six she took him one day to visit some relatives of hers; at sunset, passing by a deserted ruin rumoured to be haunted, Zein had suddenly become nailed to the ground and had begun shivering as with a fever. Then he let out a scream. After that he took to his bed for several days, and on recovering from his illness it was found that all his teeth had fallen out – except for one in his upper jaw and one in the lower.[175]

Hani Fakhouri is an anthropologist who investigated the customs and mores of the Egyptian inhabitants of Kafr el-Elow, a village situated south of Cairo, on the banks of the Nile. As part of his description of the *zâr* ceremonies persisting in the village, despite government proscription, he recounts the story of a patient who contracted her illness in a place associated with the presence of evil spirits:

> This is a woman in her thirties who, at the age of twelve, was hit by her brother in the privy of her home. As a result of the blow she felt nause-ated, her face was swollen, her eyes stared, and she refused food. A *shaik* consulted by her mother attributed the child's condition to possession by a *rieh* (spirit of a bathroom) and recommended that the girl attend a *zar*. The mother refused to comply with his advice, however, and the girl's sickness grew worse daily. Often she felt that people were jumping on her when she was in the bathroom. Finally, the girl's grandmother took her to a *zar*, and for three consecutive weeks thereafter the girl visited Mari Guirguis and Amir Tadros Churches as the *zar* practitioner had ordered, running about kissing the crosses and statues each time. After completing the church visits, she regained her appetite and began to act normal. Now, whenever the patient feels nervous or aggressive, she attends a *zar* ceremony.[176]

The main purpose of the *zâr* ceremony is to lead each afflicted female into a stable relationship with the particular spirit inhabiting her. The widespread occurrence of such ceremonies, and their equiv-alents in other countries, reflects a conviction about the possible pollution of certain spaces on earth by spirit beings.

A few months ago I was approached by Mr. K., a gentleman living near the church in London where I work as a pastor. I had grown to know this Muslim family over the previous four years, having helped them with some educational issues to do with their son. Mr. K.'s request of me now was not about schooling but about trouble in his house. "Our children sleep every night in our bedroom with us, because they are frightened of noises on the stairs. Someone bangs up and down the steps. There is a bad odour in the house in certain places. Sometimes I wake up feeling as if I am being suffo-cated by something sitting on my chest. I am very frightened. None of us can sleep properly any more. My brother, when he comes to stay, has this experience also. Can you please help?"

A colleague and I spent an evening at the house, reading the Bible and praying in Jesus' name through the rooms of their home. All the family was present. We discovered that we had not been the first port of call for assistance. The imam of the mosque that the family occasionally attends had visited several times. He had recited the Qur'ân, given them printed verses of the Qur'ân to put up round the home and urged them to pray constantly. His ministrations had evidently not produced the desired effect. Since the prayer-visit of my colleague and myself, the infestation seems to have diminished and the family members sleep better at night.

The reclamation of "space" for God is a constant theme of the Bible, extending from its first pages, with the memory of God walking in a garden alongside his human creation, to its last pages, with the vision of a city in which the Lamb is seen wherever one looks. Between memory and vision is rendered the saga of salvation: can God and man live together or is the contamination too great? How might God and man once again be enabled to share the same space?

I'm thinking once more of the outbreak from heaven as it is dramatised in Mark's Gospel. Space is a strong referent in the first eight chapters of this Gospel – before Jesus begins his journey to Jerusalem. Water travel features quite considerably as Jesus is conveyed back and forth across lakes. We soon discover in these fast-moving paragraphs that Mark is leading us to and fro between Jewish and Gentile territory. Jesus exorcises a Jewish man in a synagogue at Capernaum (Mark 1:21–28); he heals a demon-possessed Gentile in the region of the Gerasenes (Mark 5:1–20). He feeds 5,000 men and their families in a Jewish area (Mark 6:30–44) and 4,000 men and their families in a Gentile area (Mark 8:1–13).

What is Mark's point? With the exorcisms there is the strong statement that Jesus will clean up an individual's life, no matter his background, no matter how deeply enmeshed in evil he has become. With the miraculous feedings, there is the wonderful demonstration that Jesus is able to supply, out of his own divine resources, the needs of all who will receive sustenance from him. But there is a deeper significance, surely; otherwise just one example from each miraculous event would have sufficed.

Interestingly, nowhere else in the Gospel does Jesus speak directly with a demonic opponent except in these two exorcisms of Mark 1 and Mark 5:

> Mark clearly intended these stories to be affiliated. In both cases, upon entering new symbolic territory Jesus encounters immediate resistance in the form of a demoniacally possessed man. Through verbal confronta-

tion and powerful exorcism he overcomes this challenge, provoking amazement and publicity. This enables Jesus to commence his widespread ministry of healing to the poor: first to the Jews around Capernaum (1:32), and subsequently, on his next crossing back to the other side of the sea (6:53–56), to gentiles as well.[177]

In Capernaum, Jesus invaded Jewish religious space – the synagogue. There, he had an argument with the current owners of that space (the teachers of the Law) about authority. The clue to what is going on here at a deeper level is given in the words of the unclean spirit: "What do you want with us, Jesus of Nazareth? Have you come to destroy us? I know who you are – the Holy One of God" (Mark 1:24). Is this voice a single or multiple entity? Is it "us" or "I"? Does the spirit speak for itself or for those it represents in the synagogue, the Jewish religious hierarchy? The people present get the point – their conclusion is that the exorcism is not an end in itself but the clincher in an argument over teaching, over authority (verse 27). In other words, Jesus is here invading a space – Jewish religious space – which has become contaminated, and is reclaiming it for God. In the encounter, the evil spirit names Jesus, or tries to, and Jesus silences it/them and expels it/them.

In the region of the Gerasenes, Jesus invaded Gentile territory; this region lay in the furthest reaches of the Roman military occupation of Palestine. There, he had an argument with a "representative" of that imperial authority. Again the clue to what is going on is given in the words of the unclean spirit: "My name is Legion for we are many" (Mark 5:9). Is this voice a single or multiple entity? Is it "my" or "we"? Does the spirit speak for itself or for those it represents as "Legion", the infesting, military occupying power? Actually, the rest of this story is filled with military imagery; the term used for "herd", for example, was often used to refer to a band of military recruits, while the pigs' "charge" into the sea suggests troops rushing into battle. In other words, Jesus is here again invading a space – this time Roman, imperialistic space – which has become contaminated, in order to reclaim it for God. In this encounter Jesus extracts the name of the evil horde before expelling it/them.

Similarly with the miracles of provision – again specified as occurring respectively in Jewish and Gentile space. The kingdom of God invades the human spaces, the areas associated with Jew or

Gentile, and offers divine provision within them for those who will receive sustenance from the hands of Jesus Christ. In the Jewish incident, the disciples twice suggest to Jesus that the solution to the hunger of the crowds is to buy food (Mark 6:36–37). Jesus' solution has nothing to do with participation in the dominant economic order. In the Gentile incident, Jesus will not accept a pious suggestion of fasting (the "going home hungry" in Mark 8:3 is literally "fasting"). He will only send them away after they have eaten and are satisfied. In both instances, Jesus is moved with "compassion" (6:34; 8:2). The Greek word is a strong word conveying the idea of having one's guts torn apart! The Jewish and Gentile masses are each miraculously "fed", not by ordinary commercial means, nor by ignoring their physical need for the sake of some supposed spiritual benefit, but by the miraculous activity of the one who is the Bread of the world. Out of his compassion for the masses on both sites, Jesus demonstrates that in him the separated communities on earth can be satisfied, can be overwhelmed, by a superabundance of blessing – real, tangible, edible blessing.

Heaven's use of time and space

God is no stranger to Middle Easterners' concepts of time and space. In recent years, examples abound of ways in which the Lord has acted in sovereign power within such constructs. His intrusions have come along lines understood as "possible" by Middle Easterners. Through those possible channels, "impossible" messages have been conveyed. Intrusions into space have taken the form of miracles, while dreams have interrupted time.

In a very moving account, Gulshan Esther tells of an intervention in her life by a vision-appearance of Jesus. Gulshan Esther had lived her life hopelessly crippled and incurable, despite a pilgrimage to Mecca and a visit to the best surgeons in London. Back home, the broken-hearted woman began desperately calling out to the Jesus she had read a little about in the Qur'ân:

> What happened next is something that I find hard to put into words. I know that the whole room filled with light. At first I thought it was from my reading lamp beside the bed. Then I saw that its light looked dim. Perhaps it was the dawn? But it was too early for that. The light was

growing, growing in brightness, until it surpassed the day. I covered myself with my shawl. I was so frightened . . .

I then became aware of figures in long robes, standing in the midst of the light, some feet from my bed. There were 12 figures in a row and the figure in the middle, the thirteenth, was larger and brighter than the others.

"Oh God," I cried and the perspiration broke out on my forehead.

Suddenly a voice said, "Get up. This is the path you have been seeking. I am Jesus Son of Mary, to whom you have been praying, and now I am standing in front of you. You get up and come to me."[178]

In a wonderful, early morning visitation, Jesus heals the cripple and blesses her. The young woman discerns a hole in his hand as he does so. Jesus teaches her the words of the Lord's prayer, which later she reads in a Bible.

The deliverance from demonisation of Mrs. H. in 1994 was described earlier in Chapter 5. The liberated lady didn't keep her new life to herself:

Mrs. H. went to visit a sick aunt. She prayed for her aunt to be healed and she was! Two days later her aunt had a dream in which Jesus appeared to her and told her that He was the one who had healed her. She told Mrs. H. about this and she led her to faith in Christ.[179]

A vision and a dream significantly interrupted these Muslims' lives, just as they interrupted the lives of many, many biblical characters. Praying for, and being interpreters of, such dreams and visions is a significant contribution for sensitive Western Christians to make to evangelism amongst Muslims today.

In 1993, a Muslim imam was propelled to faith in Christ by a miracle which reveals God's sovereignty over "space":

While on a trip to one of the holy sites [in Mecca/Medina], he struck up a conversation with the bus-driver. The driver gently but firmly rebuked him for wasting his money on the pilgrimage and told the imam that God wanted to know him personally as a friend and not at a distance through rituals. The imam wanted to know more but when he returned to the bus after touring the site, there was a new driver. Doubts and questions about Islam filled his mind for the rest of his time in Mecca. He could not forget the bus-driver's words and wondered, "If Islam is not the true faith, what is?"

A few days after his return to S.E. Asia, the imam visited the home of a Chinese Christian friend. On the wall he was startled to see a picture of the bus-driver he had talked to in Mecca!

"Do you know that man?" he asked his Chinese friend.

"Yes," his friend replied, "that man is Jesus!"

In a state of shock the imam told his friend about his experience in Mecca. Immediately a sense of his sin swept over him and with his friend's help, he repented and believed in Jesus as Lord and Saviour.

The imam then went and shared his experience with his family and they too confessed Jesus as Lord.[180]

God has no problems with views of time and space which differ from the Western preferences. The potency of the techniques used by "Jesus" in the examples described here lies in the Holy Spirit's appropriation of concepts of time and space already functioning in the worldviews of the Muslims concerned.

Non-Western Christians are perhaps more readily accepting of constructs of reality in which the kind of occurrences illustrated here make sense. Western Christians who admit the possibility of the sun's shadow being reversed in answer to Gideon's prayer, or the overruling of the laws of thermodynamics in a Babylonian fiery furnace, should make potential co-labourers in cultures closer to those of the Bible than our own secular humanist model. In those cultures, time and space speak loudly of the values held tenaciously by the people concerned. Can we hear what they are declaring?

CHAPTER SEVEN

LANGUAGE AND SILENCE

God gave the Frenchman a head, the Chinese hands
and the Arab a mouth!

Arabic is the Arab's greatest treasure and he knows it! The language
of a peninsula's daily communication was transformed in the
seventh century to become the direct source of spiritual nourishment
for generations of Muslims.

Prophet Muḥammad was reputedly illiterate, yet he recited a text
which has sung its way into Arabs' hearts through the centuries:

> The Qur'ân is a living proof of the existence of Allah, the All-powerful.
> It is also a testimony of the validity of the Islamic way of life for all
> times. Arabic, the language of the Qur'ân, unlike the languages of other
> revealed books, is a living, dynamic and a very rich language . . .
>   The superb style of the Qur'ân has a tremendous effect on its readers.
> It totally changes the pattern of life of those who believe and practise its
> teachings. It leaves a soothing effect on the mind of the reader, even if
> he does not fully understand its meaning.[181]

Whatever their native tongue, Muslims the world over are content to
recite the Qur'ân and say their prayers in Arabic. Indeed, it is a
prerequisite for participating in the *baraka* of the Book that it be read
and recited in Arabic:

> The efficacy of canonical prayers, litanies, invocations, etc. is contained
> not only in the content but also in the very sounds and reverberations of
> the sacred language. Religion is not philosophy or theology meant only

for the mental plane. It is a method of integrating our whole being including the psychical and the corporeal. The sacred language serves precisely as a providential means whereby man can come not only to think about the truths of religion, which is only for people of a certain type of mentality, but to participate with his whole being in a Divine norm. This truth is universally applicable, and especially it is clearly demonstrated in the case of the Quran whose formulae and verses are guide posts for the life of the Muslim and whose continuous repetition provides a heavenly shelter for man in the turmoil of his earthly existence.[182]

Language of heaven!

Apologists for Islam in the late 20th century employed computer-aided analyses of the use of the alphabet in the Qur'ân as "proof" of its divine inspiration.[183] At the heart of this methodology is a conviction that Arabic is indeed the language of heaven and that the words "sent down" via Muḥammad are a reproduction of the Book "inscribed" above. Qur'ânic Arabic is God's own tongue! Such recognition of the language of the Qur'ân as the Word of God (*kalâm allâh*) throughout Muslim history has, in the words of one recent analyst, "turned every religious scholar into a linguist and made the mastery of the divine language the single most important prerequisite for intellectual and artistic accomplishments".[184] The language forms in effect the reservoir of religious knowledge and the latter can only be acquired via a proper knowledge of the former. Argued in reverse, this view has caused considerable *angst* to non-Muslim Arabic-speaking minorities; they are likely to be given the message that because they do not know the Qur'ân, they do not know the Arabic language either!

Sayyid Qutb, inspirer of many Middle Eastern Islamists,[185] wrote a commentary on the Qur'ân while he was kept in solitary confinement within an Egyptian jail by President Nasser. His consolation for the internment he experienced from 1954 to 1964 lay, he felt, in the daily reassurance of abiding "in the shade of the Qur'ân". He was critical of Muslims in the world around him who did not seem to live in that shade, despite the fact that they were at liberty to do so. His long commentary, entitled *In the Shade of the Qur'ân*, was aimed at helping his fellow Muslims to live and practise "true" Islam in the same way that the early generations of Muslims had done.

The final volume of Qutb's commentary deals with Suras 78 to 114. The author introduces his exposition with these observations:

> This thirtieth part of the Qur'ân has a special, distinctive colour. All the *surahs* it includes are Makkan, except two . . . Although they vary in length, they are all short. More significant, however, is the fact that they form a single group with more or less the same theme. They have the same characteristics of rhythm, images, connotations and overall style. They are, indeed, like a persistent and strong knocking on a door, or loud shouts seeking to awaken some people who are fast asleep, or some drunken men who have lost consciousness, or are in a night club, completely absorbed with their dancing or entertainment. The knocks and the shouts come one after the other: Wake up! Look around you!

Think! Reflect! There is a God! There is planning, trial, liability, reck-
oning, reward, severe punishment and lasting bliss. The same warning is
repeated time after time. A strong hand shakes them violently . . .

This is how I feel when I read this part of the Qur'ân. It puts strong
emphasis on a small number of highly important facts and strikes certain
notes which touch men's hearts.[186]

As Qutb here demonstrates, the language of the Qur'ân provokes
feeling. The poetry as well as the point of the text awakens the
emotions. A well-known *hadîth* says: "Nobody can escape the pleasure of the Qur'ân." Al-Ghazâlî asserted that some passages of the
Qur'ân can induce ecstasy in the listener. Ask any Muslim, especially an Arab, and he will quickly discourse on the divine quality of
the Qur'ân. The music of the verses, as much as their message,
convinces him that God must be its originator. Indeed, the Arabic
root *qirâ'a* (from which "Qur'ân" is derived) means to recite or read
aloud. The Qur'ân is intended to be a recitation. How a listener feels
as he hears the suras being chanted is as strong a proof of divine
inspiration as any analysis of its content. The inimitability of the text
declares its absolute uniqueness. The philologist al-Thaᶜâlibî (died
AD 1038) expresses what all Muslims know in their hearts:

Whoever loves the Prophet loves the Arabs, and whoever loves the Arab
loves the Arabic language in which the best of books was revealed . . .
Whomsoever God has guided to Islam believes that Muḥammad is the
best of Prophets . . . that the Arabs are the best of peoples . . . and that
Arabic is the best of languages.[187]

Oral tradition is a major source of enculturation for Arabs and many
other Muslim peoples. After the Qur'ân, which many folk learn by
heart, the records of tradition (*hadîth*) convey the details of Prophet
Muḥammad's sayings and doings. Those Traditions were conveyed
by word of mouth for many decades until sifted, authenticated and
recorded in writing for posterity. A major aim of nearly all Muslims
is to emulate the Prophet by living their lives in imitation of his. The
Traditions, consequently, are of critical importance in shaping daily
mores. That importance is enhanced by the fact that the Traditions
authenticate themselves, as the following example demonstrates:

Narrated Jabir bin Abdullah: Some angels came to the Prophet while he was sleeping. Some of them said, "He is sleeping." Others said, "His eyes are sleeping but his heart is awake." Then they said, "There is an example for this companion of yours." One of them said, "Then set forth an example for him." . . . Then they said, "His example is that of a man who has built a house and then offered therein a banquet and sent an inviter (messenger) to invite the people. So whoever accepted the invitation of the inviter, entered the house and ate of the banquet." Then the angels said, "Interpret this example to him so that he may understand it." . . . And then they said, "The house stands for Paradise and the call-maker is Muḥammad and whoever obeys Muḥammad, obeys Allah; and whoever disobeys Muḥammad, disobeys Allah".[188]

Qur'ân, *hadîth* and commentaries are the currency of Islamic theologians especially, but ordinary Muslims possess other treasures as well. Those treasures are expressed in a variety of heart-languages and through a multiplicity of art forms.

Shahrokh Meskoob is one of Iran's leading contemporary authors and cultural historians. He has presented in book form a series of lectures given in Paris a decade ago concerning Iranian nationality and the Persian language. The core of Meskoob's analysis of hundreds of literary, religious, and mystical works by Persian-speaking authors from the tenth to the end of the 19th century consists in his assessment of the role of three major groups in the spread and flourishing of Persian in the Iranian cultural world. Those groups comprise the courtiers and bureaucratic officials, the religious scholars (the *ulama*), and the Muslim mystics (the Sûfîs).[189] Not surprisingly, he concludes that the *ulama* contributed least to the development of Persian because they wrote mostly in Arabic. Huge contributions, by contrast, were made by Sûfî poets and authors and by those in employment of the royal court and the state bureaucratic apparatus. Inasmuch as the Persian language is identified by Meskoob as one of four major elements contributing to Iran's cultural identity,[190] the significance of Sûfîsm and the development of bureaucratic systems using local language cannot be overstated. Being an Iranian Shîᶜa Muslim is not just about niceties of theology or early Islamic history, but about the development of language and the emergence of the "soul" of a people.

Folk stories and legends persist and are told and retold down through the generations. Very popular, throughout the Muslim world as a whole, are the tales of Mulla Nasrudin. Superficially, the Nasrudin stories function as jokes. They derive, however, from the Sûfî mystic tradition and can be appreciated at different levels. There is the humorous incident itself. There may be a moral to the tale. There may also be something deeper that helps project the Sûfî, the initiated mystic, towards enlightenment:

A kinsman came to see the Mulla from somewhere deep in the country, bringing a duck as a gift. Delighted, Nasrudin had the bird cooked and shared it with his guest. Presently, however, one countryman after another started to call, each one a friend of the friend of the "man who brought you the duck." No further presents were forthcoming.

At length the Mulla was exasperated. One day yet another stranger appeared. "I am the friend of the friend of the friend of the relative who brought you the duck."

He sat down, like all the rest, expecting a meal. Nasrudin handed him a bowl of hot water.

"What is this?"

"This is the soup of the soup of the soup of the duck which was brought by my relative."[191]

The point, for the Sûfî, of this story is that internal experience cannot be transmitted through mere repetition. To assume that it can, leads only to perpetual dilution. It has rather to be reinvigorated from its source. The point is one that we would all do well to heed!

Nasrudin and his wife woke one night to hear two men fighting below their window. She sent the Mulla out to find out what the trouble was. He wrapped his blanket over his shoulders and went downstairs. As soon as he approached the men, one of them snatched his one and only blanket. Then they both ran off.

"What was the fight about, dear?" his wife asked as he entered the bedroom.

"About my blanket, apparently. As soon as they got that, they went away."[192]

What is the deeper meaning of this comic incident? A mystic who is gaining insight into the true nature of existence stops asking questions which presuppose a rational answer. He realises that situations can be changed by events which apparently have no relevance to them. For most Muslims, the Nasrudin stories are a delightful part of their rich heritage in oral literature.

Songs and poetry are other important facets of that oral literature. Versification is used by street vendors throughout the towns of the

Music and movement

Muslim world to advertise their wares. Children employ rhymed couplets, especially rude ones, to tease one another.[193] Folk songs are very popular, often expressing melancholy themes. Middle Eastern musical scales differ from the Western norm, being built out of quarter-tones rather than semi-tones, and lend themselves to a variety of modes, rather than just the major/minor possibilities of Western music.[194] Often there are set patterns of melodic sequence in a song, rendered alternately by instruments and vocalist. The aim of the artiste is to decorate each phrase on solo instrument or with the human voice. Applause erupts at specially contrived trills and passing notes. The traditional world of Middle Eastern music, undefined in terms of "beginning", "middle" and "end", provides an outlet for extended, creative expression. As a result, the interpreter of music is often more famous than the composer. It is said that Abd al-Wahhâb, one of Egypt's recent famous singers, emerged into the limelight at a concert in Tanta in which, feeling inspired, he improvised above the orchestra for an hour or so.[195] When Umm Kulthûm (died 1975) gave her legendary concerts, she would be asked by the audience to repeat the same stanza up to 19 or 20 times; every repetition had its own improvised melody, each different from the others. A song of 20 minutes could take more than an hour to perform. Joe Pierce offers a translated example of a typically sad, but popular, Turkish folk song:

> I am sick and cannot hold my pencil in my hand.
> I wonder if I can see my birthplace.
> Give my regards to my father.
> Look at my picture and cry.
> If my father asks, "Where is my [name of the singer]?"
> Don't tell him where I have gone.
> The world is like a gear turning backwards.
> Whoever is waiting for me will look down the road and cry.
> In the distance I see Çankira mountain.
> There is a big cemetery near the hospital.
> They will write [name of the singer] on the tombstone.[196]

Poetry comes to the forefront of public celebration during the festival marking Prophet Muḥammad's birthday. Muslims gather publicly to hear recitals of various paeans of praise, celebrating the Prophet's life. In the Arab world, al-Bûṣîrî's "Mantle" poem is one of the most popular recitations. It was composed by al-Bûṣîrî after he was miraculously cured from a paralysis. One night, Prophet Muḥammad appeared to al-Bûṣîrî in a dream and covered him with a striped mantle. When al-Bûṣîrî awoke in the morning, he was cured. In gratitude, al-Bûṣîrî composed "The Mantle" in honour of the Prophet. Part of the poem runs:

Our Prophet, who issued commands and prohibitions, and
    there is no one
    More justified than he to say: "No" or "Yes!"
He is [Allah's] beloved, whose intercession is to be hoped
    for,
    Against each terror among the oncoming terrors.
He summoned [the people] to Allah, and those who attach
    themselves to him,
    Are attaching themselves to a rope that will not break.
He surpassed the [other] Prophets in physical and moral
    qualities,
    Nor did they approach him in either knowledge or
    magnanimity.
All of them seek to obtain from the Apostle of Allah,
    A ladle-full from the ocean or a sip from the continuous
    rains.
They will stand before him at their ranking places,
    Like diacritical points of science or vowel signs of
    wisdom.
He is the one whose interior and exterior form were made
    perfect.
    Then the Creator of men chose him as a beloved friend.
Far removed [is he] from having any partner in his good
    qualities,
    For in him the essence of goodness is undivided.
Leave aside what the Christians claim for their Prophet,
    And by what you will judge and decide what there is in
    him to be praised.
Ascribe to his person whatever nobility you may desire,
    And ascribe to his dignity whatever grandeur you please.
For verily, the excellence of the Apostle of Allah has no
    bounds,
So that a speaker might tell of it with his mouth.
Were his miracles in accord with his dignity, by their
    grandeur,
His name would, when pronounced, resuscitate decayed
    bones . . .[197]

In the Turkish-speaking world, Chelebi's *Mevlidi Sherif* ("Birth-
Song of the Prophet") is frequently chanted at celebrations
honouring Prophet Muḥammad. The poem is especially memorable

as words in Turkish sentence structures rhyme internally anyway.[198]
Both al-Bûṣîrî and Chelebi give penetrating exposés of the sinfulness of humanity and mankind's helplessness before God but for the
intervention of a mediator. Chelebi's moving delineation of
Muslims' hypocrisy conveys in a few rhymed meters what it would
take years for a Western Christian missionary to communicate:

> So come, let us confess our sad rebellions;
>   With secret moan and bitter groan repenting.
>
> Though life should last however many seasons,
>   Death shall one day become our sole employment.
>
> So let us now defeat death's pangs and sadness,
>   By evermore entreating: God forgive us!
>
> Our deeds have ever been of God unworthy;
>   We know not what may be our last condition.
>
> Our worthless course have we not left nor altered,
>   No preparations made for life eternal.
>
> Our names we make to shine before the people,
>   But secretly our hearts we all have tarnished.
>
> Each breath sees us commit sins by the thousand,
>   Yet not once in our life repent we one sin.
>
> Yielding to self we sin and know no limit –
>   What shall we do, O God, how make repentance?
>
> No one of us but knows his heart's sedition,
>   Yet we have come, thy mercy to petition.
>
> We hope for grace to make a good profession,
>   For Mercy's touch, and Ahmed's intercession.[199]

The intention of both al-Bûṣîrî and Chelebi is, of course, to demonstrate the more strongly how Prophet Muḥammad is special to God
and thus the only and sure hope for his community. Muslims weep
at the recitations – both for their own sinfulness and for the wonder

of possible mediatorship on their behalf by the Prophet. In these poems lurks a strong statement of the need for some kind of mediatorship between a sinful Muslim and a holy God.

The story of Joseph, expounded in Sura 12 of the Qur'ân, has given rise to one of the greatest allegorical love stories in Islamic literature. Yusuf Ali claims that "in almost all Islamic languages the romance of Yûsuf and Zulaikhâ has justly attracted much attention in mystic poetry".[200] Zulaikhâ is a beautiful princess, daughter of a king of the Maghreb. In her youth she dreams of a handsome young man and falls in love with him. In her dream this young man will only identify himself as *wazîr* or ruler of Egypt. Zulaikhâ consequently refuses all other offers of marriage when she is older, eventually persuading her father to approach the *wazîr* of Egypt and arrange her marriage to him. This is done and the princess finally arrives in a great procession to marry the man of her dreams. There she discovers that the real *wazîr* of Egypt is not the character of whom she had dreamt in her youth. What to do? A voice comes to her from the unseen world – these are the words in Jâmî's version:

> "True this is not thy love! But thy desire for thy true love will be satisfied through him. Fear him not. The jewel of thy virgin honour is safe with him. If a great sleeve is shown, but there is no hand within, what is there to hold a dagger?"[201]

The *wazîr* turns out to be a eunuch. Zulaikhâ (safely) marries him and spends her days in Egypt in outward splendour and inward grief, learning about true love in which selfish desires are denied. Eventually Yûsuf turns up in Egypt, slave of a foreign merchant. Zulaikhâ sees him, recognises him as the man of her dreams, and helps her husband to purchase him. She then schemes to entrap Yûsuf and enjoy his love, as per the qur'ânic story. While Yûsuf spends his ensuing years in prison, the *wazîr* dies. Zulaikhâ by now has aged, losing her beauty in the process. But her immature love has been purified: she grows to be meek, lowly and sincere. Zulaikhâ is now a widow; Yûsuf, released, becomes *wazîr*. At Yûsuf's prayer, Zulaikhâ's health, youth and beauty are restored and they are married in pure and true love. The allegory is about true and false love; it offers suggestions about a divine love that transcends all human love:

> How blest is he who can close his eye
> And let the vain pageants of life pass by!
> Untouched by the magic of earth can keep
> His soul awake while the senses sleep;
> Scorn the false and the fleeting that meets the view,
> And see what is hidden and firm and true![202]

Majnûn (literally "the Mad") is another well-known legendary figure of both Arabic and Persian poetry. He represents the absolute madness of love. His real name is Qais and his love for Laylâ constitutes love for its own sake, no matter the beloved's qualities. Qais ends up as Majnûn – tormented with love. His feelings for his beloved become a parable of the love that humans may bear towards God. The Sûfîs, especially in Persia, adopted this kind of love poetry as a means of expressing their love for God, a love that sacrifices everything in its quest for union with him. Ahmad Shawqî was born in Egypt in 1868, suffered exile from his native country, but returned in 1920, a gifted poet and budding composer of lyrical drama. His most celebrated work is his *Majnun Layla*, in which he retells the story of Qais' unhappy passion.[203] In doing so he draws on the version of the story as it is recounted in the *Kitâb al-Afghânî*, the principal extant source for early Arab lore. Here, in translation, is Qais' description of his beloved as it is delivered in the second act:

> Layla! A voice called Layla, and it stirred
> A mad intoxication in my breast.
> Layla! Go, see if the sweet sound shakes the desert,
> And if a David sings there to his lute.
> Layla! A call for "Layla" fills my ear,
> A loud enchantment echoing in the hearing.
> Layla! She echoes in my ear and soul,
> Like warblers' song that echoes in a thicket.

Riddles, sayings and proverbs contribute their wit to the bank of oral literature that funds Arab and other Muslim cultures.

The impact of words and emotions counts for far more than the written transmission of facts in many Middle Eastern languages. Helen Watson, a fellow in anthropology at Cambridge University, conducted in-depth field research among women living in the City of the Dead, Cairo. One day, as she was busy making laborious research notes, one of her informants quizzed her: "Words from the heart are more alive than your scribblings. When we speak, our words burn. Do yours?"[204] Indeed, in Arabic, the word *kalama* means "to speak"; the associated noun *kalm* means "wound" or "slash". Watson observed first-hand, in this poor area of Cairo, the power of a story to entertain, teach, bind a community together and get under someone's skin:

> Storytelling is a highly-charged emotional activity which pays little heed to open wounds inflicted by real life. Storytellers are not bound by the rules of polite society and conversation and their tales are expected to be provocative, evocative and exciting. They must stir the members of the audience and touch raw nerves. The portmanteau of sensitive information at a storyteller's disposal is opened indiscriminately and used to flavour her tales with subtle, yet penetrating, references to the other women present.[205]

She quotes a series of stories, some made up on the spot, others reworked traditional tales, and offers some insight into the pointed relevance within the community of women of each tale. The record is fascinating. At the end of one particularly provocative performance, entitled "The Singing Bird", she notes:

> The tale's triumphant conclusion was greeted with cheers. Everyone tried to do the impossible – to flatter the storyteller and not go cross-eyed trying to see both Oum Mustafa's and the Sheikha's reaction at the same time.[206]

The story had been mediatorial, and it worked its magic, for Oum Mustafa and the Sheikha, embroiled in an argument and sitting in opposite corners of the room, were brought to reconciliation through it.

Mariam Behnam grew up and lived in southern Iran until 1979 when she moved to Dubai. As a child she loved the popular stories repeated in her Bastaki dialect. Gradually, she collected many of these tales, favourites of adults and children alike. One example from her collection is repeated here. It derives from Sheikh Saadi of Shiraz, a story-composer who came to be known simply as Sheikh-e-Shiraz. This is the Sheikh's story of two dervishes:

Once upon a time two dervishes (holy people) were travelling together. One was lean and ate very little and the other was fat and robust and ate all the time.

On the way, they entered an unknown land. The authorities there were on the look out for some evil spies, who were supposed to be disguised as dervishes. Unfortunately, these two fitted the description, so they were captured by mistake and thrown into a cell, where they were left to die.

However, after two weeks, the real culprits were caught. The authorities realized their mistake and rushed to the prison to rescue the two dervishes, whom they had locked up and totally neglected. To everyone's surprise, when they opened the door they found the lean man was still alive and breathing, whilst the fat man was long dead. The Hakim was brought in to examine the two dervishes.

He explained this strange occurrence to the rescuers, "You see, the fat man didn't survive because he was too dependent on food, while the lean man did not need that much nourishment and thus he survived the two weeks by praying to the Lord and meditating."

Therefore the story ends with Sheikh Saadi's couplet, "The man who eats continuously, finds it very difficult to curb his appetite when there is lack of food."[207]

Since time immemorial, comments Behnam, the telling of stories such as this has been an important part of culture on both sides of the Persian Gulf; even adults have spent hours listening to their elders narrating them.

In his novel *The Legend of the Thousand Bulls*, Turkish novelist Yashar Kemal describes the sad disintegration of a nomadic Yörük tribe. This is a powerful story describing the pathos of modernisation overcoming traditional ways for such a community in Turkey. Kemal well illustrates the power of fanciful thoughts, beautiful sentences and delicate phrases that lead the speaker of them to be convinced that others will naturally yield to their force. Sadly for the Yörük, the new Turkey no longer allows that to happen!

The Yörük nomads live by a legend which says that each year on a night in May, two heavenly stars meet. At that instant, earthly life hesitates and whoever sees the joining of the stars and makes a wish can be sure that their wish will come true. As the novel opens, the tribe is encamped in a mountain valley. The elders are trying to impress upon everyone the importance of not making a selfish wish. The prime need of the community is that when winter approaches and they have to move down to the Chukurova plain, they will find land where they can winter their flocks. For several years now, their situation has been getting increasingly precarious. This winter it has become critical. Their only hope lies in a star-born wish.

Of course, in the event, various protagonists of the novel make selfish wishes as they watch the stars meet. When the winter months approach, the tribe is once again moved on from place to place, unwelcome in the plains. Eventually, the tribespeople reach the point of disintegration. In a last desperate attempt at self-preservation, they pin their hopes on a beautiful sword that their blacksmith, Haydar, has spent all his working life forging. The blacksmith travels to the nation's capital to present the sword to a high official, confident that the man will proudly accept the wonderful gift and in return give land to the tribe. The reader knows from the outset that the idea is quaint and ridiculous. But Kemal captivates his audience with his description of the way the tribe, and blacksmith Haydar especially, thinks about the solution to all their problems. With the survival of the tribe resting on the precious piece of metal in his hands, Haydar sets himself to wait on the government official. As he waits, he dreams of the coming audience in exaggerated terms:

> They have told Ismet Pasha . . . They've told him that Haydar the Master Blacksmith of the Holy Hearth has finished the sword he's been fashioning for him these last thirty years. How glad Ismet Pasha is! His white moustache twitches with pleasure. The Master of the Blacksmith's Hearth, the last, as the Hearth is dying out after ten thousand, a hundred thousand years, Haydar, the last sage of all, has made a sword for him with all the craftsmanship, the polished skill of a ten-thousand-year-old tradition . . . This sword has been forged not in thirty years, but in ten thousand, a hundred thousand. And it will never be made any more . . . Ever since iron exists this sword has been forged, and the last one of all falls to Ismet Pasha's lot. What more does he want! . . .
>
> Oh, he'll be glad Ismet, when he sees the sword! "Rise, Haydar," he'll cry. "Rise at once. It's we who ought to kneel at your feet. Pashas like us, they come and go by the score, but Haydar, the Master Blacksmith, comes only once to this earth, and when he goes he never comes again . . ."[208]

Not long after these musings, the poor master blacksmith is traumatised by the shock of rude dismissal. The Pasha glimpses the sword, briefly humours the nomad, then jumps into his chauffeur-driven limousine and disappears. Haydar rides in a trance back to his people to confess the end of their hopes and dreams. The tribe despairs and its disintegration quickens. Even in English translation, the force of the dream-words conveys the pride of Haydar and the clash of two worlds far removed from one another – that of the tribespeople and that of the national politician.

The Egyptian novelist Taha Hussein in many ways mirrored in the Arab context the role that Yashar Kemal played in influencing the modern Turkish literary tradition. Taha Hussein was seventh of the thirteen children of his father. He came from a very poor background. He was also blind. In the first volume of his three-part autobiography, Hussein describes his childhood years in Upper Egypt up to the time when he went as an impoverished, blind student to al-Azhar University in Cairo.[209] Hussein's realism is evident in the honesty and detail with which he records his rural origins. His paragraphs capture the sights and sounds of Upper Egypt, of noisy Cairo, of family quarrels and people's different characters with such precision that it is hard to believe that the author is blind. The reader weeps at the tragedy of a little girl's death during one of the Feasts, laughs at the antics of young boys pretending to be magicians, senses the fear of a father's anger and the intense joy of a student acquiring knowledge.

Just as with their oral and written literature, so one of the main aims of everyday conversation amongst Arabs is to engage the emotions. The Arabic language provides the tools for assertion and exaggeration. Indeed, not to indulge in overstatement is likely to lead to miscommunication. A bald statement in matter-of-fact language will often be seen as implying the contrary to what is being said. Words at face value cannot really be meant: they do not tug at the heart. Real language is far more engaging. In it, God is called upon constantly. He is invoked in every conceivable greeting and made the guarantor of nearly every oath. Speech is by design flamboyant and impulsive. The imagination is in gear as phrases are savoured and offered to an audience of one or a hundred.

The lights go out in a Cairo suburb because the electricity system is overloaded. Flats are left in darkness and meals are interrupted. A host immediately utters a beautiful phrase which engages the guest in his home, reassures him and allows the speaker permission to go and find some alternative source of light. He says: "Your light is sufficient!"

In order to come out with the appropriate saying at the right moment, memories are developed from childhood. Middle Easterners know how to speak, what to speak, when to speak. One observer refers to this characteristic as shared access to "prefabricated wisdom".[210]

There are polite forms of address (rather like the difference between *tu* and *vous* in French). When I worked in the Episcopal

Waiter with a word!

Church in Egypt, an Egyptian clergyman was elected as the new bishop of the diocese. One Western colleague would address him as *Yâ Muṭrân* (literally "O Bishop") and all the Egyptians would laugh. It was simply that there was another way in Arabic of showing the deference to the bishop which the Westerner intended. The way he chose to do it was rather like saying "Queenie dear" to Her Royal Majesty.

Speech, then, is a primary conveyor of emotion. William Beeman, a sociolinguist, has analysed how emotion is communicated in Iranian culture through various genres of language use. His starting point is an observation that "there are few societies which take the obligations of status as seriously as Iranian society".[211] As a result, there are specific ways of speaking "up" or "down" to people, or of addressing someone on equal terms. Language use depends on the respective status of the parties involved. Changes in such relative status can be indicated by intensifying the use of language (flattery or rudeness) or by withdrawing from norms of conversation – referred to as being *ghar* with someone. Beeman comments that the dealings between Iran and the United States in the 1980s over the taking hostage of US diplomatic personnel "was a clear case of refusal to communicate directly. Only when the United States recognized the need for an intermediary was the impasse broken".[212] Beeman gives an example of the processes of "intensification" in language use:

> Two office workers are involved in a heated but polite discourse. One makes a disparaging remark to the other. The second man's reaction is immediate. He rises, and suddenly lunges for the first man. He begins shouting and using foul language and must be restrained by the others. The angry man is quieted and persuaded to make up the quarrel. The two men kiss on the cheek, and calm is restored. Later a spectator, queried about the quarrel, replied, "He had to behave like that – his honor (*qeirat*) was offended, and that was the only proper way to show it." When the man who was attacked was asked about his feelings toward the angry man, he said, "Oh, now we will be closer than ever."[213]

Language is freighted with far more than superficial meaning. In status-focused cultures where honour and shame are major components of the culture, language becomes the means for trading in relative kudos.

There are both formal and informal verbal channels for the expression of feeling in Muslim cultures. At times of darkness and despair, males are not afraid to cry and show their sadness. It is not unmanly to weep, especially under heavy affliction. I remember a university professor, an ex-general, falling on my shoulder with heavy sobs as I shared with his family in the sadness of his brother's dying. When his only son soon followed his brother to the grave, his letters to me were full of dark despair. There was no shame in his expressing to me how he felt. Whenever I prayed with him or wrote back to him, seeking to encourage him, he thanked me for being his "angel of light". Expansive, expensive phrases characterise the way all Arabs tend to speak.

Children learn at an early age to speak in exaggerated ways. In his book describing the processes involved in growing up within an Egyptian village, Hamed Ammar illustrates the way in which youngsters battle verbally with one another to express their pride in their own family:

> One child said: "My father is better than yours; he never worked for someone else, and his turban has always been white. My people are all leaders (sheikhs)." The other boy retorted: "All your people are liars and deceivers. We offer a larger tray of food for guests and on funeral occasions than yours. Your cow is 'rotting' and its bones are sticking out from starvation. What is the use of just talking?"[214]

Verbal battles in adult life are particularly noticeable after car accidents. They are public, boisterous affairs, usually requiring the intervention of a mediator before they can be settled. Threats are made and countered with increasing ferocity. The abuse which goes on is intended to intimidate and win the argument, whatever the details of who was legally in the right or wrong. Usually, the words act as substitutes for actions and the mediator is allowed to save each participant's pride without the risk of threats turning into actual physical fighting.

Amongst many factors which provoke anger is gossip, especially talk about the reputation of the sexual honour of a man's womenfolk. Primary purveyors of gossip are women – thus they come to be power-holders in societies where shared information or defamation can be so damaging.

Overexaggeration and overemphasis led to massive miscommunication between the Arab protagonists in successive wars against Israel during the 20th century. Geoffrey Furlonge quotes the reminiscences of Musa Alami, a Palestinian Arab leader in the years up to the war of 1948. On the eve of that war, Alami visited various Arab capitals to canvas support for the Palestinian cause. In Damascus, the president of Syria is purported to have told him:

> I am happy to tell you that our Army and its equipment are of the highest order and well able to deal with a few Jews; and I can tell you in confidence that we even have an atomic bomb . . . Yes, it was made locally; we fortunately found a very clever fellow, a tinsmith . . . [215]

Speech can often be very flowery, sycophantic and "over-the-top". It can equally well be very coarse, interspersed with obscene words and gestures. The aim in such crudity is to shame a person. Extremes are reached in calling a man a "pimp" or a woman a "lioness". Insult a man's mother and you will likely be in grave trouble!

Language is pure and profane – orisons and oaths issue from the same mouth in quick succession! Through language use, personhood is expressed in a far more overt way than amongst Westerners. There is no shame in the open declaration of emotion. Speech is generally loud, constant and provocative. It is intended to arouse feeling as much as to express it. Sharing of the Gospel will best be packaged in emotive terms if it is to touch the heart of the Middle Easterner in an effective way.

The intrinsic beauty and authority of the Bible, translated appropriately into Muslims' heart-languages, cannot be underestimated for their potential impact. For many Muslims, exposure to the emotive tale of lost humanity and patient, self-sacrificing God has melted their hearts. One British Muslim describes her experience of being on the receiving end of the Bible's force:

> Christine had been my friend for years. She had often tried to talk about Jesus, but frankly I wasn't interested. I may not have been a very religious Muslim, but I knew (or so I thought) that Christianity was not the Right Way. Then I went through a difficult time. My mother was very ill, my sister's marriage broke up, and I had problems at work. Christine was away at the time, but she started sending me these beautiful verses. I

found them so comforting. When she came back, I asked her where she found them. Did she write them herself, or what? "They're from the Psalms," she said. "You know – in the Bible." I was shocked. I'd been told I would be cursed if I read the Bible, and here I was, being blessed by it.

That was just the beginning. I asked for a Bible, and have never looked back . . .[216]

Similarly Afarin, an Iranian Muslim:

I told them I was looking for a Bible, and they handed me their own. I took it and looked at it in awe. It was the first time I had held a Persian Bible in my hand. It was in my mother tongue and it felt such a very precious thing.

After they had gone, I started to read that Bible. I read and read the gospels, because they are about Jesus. I was so hungry to know more about Jesus, the person who had comforted me when I needed help so badly.[217]

"Getting entangled is easy; the difficulty is getting out"

In tension with the theme of words, of emotive language, is the theme of silence. Silence is an important aspect of Arab mentality, for example. Self-control and discreetness are exemplified in the way in which Arabs seldom come straight to the point. Discussions beat around the bush employing all kind of euphemisms, allusions and subtle references. Language can conceal as much as expose. The Arab lives in a society where a person's reputation counts much more than the literal truth, where people's opinion of him affects his position in the society of which he is a part. What is not said is therefore as important, perhaps more important, than what is said.

Silence is a means of concealing information which might lead to a loss of honour. Even serious shame-bearing incidents can be accommodated if silence about them can be maintained. In Uris' book *The Haj*, Ishmael, the eldest son of the family, uses this stratagem to hide a potentially damaging betrayal of his honour and trust. One day he catches his sister and her boyfriend in a compromising position. The couple are both fully clothed but their behaviour is unacceptable. Eventually a solution is arrived at –

mainly because the brother loves his sister so much, after all that
they have been through together as refugees. There is no way that he
can summon up the emotional energy to kill her, nor even to evict
her. A plan is agreed which ensures that the three of them are the
only persons ever to know about what had occurred. The boyfriend
leaves for another country, the girl is allowed to remain in the family
and Ishmael retains his public image as protector of his sister.[218]

Arguments in public are won by forcing the opponent to lose his
temper. The weaker person erupts, unable to keep silence. By implication, therefore, his case in the argument is less valid. The winner
sits, quietly stroking his beard. The audience laughs, knowing who
has come out on top!

Arabs dislike revealing information deemed to be personal. Place
of birth, age, occupation, parents, wives and children are perceived
as private matters, not to be talked about with strangers or officials.
Reluctance to disclose more than what is absolutely necessary is part
of the game of everyday public engagement. A passenger in a taxi,
for example, will not tell the driver his precise destination but will
direct him as the journey progresses. Exposure of too much personal
information would give the driver knowledge, hence power, over the
passenger. It might also challenge fate if a specific prediction of the
journey's end is pronounced. A taxi driver therefore asks a new
customer, "Where to – if God wills?" and the new customer
responds by offering directions as the ride proceeds.

Often, a huge chasm exists between the role that an Arab will play
publicly and how he acts in private. While he may be flamboyant and
noisy in the external world, he carefully conceals his private world.
Perhaps this facet of the Arab's make-up helps explain what is often
seen as hypocrisy by Westerners. How come, when overseas, Arabs
are frequently seen as playboys, drunkards or gamblers and yet,
when at home, they act as faithful, orthodox Muslims? How come,
even at home, some Arabs can publicly condemn the consumption of
alcohol while privately they consume it? The issue revolves around
what is known about a person and by whom. Amongst Shîᶜa, as we
have noted, the doctrine of *taqîya* (pretence) makes a theology of
this trait. In certain circumstances it is God's will that Muslims
pretend to be other than who they really are. In Iran, under the Shahs,
the clerics dissembled allegiance to successive regimes against
which they plotted in secret. Internally, there was no surrender,

although outwardly it looked for most of the time as if the mullahs supported the status quo.

Arabs can be quite reserved about demonstrating joy or happiness. While the release of pent-up emotions of grief or pain are acceptable, feelings of joyfulness are to be carefully managed. It is undignified to "laugh one's head off" in most Arab cultures. Public demonstration of love and affection, apart from same-sex kissing of the cheek or holding of the hand, is rarely seen. Indeed, it is often assumed that public expressions of rudeness by a man towards his wife actually indicate that, in fact, he loves her. A woman, when she is getting married, tends traditionally to be restrained about showing pleasure. Open joyfulness at such a moment could easily be misinterpreted as a declaration of the bride's relief at leaving her father's home. Personal happiness must not be shown to be enjoyed at the expense of group loyalty or commitment to kin.

Silence has mainly to do with the concealment of facts. Secrecy about facts is compensated by openness about feelings, especially those to do with pain or sorrow. The Middle Easterner's preferred way of functioning is thus the opposite of most Westerners'. We trade in facts to our hearts' content but find it very difficult to identify or express our feelings. For the Britisher, moreover, the "stiff upper lip" mentality makes the admission of feelings of rejection, hurt or pain well-nigh impossible. The Arab has no such inhibition. For him, facts withheld and emotions expressed reflect important concerns – about the norms of honour, shame, personhood and group identity. Learning to function within those norms is important if Western missionaries are to be effective conveyors of Christ's life in Middle Eastern contexts.

How many Western Christians have been confused by volatile shifts from expressions of extreme friendship to those of strong enmity in Middle Easterners whom they understand to be "brothers in Christ"? Relationships quickly become deep, with the exchange of confidences and the undermining of personal privacy. Suddenly, misunderstanding or jealousy turns those friendships sour and one discovers that one is no longer a bosom friend, but an enemy. The Westerner searches his mind for the "facts" of the case, seeking some stable ground from which to evaluate what is going on in the relationship. The Middle Easterner lives each emotion in turn to the full, ready and eager for the next change of expression.

Poems from heaven?

The Bible comes to us in the guise of Semitic thought-forms. Poetry and poetic passages fill its pages from the first chapter of Genesis to the last chapter of Revelation. We quickly discover, in the first

". . . a drop in a bucket . . ."

creation narrative, the careful coupling of the rhyming adjectives *thôhû* (formless) and *vôhû* (empty). The Wisdom literature continues the trend towards poetry and proverbs, as do the Old Testament prophets. In the New Testament, the songs of Mary, Anna and

Simeon and the intimations of hymns belonging to the early Christian communities are mirrored by the great choruses of praise chanted by angelic and saintly hosts and entrusted to John to record in earthly phrases.

The majority of the narrative of the Bible, meanwhile, is couched in rural concepts and metaphors. In the latter part of the book of Isaiah, for example, the Lord seeks to comfort a people who are lost in exile. The Lord declares his sovereignty over the nations in terms easily understood by those living in a pastoral setting:

> Surely the nations are like a drop in a bucket;
> they are regarded as dust on the scales.
>
> (Isaiah 40:15)

The picture employed here is of a girl fetching water in a container from a well or river. As she hoists the pitcher to her head and trudges back home, a few drops slop over the edge and drip down. The "nations" are like those drips to the Lord. They are no threat to him! Don't worry about them, little Israel-in-exile! Or a man goes to the market to buy flour. The amount he wants to purchase is weighed out on scales and poured into his container. A tiny film of dust is left on the tray in the scales. That flour-dust is viewed as insignificant by both parties to the transaction. The Lord sees the "nations" as the seller and buyer see the leftover film of dust on the tray. They too are irrelevant to the actions the Lord is taking on behalf of his repentant people. The pictures give a touching yet powerful image of the sovereignty of the God who wills to comfort his people and end their exile. A rural community cannot but get the point.

Many of Jesus' parables are based on an understanding of nature. Others rely on the various relationships which Jesus knew from his Palestinian background – householder, servant, moneylender, merchant, friend, widow, shepherd, housewife, judge, bridegroom, housebuilder and so on. Parables are stories which relate self-evident truths from everyday life in order to illustrate new truths – in Jesus' case, about the kingdom of God. According to Mark 4:33–34, Jesus made extensive use of parables in his preaching. The stories make telling points precisely because Jesus' audience understands the implicit details of each natural situation.

Telling a story

Westerners are raised on syllogisms and constructs of truth that are propositional. We are brought up to believe that to be convincing in communicating, we need to employ facts, arguments and logic. For us, "story" carries the connotation of make-believe or fantasy. Stories are for children, almost by definition – until a J.K. Rowling takes us by surprise and editions of *Harry Potter* volumes need to be supplied with adult covers. Still, it remains somehow hard for us to believe that an anecdote could make as pungent a point as three logically connected paragraphs.

In many respects, the parables of Jesus take on the appearance of riddles for a Western readership because the point of contact, which was obvious in the original situation, is lost across the cultural divide. For many Muslim peoples, however, both the parable form and the content of the biblical stories are easily accessible.

Storytelling should not be feared by Western missionaries to Muslims. Martin Goldsmith is a past master at what he calls "parabolic preaching". Here is one of his favourite stories, usually told with plenty of embellishments in taxis and coffee-houses along with his winsome smile:

> There were once two Muslim men who went to the mosque to pray. The first man was a devout Muslim who had been to Mecca on pilgrimage, prayed regularly five times a day and was known in the community for his piety. He went to the mosque that day with total confidence, for he knew all the prescribed rituals of how to wash himself before entering the mosque, as well as the set movements and words of the prayers. He entered the mosque, went straight to a prominent place in the centre towards the front and performed his prayers with absolute perfection. But while praying, his thoughts wandered to the pretty girl who lived next door and he pictured to himself her shapely figure.
>
> The second man to come to the mosque had lived a thoroughly rotten life of moral degradation. Having not prayed for many years, he had forgotten the details of the outward ritual of washings, prayer movements and even the words one recited in prayer. But he was deeply aware of the evil of his behaviour and longed to get right with God again, start a new life and make amends for all he had done until then. Shyly he approached the mosque, dipped his hands in the pool of water to wash his hands and face, left his sandals outside the mosque and slipped

quietly in. Feeling a bit out of place he went behind a pillar in the hope that no one would see him. Deeply moved with a spirit of repentance he abandoned any attempt to remember the set words and movements of prayers; so he turned to God with simple words of his own.

With which man's prayers was God pleased?[219]

Sally Sutcliffe describes how the singing of a Christian song facilitated the communication of a gospel message to a British Muslim family in a manner that surprised and delighted her.

One day I visited a family who were going through a hard time. I wanted to communicate the peace of the Lord Jesus and the joy of his salvation. Yet my Punjabi and the mother's English were both insufficient for the task. I remembered an Urdu Christian praise song sung in Asian Christian fellowships, called *Khushi, Khushi Manao* (Rejoice, rejoice!). The song tells how Jesus came to save us, how he suffered on the cross and died, but rose again; he's now our Lord. Let's praise his name! The mother perked up and joined in, singing the words and tapping her foot to the joyful tune. She kept singing it to herself long after I'd stopped singing. I was amazed that this strict Muslim was singing about the salvation of Jesus! A thousand theological discussions with her about the cross of Christ could not have conveyed the message as effectively as this song did. Singing a song is, of course, a million miles away from trusting her life to the Lord Jesus (and could I imagine her ever coming to church?), yet a seed may have been sown in her heart.[220]

The use of storytelling, singing, parables, proverbs and poems, she concludes, are especially appropriate in the world of women – where instinct is highly developed – and in the world of children – where imaginations are hungry and fertile.

Language in most Muslim societies is the vehicle for communicating far more than just facts, ideas or theories. Speech can bite, get under the skin and tug at the heart. Silence, or speech withheld, conveys strong messages about status in an honour/shame culture. Who is coming out on top, gaining honour or dispensing shame, in the talk vacuum? Words are creatively dished up or carefully rationed in cultures where language and silence are held in tension. Can we learn appropriate ways to speak and the right time for keeping quiet?

CHAPTER EIGHT

BROTHERHOOD AND RIVALRY

I and my brothers against my cousins;
I and my cousins against my tribe;
I and my tribe against the world.

The concept of brotherhood is very important to Islamic communities. We have already seen the importance of the collective (the "group") over against the individual. We now need to investigate some of the tensions between different expressions of collectivity.

Brothers indeed!

Belonging to the *'umma* (the brotherhood of Islam) is the privilege of every Muslim. The *'umma* has connotations similar to the Christian concept of the Kingdom of God. In its origins, Islam implied a transformation of seventh century Arabian society. The various loyalties of Bedouin clans were to be consolidated in a new kind of community – the *'umma*, or brotherhood. In that new community, a supreme sense of religious allegiance was to eclipse all other loyalties though without abolishing them. A common law and a political authority were to control public and private affairs. In a way, the *'umma* redefined the meaning of "tribe" to include religious rather than blood brothers. In the development of a theological basis for this shift in emphasis, it was emphasised that all Muslims are equal before God. The only criterion for honour became zeal for the new faith rather than membership of a particular family or clan:

> . . . Verily
> The most honoured of you
> In the sight of God
> Is (he who is) the most
> Righteous of you.

> (Sura 49:13)

It is an irony that those who followed Prophet Muḥammad out of their city of Mecca, in *hijra* or "emigration", broke kinship ties in doing so. Obedience to the new religious faith came to be stronger in them than loyalty to the old order – the call to Islam was significantly counter-cultural. No wonder the protagonists in this shift of loyalty are especially celebrated! The early Muslim converts in Mecca were sent ahead by Muḥammad to Yathrib (known since as Medina): they were the heroic *Mûhâjirûn* or "emigrants". They were received by their co-believers in Yathrib: the brave *Anṣâr* or "aiders". The Prophet ordered every man among the *Anṣâr* to choose a *Muhâjir* and take him as a brother with all the legal implications of that act, including the right of inheritance – a right later rescinded in the Qur'ân. The pact of brotherhood established in this shift of loyalty away from tribal solidarity towards solidarity in faith was the firstfruits of a new "brotherhood in God" in which the Islamic community was to resemble "a compact wall whose stones are welded together" as a famous *hadîth* puts it.[221]

The new solidarity in faith is based on piety or righteous living (*taqwâ*) and manifests itself in appropriate actions (or *birr*). Sura 2:177 summarises what it means for a righteous and God-fearing man to live out his life with integrity. The emphasis of this revelation is on the acts that declare the righteousness of the person performing them:

> It is not righteousness
> In pain (or suffering)
> And adversity,
> That ye turn your faces
> Towards East or West;
> But it is righteousness –
> To believe in God
> And the Last Day,
> And the Angels,
> And the Book,

And the Messengers;
To spend of your substance,
Out of love for Him,
For your kin,
For orphans,
For the needy,
For the wayfarer,
For those who ask,
And for the ransom of slaves;
To be steadfast in prayer,
And practice regular charity;
To fulfil the contracts
Which ye have made;
And to be firm and patient,
And throughout
All periods of panic.
Such are the people
Of truth, the God-fearing.

Figure 16 summarises the actions required here in the community of faith in order for its members to be demonstrating true righteousness.

Figure 16

Acts of birr *demonstrating righteousness according to Sura 2:177*

Aspect	Action
spiritual aspects of *birr*	faith in a single God
	belief in Last Day, in angels, in the Book, in the prophets
expenditure in the name of *birr* [i.e. different from *zakât*]	for kin in need, orphans, the destitute, travellers lacking resources to continue their journey, beggars, slaves needing to be freed, prisoners needing to be ransomed
spiritual and social solidarity arising from *birr*	steadfast prayer, patience in adversity
	zakât, honouring of contracts

During the critical years at Medina, Prophet Muḥammad strove to mould a community based on shared religious beliefs, ceremonies, ethics and laws. In one interpretation of the revelations given while Muḥammad worked in Medina, the Qur'ân can be seen as giving detailed guidance for many areas of life in this readjustment away from a purely tribal interpretation of community. It is significant that the Islamic calendar starts from the beginning of the formation of the 'umma in Medina in AD 622, rather than, say, from the birth of the Prophet or from the time he began to receive revelations.

At a ritual level, the details of piety and socio-religious duty were delineated in the Qur'ân. The famous "five pillars" of Islam – ritual prayer (ṣalât), almsgiving (zakât), pilgrimage (ḥajj), the fast of Ramaḍân and the obligation to bear witness to God (shahâda) – are acts to be performed by all Muslims. Most of the requirements of these acts of piety are to be fulfilled in community, at the same moment, as, for example, with prayer:

> The mosque enables Muslims to meet five times a day on terms of perfect equality and in a spirit of brotherhood, all standing in a row before their great Maker, knowing no difference of colour or rank, all following the lead of one man. All differences and distinctions are, for the time being, obliterated.[222]

Many Muslims, throughout the ages, have felt the oneness that comes from praying together, fasting together or going on pilgrimage together:

> The impact of this enormous gathering [for the "Standing" at Arafat] cannot be over-emphasized. The coming together of men and women, regardless of sex, nationality, race or social obligation, is the very object of this ritual . . .
>
> At Arafat, during his Hajj al-Wada (Farewell Pilgrimage), the Prophet, in his last sermon, stressed the importance that Islam attaches to the principle of equality – equality without social distinction . . .
>
> This brotherly communion is the keynote of the Station at Arafat.[223]

The Qur'ân also addressed the problem of structuring the new, religiously bonded community. Family law, as it has emerged in Islam, is deduced from revelations given to sort out a variety of practice in pre-Islamic Arabia. The distribution of property, the protection of women and the guardianship of children were primary areas needing to be rationalised in a society in which no one set of customs was universally accepted. The Qur'ân came down in favour of strengthening the patriarchal agnatic clan. From that perspective, rules were made against incest, against divorce (apart from some situations),

Together to pray

against polyandrous marriages, against the relegation of women and children to the categories of mere chattels or potential warriors.[224]

Other areas of communal living were dealt with in the Qur'ân. Norms for business transactions were defined, including prohibition of usury. Ways of conducting wars were detailed so that the men fought as one. Leadership of the community was carefully exegeted in new terms. Now, the head of the *'umma* had power to arbitrate because he represented the will of God rather than tribal custom. A replacement for tribal tradition was gradually provided in the *sunna*, the authoritative example of Prophet Muḥammad. It was to this historical source (recorded in the *hadîth* literature) that subsequent leaders appealed in making decisions.

Ira Lapidus summarises the achievement of qur'ânic revelation and prophetic leadership in these words:

> In a fragmented society he integrated the otherwise anarchic small clans into a larger confederacy on the basis of religious loyalty, built a state structure through which political and economic order might eventually be achieved, and resolved the conflict of Bedouin familial and Meccan commercial values in a new religious point of view. Islam fused tribal society, the monotheistic religious mentality, with a religious community, trading confederacy and political organisation to create a new society.[225]

In that new society, the quest for salvation was to succeed through positive action, a methodology that has remained at the heart of Islamic faith ever since:

> And say: "Work (righteousness):
> Soon will God observe your work,
> And His Apostle, and the Believers:
> Soon will ye be brought back
> To the Knower of what is
> Hidden and what is open:
> Then will He show you
> The truth of all that ye did."
>
> (Sura 9:105)

Positive acts of solidarity, however, can prove subject to the fluctuations of people's fervour and piety. Islam therefore specified three required kinds of relating to the brotherhood of believers. Chadly Fitouri summarises these mandated actions as expressions of "diffuse solidarity" (*takâful*), expressions of "institutionalised solidarity" (*zakât*), and expressions of "subsidiary solidarity" (*waqf*).[226] His analysis is depicted in Figure 17. By "diffuse solidarity", he refers to the fact that all property belongs ultimately to God, not to humankind. A human being is but a vice-regent to the divine owner of all and therefore cannot back away from accepting responsibility for his or her fellow dwellers in God's world. Concern for kin, for neighbour, for guest and for the needy are emphasised in this concept of maintaining solidarity. Verses of the Qur'ân are offered in support of three of these concerns. Responsibility for hosting is backed up by a *ḥadîth* from al-Bukhârî:

> He who believes in God and the Last Day must treat his guest with defer-
> ence. He must honour him for a day and a night. Hospitality lasts for
> three days and everything subsequent will be considered as alms; a guest
> must not impose himself on his host to an importunate extent.

Figure 17
Fitouri's summary of specified acts of Islamic solidarity

Solidarity	Meaning	Detail
takâful diffuse solidarity	a human being as God's vice-regent has responsibility for neighbour dependent on individual conscience	kinship right (Sura 17:23–24) neighbourhood right to utensils (Sura 4:36) right to hospitality right to alms (Sura 2:262)
zakât institutionalised solidarity	redistribution of wealth between members of a society administered by state from Sura 9:60 "pillar" of Islam	direct benefit to: • poor • needy • tax officials collecting tax • those won to Islam indirect benefit to: • slaves/prisoners of war • people burdened by debt • volunteers for holy war • travellers with not enough money to continue journey
waqf subsidiary solidarity	goods/funds held in religious trust	family *waqf* public *waqf*

In this concept of diffuse solidarity, several of the major themes of this book find themselves under consideration. Expressions of mutual concern exercised in this sense are very much left to the individual's conscience. By "institutionalised solidarity", Fitouri refers to the requirement for *zakât* to be paid. As a religious requirement –

one of the pillars of Islam – the gains which a person makes are purified through the process of freely redistributing a portion of them.
That way, the gain is made lawful or *ḥalâl*. Eight categories of
persons with right to *zakât* are deduced from Sura 9:60:

> Alms are for the poor
> And the needy, and those
> Employed to administer the (funds);
> For those whose hearts
> Have been (recently) reconciled
> (To Truth); for those in bondage
> And in debt in the cause
> Of God; and for the wayfarer:
> (Thus is it) ordained by God,
> And God is full of knowledge
> And wisdom.

Some gain their benefit directly, some indirectly. By "subsidiary
solidarity", Fitouri refers to goods held in mortmain or religious trust
– known as *waqf*. These might relate to the preserving of family
interests or funds for religious or charitable foundations in the public
domain.

A sense of brotherhood has often been renewed, in the history of
Islam, in the midst of discrimination and shame. After Napoleon's
invasion of Egypt in 1798, one effect of colonisation by European
powers was to reawaken a sense of the brotherhood of Muslims.
Heart-searching as to why Muslim peoples should have become so
dominated by the irreligious or unfaithful gradually led to a new
sense of common purpose – as Muslims.

In the last part of the 19th century and the first half of the 20th
century, many leaders of Arab nationalist causes sought to identify
Arabism with Islam. Sayyid Jamâl al-Dîn al-Afghânî (1838–1897) is
broadly acknowledged as the father of modern Muslim nationalism
and pan-Islamism (a striving for the political union of all Muslims).
He, supremely, stirred in Muslims the consciousness of their incipient strength despite the outward humiliation of colonialism. Middle
Eastern disciples of Afghânî began a movement, with its own journal, which carried the ideas of Muslim reformism throughout the
world from North Africa to South-East Asia. In his tract on *Islamic*

Solidarity, Afghânî attacks the attitude that ethnic identity is the basis for state-building. The individualistic racial solidarity which existed during Afghânî's lifetime and which guaranteed the rule of some races over others was a philosophical approach which could be validly opposed from an Islamic perspective. In that perspective, according to Afghânî, "faith" relations are much more binding:

> That is the secret of the aversion which Muslims have for manifestations of ethnic origin in every country where they live. That is why they reject all clan loyalty with the exception of Islamic sentiment and religious solidarity. The believers in Islam are preoccupied neither with their ethnic origins, nor with the people of which they are a part because they are loyal to their faith; they have given up a narrow bond in favour of a universal bond: the bond of faith.[227]

Whether Muslims have ever really lived by the ideal proclaimed with such conviction by Afghânî is a moot point. Nonetheless, the viewpoint he was promoting contributed towards a unity-in-opposition amongst colonised Muslims at the end of the last century. A reformed Islam, with its primary emphasis on religious brotherhood, became a strong motivating force, with Muslim nationalism its surface expression, for a rejection of European colonialism and a struggle for independence. "Islam" emerged as a powerful rallying cry in the rise against imperial, occupying forces. The vocabulary of such Muslim nationalism was infused with words such as *'umma* (brotherhood) and *milla* (identity by religious community).[228]

More recently, the concept of *'umma* has been emphasised by the ideologists of contemporary Islamic reform movements. Sayyid Qutb, interned leader of the Muslim Brotherhood during Nasser's presidency, was put on trial in Cairo in 1965. He was charged with plotting against the state. Qutb admitted the charge, arguing that resistance against a regime which was un-Islamic was the duty of a true Muslim. Loyalty to the brotherhood of Islam (the *'umma*) should come above obedience to the Egyptian homeland (*watan*). Belonging to the fellowship of Muslims everywhere was more important than membership of a particular earthly state. Qutb quoted the Qur'ân in support of his case:

The Believers are but
A single Brotherhood:
So make peace and
Reconciliation between your
Two (contending) brothers;
And fear God, that ye
May receive mercy.

(Sura 49:10)

Indeed, Qutb identified the Egypt of Nasser as effectively non-Muslim. He called it a society of "ignorance" (a *jâhilî* society), reflective of the Days of Ignorance before Prophet Muḥammad appeared with his revelation from heaven. Such a society, led by such a leader, was to be rejected. In its place, the true believers were to form a "state within a state", a community (*jamaᶜa*) living truly by the tenets of the Qur'ân. In order to achieve this, believers were to withdraw from the society of ignorance in imitation of Prophet Muḥammad's exodus (*hijra*) from Mecca to Medina. In the small, separated cells of believers, the real Muslims were to practise Islam as God intended and prepare the way for when that proper Islam was to be inaugurated within society at large. At his trial, Qutb declared:

> We are the umma of the Believers, living within a jahili society. Nothing relates us to state or to society and we owe no allegiance to either. As a community of believers we should see ourselves in a state of war with the state and society. The territory we dwell in is Dar al-Harb [House of War].[229]

The strong sense of brotherhood generally felt within Muslim communities colours their perspectives on sin. We have already discerned a strong shame-flavour to Muslims' concepts of falling short. There are other important implications for the perception of wrongdoing in relationship-oriented cultures. Most serious sins are those made against the kinship group. Incest, for example, constitutes a strongly distasteful offence. Failure to respect authority, especially if a son disobeys a father, amounts to a major sin. The use of magic or sorcery against one's own kin group or the abandoning of one's inherited faith for another faith – these constitute strong sins against the group. By contrast, offences against those not within the kin-group are seen as less significant:

Being mean and inhospitable to your own people is a great sin because it touches the very solidarity of the group. On the other hand, murder or rape of members outside the group is of little significance.[230]

For Westerners, murder or rape or theft are seen as major sins – they are aggressive acts against an individual's life or well-being or property. By contrast, lack of hospitableness or meanness of spirit or anger are not seen as such big deals by Western Christians. Conviction of sin is the Holy Spirit's prerogative but most of us most of the time expect the Spirit to function via our own culture's definitions of what constitutes major or minor sin.

Aiming for the top

In contrast to the strong sense of brotherhood and belonging described so far in this chapter, it must be recognised that a powerful process of challenge goes on constantly in many Muslim societies. Every man sets out on a career by virtue of who he is, who his family is, and what honour he is entitled to. He is in competition with everyone else. His family competes with other families. When places at university are limited in number, when the job market is stretched to capacity, when there is only so much good to go round, there develops fierce competition between "brothers".

Those holding power do all they can to protect their place of privilege. For them, everything is at stake in any challenge to their position. Those seeking power strive carefully to accumulate standing. Challenges to prevailing orders of power and privilege are often accomplished violently, as we have seen. An under-the-surface rivalry continues through the web of various family and clan relationships, emerging every now and then in public victory or ignominious defeat. As Gerald Butt concludes, "Differences and quarrels. It's very easy to get the impression that there is nothing else to talk about in the Arab world."[231]

In the early development of Islam as an expanding force, as we have seen, a new layer of distinction came to eclipse former tribal renown. Kinship with the Prophet became the main touchstone of nobility. Hence, descendants who can boast a Hashemite, Alîd, *Muhajirûn* or *Ansâr* connection in their family tree are accorded superior status. Similarly there has developed a cultural pecking order favouring Arab over non-Arab, and city-dweller above desert-dweller, because of the esteem accorded to Muḥammad (both Arab and city-dweller) by the whole Islamic community.

Each locality knows its own hierarchy of privilege. The typical village has a headman who is commonly linked with the community's most powerful family. Such power is determined by wealth, family size and prestige. In her novel *God Dies by the Nile*, Nawal El-Saadawi paints a picture of life on the remote banks of that river. The main character, Zakeya, is a simple peasant woman who lives with her two pretty young nieces. The girls arouse the lust of the village mayor who plans to abuse them. He involves the chief of the village guard and the sheikh of the mosque in his criminal activities. There seems to be no power to stop the evil, for there is no power beyond the mayor's. No one in the village can rival him. The girls accordingly suffer abuse and exile at his hands and the little family group is destroyed.[232]

In Arab society, it frequently seems to be the case that more authority is exercised than responsibility shouldered. It is not uncommon for men with power to abuse or misuse their position. The point of privilege is that it is there to be exploited and enjoyed. The concept of a "benevolent dictator" is as much a misnomer in reality as it is a theoretical contradiction in terms. Zakaria Tamer, in his short story *A Lone Woman*, describes the seduction of the beautiful young Aziza by her local sheikh. The sheikh is supposedly invoking *jinn* which will bring back to Aziza her husband who has absconded as a result of a spell put on Aziza by her in-laws. In the darkened room of the sheikh's house, the man uses his socio-religious authority to manoeuvre Aziza into submission to his sexual advances. The sting in the tale, in a way, is that in the lovemaking the young woman is fulfilled sexually (though innocently, because she believes that it is the *jinn* that are making love to her) in a way she had not known before.[233] Nonetheless, the incident illustrates a reality only rarely acknowledged but surely commonplace – the abuse of females by those with authority over them and access to them.

In the post-independence era, many Muslim (Arab and other) nations have developed as dictatorships in which the country's wealth and control of its financial policies has become concentrated in the hands of a few "great" families. Indeed, some observers have caricatured Arab states as being simply "tribes with flags". The founder of Saudi Arabia stage-managed a tribal coalition through marriage and other means, and Saudi politics since then has largely been a matter of tribal politics with Sudairis opposing Shammars and other tribes. Some 18 major tribes have controlled the manner of Libyan development while some 500 tribes live in the Sudan with the largest of them encompassing 12 per cent of the country's population.[234] Within Iran under the late Shah, it was estimated that there were some 40 national élite families holding power in the country. Huntington makes the point that the nation state has never really worked as a concept for Arab societies. Rather, "the small group and the great faith, the tribe and the *ummah*, have been the principal foci of loyalty and commitment".[235] Often a single tribe rules, even a small tribe with strong connections, as with the minority Sunni group that supported Saddam Hussein in Iraq or the Alawi group supporting the Assad family in Syria. Salah Khalaf concludes that "the whole political history of Lebanon may be viewed as the history of a handful of leading families competing to affirm their name, power and prestige in their respective communities".[236] There is no exposure nor censure of those extended families as long as they remain united and powerful against all rivals.

As a consequence, absolute tribal rule begets conspiracies and rivalries on a massive scale. How else are dictators or ruling tribal groups to be overthrown? Revolutions galore punctuate the history of Muslim nations since independence. David Pryce-Jones, in his incisive book on the Arabs, lists some of the plots and counter-plots that have marked Middle Eastern politics in recent decades:

To the long line of murdered, deposed or exiled power holders, to Sultan Abdul Hamid and his successor, to Khedive Ismail and his heirs down to King Farouk, last of the descendancy in 1952, were added Shah Reza Pahlavi of Iran, deposed in 1941; his son Shah Muḥammad Reza, deposed in 1979; King Feisal II of Iraq, who was murdered with his family and his prime minister in 1958 and their corpses then defiled in the streets; the Imam of Yemen; the sultan of Oman, deposed by his son Qabus; King Idris of Libya; King Abdullah of Jordan, killed in 1951; and King Feisal of Saudi Arabia, shot dead in 1975 by a young relation. And to them was added the next generation of power holders, Qassem in Iraq, shot by the brothers Aref, one of whom was then deposed and the other killed in a helicopter crash; Ibrahim Hamdi of north Yemen, murdered in

1977 with his brother Abdullah by Ahmed Hussein Ghashmi, who himself nine months afterward was blown up by a bomb in the briefcase of an envoy sent by the president of South Yemen; Husni Zaim and President Shishakli and Salah al-Bitar and dozens more in Syria; Riad as-Solh, prime minister of Lebanon; Anwar Sadat in Egypt; General Abboud in Sudan, where his successor General Nimeiri was in due course deposed – not to mention the twists and turns whereby King Hassan of Morocco and King Hussein of Jordan have both escaped more attempted assassinations than can be correctly counted, whereas General Oufkir or Mehdi Ben Barka, both Moroccan challengers, met strange deaths, and innumerable Arab officers everywhere have been hurried from specially convened tribunals to the firing squad.[237]

Many people have found themselves victims of the violent fallout from such plots and counter-plots. The world looked on in horror in 2003 as mass graves were uncovered in the fields of Iraq: resting places for untold numbers of objectors to the Baathist regime who met untimely deaths at the hands of Saddam Hussein's executioners. Already known about his regime's violence was the infamous Anfal campaign of the 1980s when over 4,000 Kurdish villages were destroyed and tens of thousands of Kurds disappeared. In Algeria in 1992, elections were cancelled and the constitution suspended because it looked as if an Islamist party was about to be voted into government. The ensuing seven years of civil war saw the taking of 100,000 Algerian lives (according to the official and therefore likely understated statistics), most of them unarmed civilians including women and children.

The resolution of Saadawi's novel about life in Upper Egypt mirrors the rivalry exegeted in Pryce-Jones' analysis of Middle Eastern political history. The old lady, Zakeya, eventually realises that it is the mayor who has wrecked the lives of her nieces. At the end of the novel, she takes her revenge on behalf of her destroyed family:

Zakeya continued to squat at the entrance to her house with her eyes wide open, staring steadily into the night. Now she never slept, or even closed her eyes. They pierced the darkness to the other side of the lane where rose the huge iron gate of the Mayor's house. She did not know exactly what she was waiting for. But as soon as she saw the blue eyes appear between the iron bars she stood up. She did not know why she stood up instead of continuing to squat, nor what she would do after that. But she walked to the stable and pushed the door open. In one of the corners she noticed the hoe. Her tall, thin body approached and bent over it. Her hand was rough and big, with a coarse skin, and it held the hoe in a firm grip as her big, flat feet walked out of the door. She paused for a moment then crossed the lane to the iron gate. The Mayor saw her come towards him. "One of the peasant women who work on my farm," he thought. When he came close he saw her arm rise high up in the air holding the hoe.

He did not feel the hoe land on his head and crush it at one blow. For a moment before, he had looked into her eyes, just once. And from that moment he was destined never to see, or feel, or know anything more.[238]

Zakeya concludes that she has murdered "God", for the mayor represents to her the ultimate authority in her life. Saadawi's point is that perhaps peasant women have to murder "God" if they are ever to know the honour, in an Arab community, of being truly human. In reality, the brotherhood (the *'umma*) means nothing for the powerless and non-privileged. They are the forgotten, the preyed-upon in a set-up which allows their abuse by various power-holders. The "God" who supports such a system of tyranny needs to be buried on the banks of a river.

When the Iraqi forces rolled into Kuwait in August 1990, they came across Hala and her husband and family. Being Bedouin, Hala and her family were traditional folk, living according to the honour code and thankful for the sense of brotherhood with all Muslims everywhere. Hala's husband was taken away and subjected to extreme torture by the invading army. Soon the soldiers came back for Hala also:

" . . . you should know what happened to us . . . The soldiers ripped my clothes. I told them I was pregnant. They laughed. Then they raped me, four of them. They left me bleeding on the floor, and kicked me in the stomach, cursing me because I was making them dirty." Hala did not know it at the time, but she was miscarrying.

"Kuwait and all its money can never bring back my honor. If water is poured onto the ground, you cannot put it back in the jug. I am not a modern girl, my honor was the most important thing I owned. It is lies what they say about Arab brotherhood, if Muslim can do this to Muslim."[239]

To this day, Hala has not told her psychologically damaged husband the truth of what she endured at the hands of fellow Muslims from the north.

The rivalry factor filters into every aspect of living. Constant assessing and reassessing of options and alliances is engaged in by individuals, families, communities and nations. At the micro-level, since there is always some risk that a man closely related may turn into a rival, it is often women – especially mothers, wives, or sisters – who are looked to as a local leader's most trusted allies within the community. Who says that Muslim women do not have influence beyond the reaches of home and family?

Individuals find "honour-justification" in whatever will promote their careers, even at the expense of others. As a consequence, little dishonour attaches to selling other people short or deceiving customers concerning the quality of goods. Cheating at gambling or bearing false witness are easily justified. The individual is, in Pryce-Jones' phrase, an artful "careerist". The killing of enemies may well be perceived in such careerist terms as the following interview from the recent Lebanese civil war illustrates:

Marwan, a sixteen-year-old enrolled in the Shia militia in Beirut, explained to the French journalist Patrick Meney how murdering the innocent in the Lebanese civil war actually enhanced him. A friend of his had been shot in the day's fighting. For the sake of revenge, Marwan simply approached a crowd of bystanders and shot one of them dead. Afterward he told Meney, "Everyone knew I'd killed this man, for nothing, point-blank. Many people witnessed it. . . . Later that was a help. They were all afraid of me, they respected me. I'd proved my will publicly. I was a real warrior. I was able to boast of my prowess, knowing I'd get away with it."[240]

In Arab society as a whole, as we have seen, "who you know" is far more important than "what you know". To the Western onlooker, the processes involved in advancement look like nepotism or favouritism. In reality, society works as a cohesive entity. The Arab, by and large, prefers to interact on a personal level in which people are far more important than certificates. Each individual wants to be treated as a special case. Bureaucracy is weighed down with the necessity for subjective, personal attention. Paperwork waits while patrons lobby behind the scenes. Rival applicants or petitioners are dependent upon many factors other than the merits of the case. For Westerners, this process is hardly understandable. The Westerner wants to be objective and treat people fairly and equally. The Middle

Resting from the weight of office

Easterner is immersed in a complex web of potential human connections, both positive and negative. What looks like evil corruption to the Westerner is merely the normal outworking of a healthy ambition in the other's culture. To the Arab, the competition which goes on in a democracy is obscene, cutting across family loyalty and respect for persons. It elevates impersonal processes at the expense of human relationships.

Pryce-Jones summarises the procedure for individual self-advancement as one of "force" or "favour". Force is the more effective but also the more risky process. You really have to be able to guarantee success. Favour is the normally preferred process and (often) money is its currency where there are no family connections available to tap into.

Perhaps the most daring exegesis of rivalry in recent years has come from the pen of Naguib Mahfouz. His *Children of Gebelawi* was written in serial form for the Egyptian daily *al-Ahram* in 1959. It caused uproar. Interestingly, only the personal friendship of the newspaper's editor with President Nasser ensured that the serial was published uncensored to the end. No one dared produce the serial as a book, however, until 1967 when it was eventually made available by a publisher in Beirut.[241]

In a parabolic way, Mahfouz seeks to show the timelessness of human despair and, by implication, the futility of belief in God. His serial about raw, hopeless, forgetful and cruel humanity is delivered in 114 sections, mirroring the number of suras in the Qur'ân. In those sections, the burden of being human in a society which functions by tyranny/rivalry is explored. Can the ministry of "prophets" make any difference on earth?

Humankind's ancient ancestor, Gebelawi (literally "Mountain Man") represents "God" or at least an idea of God that people have created and handed down. Gebelawi reputedly lives in a great house on the edge of town. People in the town, meanwhile, are tyrannised by governors who flout Gebelawi's will. Gebelawi doesn't intervene directly but relates to his subjects via chosen leaders. Those leaders represent, in Mahfouz's parable, various prophets easily recognisable by their characters and actions. Gebel (Moses) is a snake charmer, Rifaa (Jesus) is an exorcist and Kassem (Muḥammad) is leader of a group of vigilantes.

Gebel (bearer of Gebelawi's own name) is the first to revolt against oppression. His actions are limited, however, intended only to liberate his own people. His rebellion is punctuated with violence and after his death no one emulates him. He is a failure. Rifaa is an odd sort of dreamer who concentrates on inner purity and happiness. His ethical rebellion comes to a bloody end when he is cudgelled to death in an ambush by a worldly leader. He also is a failure. Kassem builds a band of rebels and eventually achieves victory, announcing the full implementation of Gebelawi's will. Harmony continues as long as the leader of the vigilantes is still with them but when he dies the people quickly forget. So he too is ultimately a failure?

The last part of the book concerns Arafa, the modern scientist. By this time, Gebel, Rifaa and Kassem are thought of as quaint legends. Yet the world is still full of oppressions. At Arafa's hand, the people of the town come to believe that Gebelawi is dead. A partnership develops between Arafa (man of science/magic), whose character rapidly disintegrates, and the Trustee (man of power), one of the chiefs who had earlier allied himself with Arafa to obtain control of Arafa's "magic" (atomic power?). The partnership is destined to go wrong because both men are rivals, seeking ultimate authority. Eventually, the politician proves more powerful than the scientist. Arafa tries to flee but he and his wife are captured and buried alive. All of Arafa's magic now lies at the disposal of the Trustee who uses it to indulge in unbridled tyranny. The final chapter (*sura*) of the novel begins:

> The news about Arafa spread through the alley. No one knew the real reasons for his death, but they guessed that he had annoyed his master and that the latter had brought him to his inevitable fate. At some time it got around that he had been killed by the same magical weapon as he had used to kill Saadallah and Gebelawi. The people took pleasure in his death, despite their hatred for the Trustee, and the relatives and friends of the chiefs rejoiced. They were pleased at the killing of the man who had killed their blessed ancestor and given their tyrannical Trustee a dreadful weapon with which to keep them for ever in servitude. The future looked black, blacker than it had ever been, now that power was concentrated in the hands of one cruel man. There was no longer the hope that a quarrel might break out between the two men and lead to both of them being weakened and one of them siding with the people. It seemed that nothing was left for them but subjection and that they must regard the estate and its conditions and the words of Gebel and Rifaa and Kassem as forlorn dreams, fit only for the storytellers' songs and not for putting into practice.[242]

Mahfouz's exposition of contemporary Muslim society highlights the processes of rivalry at its worst, blocking out the memory of alternative concepts of community as depicted by Moses, Jesus and Muḥammad. Political power-holding, backed up by the "magic" of science and untempered by any submission to God's will (God being effectively "dead"), leads only to a mindless tyranny. The people are condemned to live in despair – not brothers but pawns in the power game.[243]

Brothers, really?

The dominant pattern of conflict in the Old Testament is that between brothers. Examples spring quickly to mind: Cain and Abel, Jacob and Esau, Joseph and his brothers, Moses and Aaron, Absalom and Amnon, Solomon and Adonijah. And then there are the co-wives! Within patriarchal families, wives quarrel: Sarai and Hagar, Leah and Rachel. Later on, Hannah and Peninnah, co-wives to Elkanah, prove to be rivals.

After brothers and wives come clans and tribes and nations. Tribes linked by progenitors grow increasingly apart: Israelites, Moabites, Ammonites, Edomites. We have already commented on some of the violence involved in such tribal or national rivalry. Perhaps now we can understand a little better why it often manifests itself in such an "excessive" manner. Why do so many people have to die in a change of royal dynasty? Why is vengeance-taking so bloody? Why the language of "wiping out", of total annihilation? The rivalry factor predicts that sufficient force must be used to make the aggressive action effective – no one is left to plot revenge or dabble in counter-alliances. Rivals and potential rivals are comprehensively dealt with throughout Old Testament history. Rivals are perceived as the major threat to personal, tribal and national security.

The New Testament concept of the kingdom of God challenged the inherited divisions of Near East society in the first century. Jews gradually came to see Samaritans and Gentiles as valid potential members of the body of Christ. The moves away from a strictly Jewish Christianity towards one which could accommodate any variety of human cultural form are carefully documented by the non-Jew, Luke.

In Acts, Luke is particular about highlighting the involvement of "the Twelve" in authenticating or ratifying the shift from Jewish to universal concerns. With the Samaritan harvest under Philip's ministry, and with the opening door into the Gentile world through Cornelius, representatives of the special associates of Jesus (the

Twelve) acknowledge that they are convinced that the Holy Spirit has included the newcomers in the kingdom. In the case of the Samaritans, the Holy Spirit is not given to the new believers (despite the conditions in Peter's earlier promise of Acts 2:38 being fulfilled) until Peter and John are present and in charge.[244] In the case of Cornelius, Peter is interrupted in mid-sermon by the Holy Spirit falling on the Gentiles in a way reminiscent of Peter's own experience on the Day of Pentecost.[245] Thus it is contrived that representatives of the Twelve are present to authenticate both shifts in the understanding of the word "brother" – now to include Samaritans and Gentiles.

Later, in the expansion of the church, Paul learns to translate the messianic message into language appropriate to a Gentile milieu, evidenced especially in his speech on Mars Hill outside Athens.[246] Eventually John specifically restates the ministry of Jesus in concepts accessible to the constructs of the Greek mind.[247]

To a large extent, by the end of the first century, the "middle wall of partition"[248] between Jew and Gentile had been broken down "in Christ" in practice as well as in theory. The process had been carefully monitored by the Twelve, promoted by Paul and Barnabas and accelerated by the pouring out of the Holy Spirit upon non-Jews.

Somewhat addressed during this period was the problem of freedom and slavery, part of the socio-economic reality of the Roman empire. Paul writes a letter to Philemon in Colosse concerning Philemon's runaway slave Onesimus. He requests the slave owner, who had become a Christian under Paul's earlier ministry in Asia Minor, to receive back his former slave, who has more recently become a Christian at Paul's hands, as a freed man.[249] The apostle also openly condemns slave-trading (1 Timothy 1:10), taking to task those who deal in the buying and selling of prisoners of war on the slave market. Paul's general exhortations to slaves themselves, however, require their continuing obedience to their human masters, in the understanding that in Christ they are already, essentially, "free".

Least attended to, in the New Testament corpus at least, was the perception and position of women in both Jewish and Roman worldviews. The practical implications of "kingdom" and "brotherhood" for the male-dominated worlds of Jesus and Paul were there, however, and the evidence of the charismatic days of Jesus' public ministry and the initial flowering of Christianity suggests that women were happily included in both discipleship and leadership.[250]

The dynamics of brotherhood/rivalry are critical with regard to the building up of the body of Christ amongst believers from a Muslim background. An understanding of the reality of these dynamics in many current Muslim cultures will perhaps take the sting out of incipient church situations in which vying for power or negotiating for position seem to occur alongside the wonder of mutual fellowship as brothers and sisters in Christ.

One missionary describes the creative way in which the Holy Spirit solved a rivalry problem amongst the leadership of a local West African church. In that fellowship of believers from a Muslim background, the individuals concerned had all been accustomed to exerting spiritual and social power as Islamic religious leaders:

> In a town where many Muslims had become Christians there was a struggle over leadership. Mullah X, the first leader and the one who had the largest following, had been bribed back into Islam. His disciples, however, did not go back to Islam with him. Mullah Y then took over the leadership. Later, due to a vision, Mullah X repented and came back. Mullah Y accused Mullah X of being a hypocrite. Mullah X's disciples wanted to use church funds to help Mullah X pay back some of the bribe he had accepted. Mullah Z, who was in charge of the money, was soon accused of squandering church funds. Then all three mullahs started fighting for leadership, even breaking bones!
>
> A mature Mullah trouble-shooter from outside was called in. He took six pieces of paper and had written on three of them "Leadership." On the other three he had written "Resignation of Leadership." He had the papers folded up and put in a dish. He then called the three Mullahs to each choose one. Each Mullah had an equal chance of choosing either "Leadership" or "Resignation of Leadership."
>
> All three Mullahs chose "Resignation of Leadership"! Everyone took this as the will of God.
>
> Next the troubleshooting Mullah asked for nominations. The group as a whole nominated two other Mullahs whom they said were honest men and had never taken sides. When the trouble-shooter asked who voted for Mullah A, all raised their hands. When he asked who voted for Mullah B, all raised their hands again. So two papers, one with "Leadership" and the other with "Resignation of Leadership" were put in a dish. Mullah A drew "Leadership" and so became the leader. The group now lives in peace, with problems, of course, but the problems are now manageable.[251]

Equivalent situations elsewhere don't always reach such a positive conclusion. Indeed, splits and the disintegration of fellowships occur instead. Nevertheless, it is healthy for us to maintain our patience. After all, if it took 1,900 years for some (Western) Christians to follow through implications about freedom/slavery to their New Testament conclusion, it need not surprise us that some of the dynamics of Muslim cultures will take a while to find transformation. Meanwhile, we might ask the Holy Spirit whether there are aspects of our own cultural background which we refuse to surrender when it comes to being "church".

If Western Christians demonstrate practically that "brotherhood" is only reserved for church services or pre-arranged meetings, it is not surprising that rivalry issues come up in the church groups for which they are responsible. If brotherhood comes to mean something approaching the reality of mutual accessibility, sharing of possessions, trusting of one another across the cultural divide, perhaps some of the rivalry patterns will be eclipsed. "Paradise without inhabitants is hell," says one Arab proverb. Visiting, praying, eating, relaxing and working together are norms to be expected in a brotherhood nexus in most Muslim cultures. Mazhar and Christine Mallouhi are convinced that spiritual nourishment can just as easily take place in a restaurant as in a church meeting:

> We need shared family experiences together with the believers. In North Africa we took a day to be with one of the believing couples from another city. We walked through parks and gardens, ate at a special restaurant and took the children to an amusement park. And while we had fun we talked. We talked about marriage, about the difficulties of raising children for the Lord in a totally Muslim society, and about what the church should look like according to nationals. An old deep hurt surfaced and the steps towards healing and putting it right were taken in the main street. They told us with tears in their eyes that they had never had such a special time before. "Christians usually have meetings; they don't have fun and social times." This casual day of fellowship had a special spiritual significance in their lives.[252]

Are Western Christians prepared to give up their individualism/privacy concerns for a different perspective on "community"? Can we learn to see church as a vital mix of daily interaction between believers rather than as meetings we go to?

In Christ there is the possibility that the spiritual reality of unity can become increasingly our experience here on earth in the nitty-gritty of relating as Christians across cultures. The New Testament experience seems to have been that the agents of the gospel needed to undergo continuing and massive conversion if the burdens of God's heart for Gentiles, slaves and women were ever to see the light of day. After all, whose conversion was the greatest: Peter's in Joppa or Cornelius' in Caesarea? Onesimus' in Rome or Philemon's in Colosse? Mary's in Nazareth or Paul's in his missionary work alongside women (see Romans 16)? Such were hard and long lessons to learn when the early Christians' expectation was that the other party (Gentile, slave, woman) needed to do all the converting.

Is the Holy Spirit asking us to hold lightly some of the dynamics of church à-la-Western-mode and allow him time to bring to birth fellowships with a different face? Perhaps, on his agenda, the brotherhood/rivalry issue will not be the first priority for transformation.

CHAPTER NINE

RESIGNATION AND MANIPULATION

Some said he was deli *(insane),*
some said he was veli *(a saint).*

Most Muslim cultures accommodate in their peoples' worldview a bewildering contrast between fatalistic, passive dependence and individualistic, active aggression. Unashamedly conversant with the supernatural, Muslims vary in their response to it. At one extreme they exhibit a simple resignation to God and fate. At the other extreme they pursue a detailed manipulation of the spirit world. The Turkish proverb quoted above uses a rhyme to emphasise that there is seemingly only a thin line between insanity and holiness. On the one hand, people are what they are because, ultimately, that is the way God has made them: insane, deformed, poor, clever, athletic, wealthy or whatever. On the other hand, people are what they manage to become: some even make it to sainthood!

The true Muslim

Submission is the basic "ought" of most Muslim cultures. The God of Islam is sovereign, beyond the appeals of created things. He may in some lights even seem coercive or capricious. There is no arguing with his will:

We believe that Allah has created the universe and He is its Absolute Controller and Regulator. Everything in the universe has a predetermined set course which we call *Al-Qadr*. Nothing can happen without the will and the knowledge of Allah. Allah knows the present, the past and the future of every creature. The destiny of every creature is already known to Allah (Suras 25:2; 33:38).[253]

The concept of predeterminism has been one of the principles of orthodox faith for Muslims from earliest days. Al-Bukhârî, in his collection of *hadîth*, dedicates a book to the subject of predestination (*Al-Qadr*).[254] Two samples illustrate the tenor of that book:

Narrated Anas bin Malik: The Prophet said, "Allah puts an angel in charge of the uterus and the angel says, 'O Lord, (it is) semen! O Lord, (it is now) a clot! O Lord, (it is now) a piece of flesh.' And then, if Allah wishes to complete its creation, the angel asks, 'O Lord, (will it be) a

"Muslim" at heart

male or a female? A wretched (an evil doer) or a blessed (doer of good)? How much will his provisions be? What will his age be?' So all that is written while the creature is still in the mother's womb."

Narrated Abdullah: Allah's Apostle, the truthful and truly-inspired, said, "Each one of you is collected in the womb of his mother for forty days, and then turns into a clot for an equal period (of forty days) and turns into a piece of flesh for a similar period (of forty days) and then Allah sends an angel and orders him to write four things, i.e., his provision, his age, and whether he will be of the wretched or the blessed (in the Hereafter). Then the soul is breathed into him. And by Allah, a person among you (or a man) may do deeds of the people of the Fire till there is only a cubit or an arm-breadth distance between him and the Fire, but then that writing (which Allah has ordered the angel to write) preceeds, and he does the deeds of the people of Paradise and enters it; and a man may do the deeds of the people of Paradise till there is only a cubit or two between him and Paradise, and then that writing preceeds and he does the deeds of the people of the Fire and enters it."[255]

The common understanding of predestination (*al-qadar*) is that the events of a person's life are determined from before conception. What is written in God's book is what his or her lot on earth will be.

Theologians have long wrestled with the delicate balance proposed in the Qur'ân between God's absolute sovereignty and humankind's free will. A typical suggestion is that verses stating that a person's will is not operative except by the will of God or that nothing takes place in the world without God's permission (*idhn* – as expressed, for example, in Sura 18:23) need to be understood in accordance with a universal view of humankind as vice-regent to God. At that universal level, human beings are certainly dependent on their Creator but they are also created free to make fundamental choices about the nature of their vice-regency.[256] For non-theologians, the everyday reality of human living colours their view of the lofty and complicated subject of divine predeterminism.

Om Gad married her first cousin and bore him eleven children, some of whom died at childbirth or shortly after. Her husband, Omar, looks after a garage in the basement of an apartment block in Giza, Cairo. He suffers from chronic back pain and often Om Gad has to do his chores for him. In looking back on 30 years of marriage, Om Gad reflects:

> This is our life, everything that happens is God's will after all. We accept it. I just hope God gives Omar time enough on this earth to place each one of our five daughters happily in some man's house.[257]

Because the sacred and secular aspects of living are interwoven, the essence of "submission" is carried over into all the details of everyday existence. Inheritance laws, marriage regulations, divorce proceedings and the broad outlines of the kinship system, with its emphasis on the paternal line and its stress on the division of the sexes, thus have religious sanction:

Sana al-Khayyat, in her study on women in contemporary Iraq, concludes that:

> ... marriage is based more on what is considered to be fate and luck than on real feelings and an intimate relationship: it is based on materialistic factors, which often causes difficulties later on in life.[258]

All the women whom al-Khayyat interviewed expressed their acceptance of "fate and destiny" (*qisma wa nasîb*) with regard to their marriage situations, however much they felt trapped, disappointed or humiliated.

In her short story entitled *Bahiyya's Eyes*, Alifa Rifaat describes the musings of an older Egyptian woman concerning various events in her life. Bahiyya is now going blind, so she writes to her daughter asking her to come and visit before her sight disappears completely. For Bahiyya, the matter of going blind is "all a question of fate and destiny". As she looks back on her life, and especially her unfulfilled teenage love for a young man named Hamdan, she reflects that what was decided for her by men in her life was also fated:

> Then suddenly all these hopes were shattered when my father came in one day and said to me: "Congratulations, Bahiyya, we've read the Fatiha for you with Dahshan." What a black day that was! I just sat where I was and cried. I didn't dare say I wanted to marry Hamdan or even to look up at my father. I was an ignorant girl and who was I to say I wanted this man and not that one? He'd have cut my throat for me. So I told myself that my destiny was with Dahshan and that was that.[259]

A strong determinism tends to underlie the Muslim's approach to daily living. There is a stoical acquiescence in all that life may bring along. An Arab, for example, never speaks of anything that he or she intends to do without adding the rider "if it is God's will" (*in shâ'a 'llâh*). By the same token, if final responsibility lies with God or fate, why need the human agent worry so much about safety procedures at work, seat belts in cars or smoking in the bedroom?

Control over the future is thus projected away from individuals. It is all down to God or fate or destiny. At the same time, as we have seen, the Arab is more oriented towards the past. So there is little motivation to plan ahead or to initiate change. The Arab is able consequently to live each day for itself, to be at peace in the midst of distressing uncertainty and to accept life without questioning it. An Egyptian couple regret the sad marriage that their only daughter is experiencing. There seems to be so little they can do to help. The daughter's husband will neither divorce her nor support her. Every now and then she arrives back at her parents' home after being beaten. Even with breaking hearts, the older couple cannot see what might be done:

> We would like our daughter to be divorced from this man. We would like her to marry someone who will look after her and care for her. We can only do what we can. The rest is in the hands of God, and everything in this world, in the end, is a matter of destiny.[260]

An Egyptian widow living in the City of the Dead on the outskirts of Cairo reflects on the change that came to her life when her husband suddenly died. She had to learn to provide for herself by running his fruit and vegetable stall with her two sons:

> I think I am a better person because I have had to go through this hardship. For one thing, work in the streets has taught me that many women don't have the easy life I took for granted when I was married to a devoted, hard-working man. I've seen a lot of things I'd rather not have seen and I've learned what it's like to feel shame, guilt and embarrassment without a man to protect you. I am a stronger woman because of all this and that is God's will.[261]

What visitor to Middle Eastern countries has not been struck by the dignity and poise of the indigenous people, most of them far worse off than the least advantaged in Western civilisations? Life is evaluated from a perspective which includes the assurance of paradise for those who submit to what is decreed. After all, "God is with the patient."

At the end of her short story *Degrees of Death*, Alifa Rifaat describes the serenity of the widow Widad as she contemplates what might have been had she married her childhood friend Mitwalli. Now both he and she are widowed and the possibility of their marrying late in life has been mooted by Mitwalli. Her musings reflect the personal peace of submission:

Though she shook her head at him, a great sadness took hold of her as she watched those large feet turn away and walk off. She thought with pain of how her life might have been had she married Mitwalli instead of Ahmed, but there is a time for everything: a time for romantic dreams, and a time for marriage and child-bearing, and a time when God has decreed that you are left alone in this world in order to prepare yourself for leaving it.[262]

Patient in waiting

The real Muslim

The cosmological map of most Muslims, however, is not limited to an understanding of God or fate "up there", with humankind "down here" acting out the destinies imposed from above. Rather, that map is crammed with a complex variety of powers and life-forms, all active and all competing for influence in the world of human beings. Those powers and life-forms are, for the most part, transempirical in essence. They are non-measurable and non-tangible. They cannot be pinned down or controlled in physical ways. They are nevertheless "real" and potent, and they share this world with humanity. In response to their awareness of such phenomena, ordinary Muslims are above all pragmatists. They pursue with energy and money whichever powers or beings might potentially work in their favour.

Such concepts of transempirical powers and beings that nonetheless share the world of human existence are difficult for Westerners (especially) to comprehend. For Westerners, such kinds of forces and persons (if they are believed to exist at all) belong to another world, the world of the supernatural. A person may choose to believe in them if he or she so wishes but they are not "evidently" present in our world. Paul Hiebert, an American missionary-anthropologist born and raised in India, came to recognise that he shared with fellow Westerners a distinct inability to scratch where most village Indians were itching. He discovered that the indigenous view of the world was very different from his own. The resultant non-understanding hinged, concluded Hiebert, on a "flaw" in the Westerner's worldview – the "flaw of the excluded middle".

Figure 18
Hiebert's summary of a Western two-tier view of reality

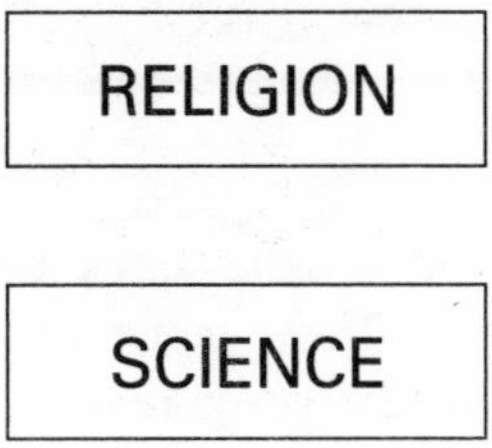

RELIGION

SCIENCE

The Western view of reality, since the period of the Enlightenment, has come to be basically two-tiered. Hiebert summarised the separate levels as that pertaining to science and that pertaining to religion (Figure 18).

Primary focus is given to science. Science provides the instrument for a Western handling of the natural or empirical world. It is based on sense experience, experimentation and proof. Secondary focus is given to religion. Religion deals with other-worldly matters, issues of faith, mystery and so on. People choose to believe what they want in matters of religion.

In India, Hiebert grew to know people who lived according to a different view of the world. For sure, there were strong concepts of natural phenomena. For sure, there were religious concepts, ideas about cosmic history, ultimate destiny and so on – matters of belief. Common to many Indians, however, was the conviction that transempirical beings and powers were real, active, and potentially harmful or beneficial to humans – in this world.

Figure 19

Hiebert's summary of a non-Western three-tier view of reality

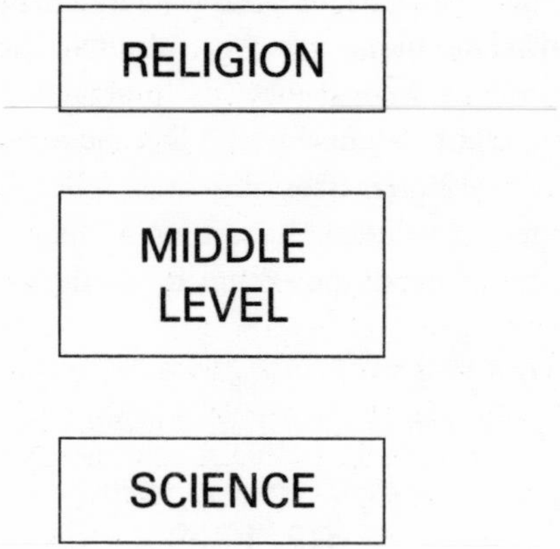

RELIGION

MIDDLE LEVEL

SCIENCE

Hiebert acknowledges that in these convictions lie concepts of reality that he did not share. Those concepts fill the "middle level" between religion and science (Figure 19). They explain present crises; they give meaning to past events; they offer hope for successfully navigating the unknown future.[263]

Many Muslims around the world share such a three-tiered view of reality. Life and death and all that lies between come down to the matter of managing, of manipulating, the beings and powers that fill that middle area of cosmological outlook.

A dichotomy therefore exists. In line with theological orthodoxy Muslims adhere at one level to the doctrine of predestination. They genuinely believe in "predeterminism" (*al-qadar* in Arabic; *kismet* in Turkish). Moreover, in terms of their status in life, often subject to the tyranny of dictatorship and economic mismanagement, they mostly feel like helpless pawns in a game of life for which their parts have been determined by forces beyond their control. One's lot is what has been fated. Yet in those areas of life over which people might conceivably exercise some jurisdiction, Muslims are anything but passive. Indeed, they are very active! Changing one's destiny is one's goal, though most Muslims wouldn't express it thus.[264]

One of the main female characters in Nawal El-Saadawi's *The Innocence of the Devil* is Nefissa. Nefissa is incarcerated in the Yellow Palace, an asylum for the insane. At night in her dreams, Nefissa takes on the character of her Aunt Zanouba, her favourite relative from childhood days. Aunt Zanouba represents freedom to Nefissa – not just the freedom of non-confinement, but the freedom of being a woman on equal footing with men. Zanouba owns such freedom because of her familiarity with the spirit world. She is called *El Alma*, "the lady who knows" – one who has access to spirit-inspired sources of information:

> During the day she saw her Aunt Zanouba sitting amongst the men. She smoked the water pipe and blew the smoke into the Headman's face. The Headman threw his head back and laughed, and the men around him called her El Alma. Her house was built of red brick. It rose two storeys higher than the house of the Headman, and was three metres higher than the House of God [the mosque]. She moved her arms and legs freely in front of the Headman. She feared no one, not the King, nor the President, nor the General. She stamped on the ground and her voice rose in song. Everyone acclaimed her name and called her Zanouba El Alma. Their eyes gleamed and their irises trembled in the whites of their eyes. Their hearts beat under their ribs and in their hearts was hidden a feeling like awe, a fear mingled with lust. She knew their secrets. She knew what was hidden, what was beyond ordinary understanding. God had revealed things to her. She read the cup and the palm of the hand. She could

decode the signs in the palm and understand the language of shells. She mingled with spirits and sirens.[265]

Saadawi's aim is to illustrate some of the cracks in the patriarchal, male-oriented world of the Muslim Middle East. She is writing in support of a movement for women's liberation. In the process she

Custodian of others' secrets?

identifies a major theme in most Muslims' lives: they are caught up in attempts to manipulate the spirit world. The universe of the "unseen" – of *jinn* and angels, blessings and curses – is familiar territory to them. Some of them, such as Zanouba, have incredible power in that world. All of them fear it.[266]

The two opposing concepts – submission to, and manipulation of, the supernatural – are resolved in the case of Zanouba with the assertion that God is the ultimate revealer, who speaks to her via palmistry and spiritism. For most Muslims, no such rationalisation is made: the spirit world is simply the more accessible realm in which to function. "God" is eclipsed in the desire to recruit other, lesser powers that can be more easily influenced. In orthodox circles, such meddling with the supernatural is of course strenuously deprecated.

I have written extensively on this subject elsewhere.[267] For our present purposes, one manifestation of the Muslim's concern for help from the "other world" will illustrate the paradox of resignation/manipulation.

Pilgrimages to shrines and the making of vows are common preoccupations of ordinary Muslims. They reveal their openness to the transempircal and their attempt to manipulate or change what is "written" (*maktûb*). Pilgrimages are undertakings of hope by people whose lives seem stamped with the heavy hopelessness of uncomfortable destinies dictated from above. Women especially, though by no means exclusively, visit shrines on a massive scale throughout the Muslim world.[268]

Tayeh Salih's short story *The Doum Tree of Wad Hamid* is about a saint's shrine in a Sudanese village. At the time of the narration, a weekly gathering of the village people at the shrine still occurs on Wednesdays. The spokesman for the village (narrator of the story) gives several examples of the significance of shrine visitation for various villagers. Included amongst them is the experience of a neighbour of his who had been ill for two months from a sudden swelling of her neck. One night, in a heavy fever, she had dragged herself along to the saint's tomb. What happened to her there is passed on in the woman's own words:

"I was under the doum tree," she said, "with hardly sufficient strength to stand up, and called out at the top of my voice: 'O Wad Hamid, I have come to you to seek refuge and protection – I shall sleep here at your tomb and under your doum tree. Either you let me die or you restore me to life; I shall not leave here until one of these two things happens.'

"And so I curled myself up in fear," the woman continued with her story, "and was soon overcome by sleep. While midway between wakefulness and sleep I suddenly heard sounds of recitation from the Koran and a bright light, as sharp as a knife-edge, radiated out, joining up the two river banks, and I saw the doum tree prostrating itself in worship. My heart throbbed so violently that I thought it would leap up through my mouth. I saw a venerable old man with a white beard and wearing a spotless white robe come up to me, a smile on his face. He struck me on the head with his string of prayer-beads and called out: 'Arise.'

I swear that I got up I know not how and went home I know not how. I arrived back at dawn and woke up my husband, my son, and my daughters. I told my husband to light the fire and make tea. Then I ordered my daughters to give trilling cries of joy, and the whole village prostrated themselves before us. I swear that I have never again been afraid, nor yet ill."[269]

Shrines are commonplace, not only in the countryside or in villages but also in towns and cities. For several years my family lived in Zamalek, Cairo, opposite All Saints' Cathedral where I worked. Just across the river from Zamalek in an eastwards direction lies Boulaq, a poor suburb of the city. Boulaq boasts a famous shrine, that of Sultan Abû ᶜAla. The shrine is housed in a side room of the Abû ᶜAla mosque that stands near the bridge between Boulaq and Zamalek:

> The holy man Abu 'Ala lived in the fifteenth century and was known for his bravery and his ability to cross the Nile River without a boat. It is said that the saint was a common laborer whose holiness was demonstrated by many miracles; for instance, at his funeral his coffin flew through the streets, eluding all who tried to catch it.[270]

To this shrine and to other similar neighbourhood shrines in Boulaq and throughout the city of Cairo, many citizens make informal and formal visits. The same is true of Meknes in Morocco, where a "pilgrimage visit" will take in attendance at the shrines of Shaikh al-Kamal and Sidi Said. Salé, another Moroccan town, is full of shrines. A local proverb simply says: "If you want to make a pilgrimage, just go around Salé barefooted."

There are two major focuses in shrine visitation: one is the mausoleum of the saint concerned, the other is the *ṣandûq al-nudhûr* or vow-box, with which most shrines are adorned. The mausoleum is a repository of *baraka*, a bank of holiness or "blessing" deriving from the saint. From the shrine's accumulation of power, the petitioner wants to withdraw enough to help his situation. The vow-box

To make a vow

is where he deposits his written vow or, if a saint has granted a request, where the pilgrim places the money previously promised in his vow.

The primary purpose in making a vow is to obtain what, in the ordinary run of events, is not obtainable. Nowal Messiri, researching amongst Nubians in Upper Egypt, describes the rationale for the shrine visitation which she discovered going on there:

In Dahmit, sheikhs were expected to render to believers certain services, for as saints they possessed *baraka* (grace, power to bless) and were capable of performing miracles (*karamât*). In return, adherents of the cult were expected to express their gratitude and recognition for such services in the form of *nafr* (vows), *ziâra* [visits] and *mawlids* [birthday celebrations], in addition to building the shrine and caring for it.[271]

Vow-making is done in two stages. The first stage is that of formulating the vow itself. This may be done privately, though it is generally held to be more efficacious to make the vow at a saint's tomb. In Cairo at every annual examination time, for example, many students will vow at Qaitbey mausoleum to make a certain number of recitations of the sura *Yâ Sîn* if they are successful. Other vows could involve small or large commitments such as making regular offerings at a shrine, building a mausoleum in memory of the saint concerned or going on pilgrimage.

The second stage is that of fulfilling the vow. Fulfilment is of extreme importance though often no fixed time is set. If a person has made a vow and not fulfilled it, nightmares or accidents tend to be interpreted as reminders of the need to make good what has been promised.

Rites of vow-making often involve a prayer, a reading or reciting of qur'ânic verses, the tying of pieces of rags or threads to the railings or doors of a shrine, or the lighting of candles. Blessing (*baraka*) is imported into the process by the prayer and Qur'ân reading. The candles and rags are reminders to the saint of the favour asked.

Motivations for vow-making are numerous. They tend to reflect the focuses of anxiety in the person, family or locality concerned. Messiri discerned seven major reasons for making a vow (*nadhr*) among the Nubians in Dahmit. They are listed here in descending order of priority: bearing a child, marriage for oneself or a member of the family, recovery from sickness, return of a relative from a visit to the city, success in school examinations for a family member and well-being of one's animals (see Figure 20).

Amongst women in the Boulaq suburb of Cairo, Evelyn Early discovered that shrines near the city cemetery – that is across the city from Boulaq – were visited to treat mental depression, to reverse sterility, to secure a spouse, or to reconcile quarrelling relatives or friends.[272]

Figure 20
Vow-making in Dahmit

Reasons for Vow	Kinds of Vow Payment
gaining a child	sacrifice of animal
marriage	whitewashing shrine
recovery from sickness	food offerings
safe return of relative	money donation
success in examinations	visit to distant shrine
health of animals	gifts of candles etc

After the fulfilment of the request by the saint's mediation, various expressions of thanks are made. These comprise the devotee's part of the bargain: the conditions of the vow having been met, the vow itself is made good. In Nubian Dahmit, the types of bargain struck with the saint were relatively simple. They included sugar cane offerings, money donations, a walk to a distant shrine and gifts of candles, rice or lentils. Larger gifts, for bigger requests, included the sacrifice of a goat or even a sheep, and the whitewashing of the shrine. The Baladi women of Boulaq fulfilled their vows by lighting candles, making meals for the poor, or offering animal sacrifices.

Different saints are approached for help with different problems. In the Dahmit region, Hamad, whose shrine was high in a mountain, was believed to be able to protect people from foreign invasion. Shelshel, whose shrine was in the fields, reputedly specialised in preventing crops from being stolen – stories circulate of thieves who have been paralysed by him for their misdeeds. Yacoub was another popular saint sought for his help in healing barrenness in women. Near the famous shrine of Imam al-Shâfiᶜî in Cairo's famous City of the Dead sit other, lesser known shrines: those dedicated to Shaykh Lizza, Shaykha Dandarawi, Sidi Qubba, Shaykha Raba'iyya, Shaykha Khadra and Shaykha Sukkariyya. Several of these saints are female. Each saint or shrine is reputed to alleviate a specific problem. Sidi Qubba, for example, is renowned for answering the prayers of aspiring brides and women who hope to become pregnant.

Sickness is a common condition leading to shrine visitation.

Many Muslims will visit both a government clinic and then a shrine. Many won't even bother troubling the clinic:

> Fathiye. About 28 or 30 years (she said maybe 15, maybe 20). Married with one boy and two girls, the eldest child being fifteen years. She is a housewife and lives in Hamoul; she was living in Cairo previously. She has been to several shrines many times. The shrines include those of Sayyid Husayn, Sayyida Zainab, and Sayyid Hakîm. She goes especially at the *mawlids* [birthday remembrances] . . . She goes for health reasons; she feels dizzy with weakness in her fingers and lower limbs. She goes also to pray that the Lord will keep evil spirits away from her. While circumambulating the tomb she asks the saint directly to cure her. When asked if the saint answered her prayer, she said that she feels comfort to such a degree that she doesn't want to leave the shrine. She pays a *nadhr* [vow-payment] at each shrine, though she cannot say what it is as that is a secret. She prays for herself and for her children. She does not pray the regular *ṣalât* [formal prayers of Islam].[273]

Vows, then, are seen as potentially powerful means of involving the activity of saints on behalf of the ordinary Muslim. They make sense in a world in which the Muslim lives out his life amidst a whole range of potentially hostile powers and a plethora of untamed beings. In the face of such transempirical phenomena, many Muslims spend much time and money seeking to keep at bay the constant threat of disequilibrium. In the absence of help from the remote God of formal faith, any help from a proven source of blessing (*baraka*) will be appropriated if at all possible.[274]

Vow-making is especially the province of women. Perhaps the shrines offer a dramatic alternative to their normal subordinate place in a patriarchal society where decision-making positions are held by males. Certainly the language of shrines is their language – colloquial dialect, not formal classical Arabic. Do women make recourse to shrine visitation in order to manipulate the world in which they lack formal power? Fatima Mernissi certainly concludes so:

> At the bottom, women in an unflinchingly patriarchal society seek through the saint's mediation a bigger share of power, of control. One area in which they seek almost total control is reproduction and security, the central notions of any patriarchal system's definition of women, classical orthodox Islam included. Women who are desperate to find

husbands, women whose husbands have sexual problems, women who have lost their husband's love or their own reproductive capacities go to the saint to get help and find solutions.[275]

Visits to saints' shrines for vow-making purposes offer a rare and powerful possibility for women especially to shape their world and their lives.

The pragmatism of Muslims in their search for sustained equilibrium in life outweighs the theological niceties of "submission". The possibility of mediators, intercessors and repositories of blessing is broadly legitimised, anyway, in the historic veneration of Prophet Muḥammad, Fâṭima, ᶜAlî and other historic figures of the faith. Muslims are rampant manipulators as much as they are humble submitters.

Seriously speaking

The Bible, and especially the Old Testament, is no stranger to the concept of vow-making. Though the references are few, they are significant in their content and contexts.

The vows that are recorded in the Old Testament are usually made by people in a state of disequilibrium. Hannah provides an early and engaging example. She is a woman who is barren, mocked by her co-wife, yet who longs to bear children for her husband Elkanah. Weeping and praying in bitterness of soul:

> . . . she made a vow, saying, "O Lord Almighty, if you will only look upon your servant's misery and remember me, and not forget your servant but give her a son, then I will give him to the Lord for all the days of his life . . . .
>
> (1 Samuel 1:11)

David exemplifies someone in an extreme state of disequilibrium who makes a vow. He is on the run from King Saul and falls into the hands of the Philistines in Gath. He acknowledges before God:

> I am under vows to you, O God;
> I will present my thank-offerings to you.
>
> (Psalm 56:12)

We are informed that this psalm was composed when the Philistines had seized David in Gath. On his release and later freedom to worship publicly in Israel, David sings:

> I will come to your temple with burnt offerings
>   and fulfil my vows to you –
> vows my lips promised and my mouth spoke when
>   I was in trouble.
>
> (Psalm 66:13, 14)

Jonah, whilst reaping the results of his disobedience, also seems to have made a vow. During his brush with death, he prays from inside the fish:

> What I have vowed I will make good.
>
> (Jonah 2:9)

Vows, as they are recorded in the Old Testament, constitute conditional promises of action or attitude. The always-bargaining Jacob well illustrates such conditional promising as he proposes a partnership with God to get him out of his earthly scrape:

> If God will be with me and will watch over me on this journey I am taking and will give me food to eat and clothes to wear so that I return safely to my father's house, then the Lord will be my God.
>
> (Genesis 28:20, 21)

Jephthah, one of the pre-kingdom judges of Israel, makes a vow-promise which he lives to regret:

> If you give the Ammonites into my hands, whatever comes out of the door of my house to meet me when I return in triumph from the Ammonites will be the Lord's, and I will sacrifice it as a burnt offering.
>
> (Judges 11:30, 31)

His only child, a girl, is the first "whatever" to come out of his home to meet Jephthah on his victorious return. After two months of wandering in mourning, she returns to her father in order for him to fulfil his foolish vow.

Vows, as recorded in the Bible, are serious affairs. They occur rarely, usually in desperate situations. The making of them is entirely voluntary, but once made they are in nearly every case binding. The one exception under Sinaitic law was the situation in which an unmarried, or married but unthinking, woman made a vow. Her husband, upon marrying her or upon hearing about her vow, had the opportunity of nullifying what she had sworn (Numbers 30:8).

Vows, once made, are to be fulfilled as soon as appropriate. Absalom's claim of needing to fulfil a vow in Hebron put enough moral pressure on King David for the monarch to permit his rebellious son to leave Jerusalem and move outside his immediate control. Equally, the strong words of Boaz, expressed in terms of a vow, must have given young Ruth a settling sense of peace as she waited out the night (Ruth 3:13). Certainly the next day, Ruth's mother-in-law Naomi knew for sure that Boaz would not rest until the issue was sorted out. Naomi understood the strength of a vow.

In the fulfilling of vows there is to be no attempt to cheat God. Deformed animals (cows or sheep) might occasionally be presented to the Lord as freewill offerings but under no circumstances will such stunted or deformed animals be accepted in fulfilment of a vow (Leviticus 22:23). At the end of the Old Testament period, Malachi pronounces people as accursed who have an acceptable male in their flock and vow to offer it but then sacrifice a blemished animal instead (Malachi 1:14). Such activity makes a mockery of the holy name of God before the nations. Neither will the Lord accept, as vow fulfilment, earnings derived from female or male prostitution (Deuteronomy 23:18).

Vows are, evidently, part of the reality of Old Testament Hebrew culture. The Lord accepts their occurrence, understanding that they are made by individuals or groups of people in severe disequilibrium. Once made, however, vows are treated by the Lord with deadly seriousness. Whoever makes a vow, with virtually no exception, is held to it. In the fulfilling of a vow, speed, honesty and concern for holiness is urged. Most significantly of all and without tolerance of any exception, vows in the Old Testament are made, or are to be made, to the Lord. There is no question of them being made to some other "mediator". They are offered to the God who has condescended to be in covenant relationship with the people of Israel and who has declared himself Lord of the nations.

Sadly, there is evidence that, late in the life of the kingdom of Judah, vows were being made by a group of Israelites to other supposed mediators. After the fall of Jerusalem, a remnant of the kingdom of Judah stubbornly make their way south to Egypt. They force the prophet Jeremiah to accompany them. In Egypt, they lapse into a rather mixed-up faith which includes the making and carrying out of vows to "the Queen of Heaven" (Jeremiah 44:25) The Lord gives Jeremiah a message condemning this activity. There is no tolerance whatsoever for the degrading of this permitted way of relating to the Lord. Vows, such solemn events in themselves, are only to be made to him.

In stark contrast with the unacceptable state of affairs exposed by Jeremiah, Isaiah prophesies of days in which Egyptians will themselves acknowledge and worship the Lord. That submission and relationship is described in terms of vow-keeping:

. . . they will make vows to the Lord and keep them.

(Isaiah 19:21)

The outsider will live as an insider before the Lord. The covenant God of the people of Israel will be the auditor of the Egyptians' vows.

Limits to manipulation?

The Old Testament largely agrees with contemporary Muslim perspectives on the actualities of the unseen world. Magic, sorcery and occult practices are demonstrably real, according to the Bible. The devil is conceived of as a personal being, heading a hierarchy of evil spirits. "Reality" involves a context greater than the merely mundane. The Lord himself, in the courts of heaven, boasts to Satan about his servant Job. Spiritual powers for good and ill abound. Curses are to be feared and blessings appropriated. Lying demons are Lucifer's children while prophet Elisha's buried bones can impart renewed life to a corpse. There is no "flaw of the excluded middle" in the biblical worldview!

Pragmatism, however, is not to be the main motive for moving "successfully" in such a world. Nefissa's Aunt Zanouba, with her new-found power amongst men on earth, gains such authority at a price. God is not her adviser as she seeks to interpret coffee grounds and "charted" palms. According to the Bible, ethical concerns for good and evil are extremely important and override mere pragmatism. Moreover, relational concerns about loyalty to humankind's Creator are even more critical in issues of "guidance". The transempirical realm is real enough. It is all a matter of living faithfully towards God in such a context.

Some Muslims who become believers in Christ experience extraordinary problems, seemingly the result of their entanglement in dangerous spiritual dynamics during former shrine visitation and vow-making. For many such believers, there is need for deliverance from bondage to powerful forces which have come to dominate their lives:

When still in her early teens, Aziza of Eastern Algeria was led to Christ. It was known that her Muslim, Berber family had been in touch with sorcerers and had visited saints' tombs from which charms and writings had been obtained.

While continuing to meet with other believers, she had begun to experience choking spells at night, along with terrifying dreams. Her attendance at Bible Studies became intermittent – she was busy studying at the time and under many social pressures because of her faith in Christ.

Later, and out of regular fellowship by this time, she agreed to marry a Muslim. She knew that in that contact she disobeyed God. In the distress of soul which ensued, she sent for a counsellor of former years. The counsellor stayed with Aziza in her room in the home of the fiancé – and while there Aziza suffered a Satanic attack manifested by extreme depression and real fears of a nervous breakdown.

Prayer in Jesus' Name, confession of sin and the ministry of the Word led to a marvellous deliverance. God enabled Aziza to escape from that situation of imminent marriage. Escape also meant her removal from the area of her fiancé's home. Later Aziza recognised that the deadening attacks of depression had been of demonic origin. Christ had brought deliverance. The Lord later brought a Christian man into Aziza's life – they are now married. She bears a clear testimony to the liberating power of the risen Lord.[276]

The transempirical world is not neutral. Neither is it up for grabs to the greatest pragmatist. It has a powerful sting in its tail, a sting which many Muslims have felt in their own lives. The temptation to indulge in the occult understandably arises in situations in which God is seen as far removed and beyond human appeal. Often, with "power-conscious" people such as Muslims, the nearness of God is first really recognised in an encounter in which the paralysing authority of the unseen world is neutralised and banished.[277] In its place, Muslims like Aziza discover in their experience that God is at hand, present and willing to be in daily relationship with his children.

The Lord's desire for such divine/human relationship is well illustrated in the way that the subject of vow-making is progressively dealt with in the biblical revelation. The burden of the Old Testament on this subject is to focus human attitudes concerning vow-making away from an "automatic" approach and towards an "engagement" type of arrangement. Care was taken, when producing the Septuagint (a Greek version of the Old Testament, often quoted by Jesus and the apostles) to use words which differentiated the narrow sense of vow-making in the Old Testament text from the common and careless proliferation of vows and votive offerings, by then ubiquitous in the Greek and Roman worlds.[278]

In the New Testament, the Greek words carefully chosen in the Septuagint were adopted and used for "calling on God". Now, however, no allowance was made for vow-making to be involved in such "prayer", despite its frequent occurrence throughout the Roman empire. Of course, as far as the New Testament is concerned, prayer to God is qualitatively different after Messiah's coming. The relationship, though still with a holy, perfect Father, is now declared to be open to all in Christ through whom there may be intimate personal knowledge of God. All the seriousness of vow-making and all the positiveness of it is transferred into a relationship with God in Christ. In Christ, the believer himself is to be the vow, the consecrated gift, the one dedicated to God. And in Christ's name, the believer may ask what he will and he shall be answered positively.

Redundant vow-boxes?

In reflecting upon the syndrome of vow-making in Muslim experience, it would seem that the cult of saint veneration which provides its rationale gradually developed to meet needs unsatisfied by the beliefs and practices of formal Islam. Submission to a remote God or impersonal fate is not enough of an answer when a woman finds herself barren or her child sick with a fever.

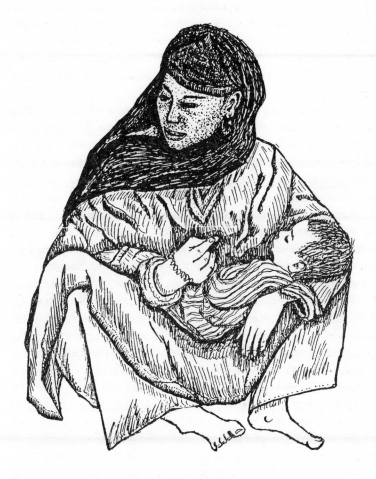

Whence healing?

The ordinary Muslim knows that her disequilibrium arises in the context of a vast world of competing beings and powers. Its cause could be one of many. Perhaps she has been cursed? Or has her familiar spirit (*qarîna*) upset her? Maybe an evil spirit is infesting her child? Or has he been struck by the evil eye? The obtaining of a saint's assistance via a process of vow-making provides one way of seeking new equilibrium either for herself or for those whom she loves.

The saint cult stands its ground in the face of orthodox criticism basically because ordinary Muslims continue to experience unanswered felt needs and because, as devotees of saints, they find the process to work.

The Old Testament is not unfamiliar with a rite of vow-making, though it insists that vows be made only to God. It protects the process with sanctions, identifying the procedure as utterly serious: vows must be properly fulfilled. The message, in Old Testament terms, is that the Lord is willing to accommodate himself to the cries of human beings in disequilibrium. The world of hostile beings and forces, human and transempirical, in which mortals find themselves at a disadvantage is real enough. The Lord will hear and respond to their vow-making, but he is nonetheless a holy God, not a pawn to be manipulated by a formula. By the time of the New Testament, the concept of vow-making as an approach to God is abrogated by a superlative alternative – namely that in Christ the answer to all human felt need is found. Prayer, now, is supremely to be the channel for intimacy between a believer and the Lord of all creation.

In terms of relating this wonderful news to Muslims, it would seem that as much emphasis must be placed on experience (their pragmatic sense) as upon conveying cognitive information about Christ. Visits to the vow-box (ṣandûq al-nudhûr) must be made redundant by their being rendered unnecessary. Jesus Christ as healer, answerer of prayer, exorciser, guide, light, peace and sustainer of mortal beings is the only Person in the world who can, in glorious tenderness and great power, replace the Muslims' inclination towards shrine visitation.

The honest words of Donna Smith, reflecting on 18 years of faithful ministry amongst women in a Muslim country, highlight the need for Western Christians to see beyond the real resignation to the equally real manipulation of their Muslim friends:

Again and again I find that the barrier against the gospel of Christ is due to women's strong attachment to folk Islam and the animistic practices it encourages. From birth to death, some "superstitious" practice binds them to the spirits. A woman goes to a saint's tomb and asks for a child:

she returns to carry out her vow when the child is born. Children are protected against the "evil eye" by many charms and amulets. Marriages are made and broken by sorcery. Sick people are healed by the intercession of dead "saints". Houses are built, fields are plowed, diplomas gained – all through the power of the saints' tombs (*marabouts*).

Victory through the powerful name of Jesus Christ must be proclaimed to break the bondage of these women who dearly guard the traditions of their ancestors. They confide in me about these practices: I long for their deliverance, but personally I have seen little breakthrough here. My present concern is to focus prayer and proclamation of the gospel for his victory over their bondage. I seek his wisdom and power in applying the message of deliverance to the lives of women in the Muslim world.[279]

Iba Zizen, a Kabyle of Algeria, grew up in a family that made regular family pilgrimages to local saints' shrines. In a wonderful way, the Holy Spirit used the experience of "making a visit" to the shrine of Sidi Ali Moussa to awaken a hunger in Iba's heart:

I made the round of the tomb seven times, as I had been taught, for seven was the magic number. Then I waited ... For what? Not for anything precise certainly. Perhaps I hoped to hear a voice, or the revelation of something hidden. But nothing spoke to me.

When later on I would consider the meaning of these excursions, I would recognise a thirst which was destined to remain for a long time unsatisfied.[280]

Later in his life, that thirst was to be quenched in a dramatic way. Iba was sitting in the office of a Roman Catholic missionary when his eyes were drawn to a picture on the man's desk. It was a photo of a sister, Sister Theresa of Lisieux, who had died some twelve years previously. The Catholic Father embarked upon the life story of this saint but Iba hardly heard him. He was wholly absorbed by something going on inside his spirit:

What I had sought while going round the tomb of Sidi Ali Moussa, and in stroking the stiff brocade, was now shining out at me from a young face and a young life ... A window into Christianity opened for me, with the possibility of a life transformed.[281]

Gradually, over many years, Iba came to own for himself the Christ whose life and light he had unconsciously sought from his youth and which he had glimpsed shining so strongly from a picture of a young nun.

What is fated and what is negotiable? To what circumstances does a Muslim simply submit, even while longing for an alternative reality? What beliefs and activities does a Muslim actively pursue in order to change prevailing circumstances? In the constant tension between these two themes – resignation and manipulation – lies the prospect of deep insight into the circumstances and heart-cries of ordinary Muslims.

Conclusion

CHAPTER TEN

SOUL MUSIC

. . . hearing oftentimes
The still, sad music of humanity . . .
William Wordsworth

One of the well-loved Mulla Nasrudin stories best expresses my feelings in drawing these chapters to a close:

Visiting a sick friend, Nasrudin was just in time to see the doctor arrive. The man was in the house for less than a minute, and the speed of his diagnosis stunned the Mulla.

First the doctor looked at the patient's tongue, then he paused briefly. Then he said, "You have been eating green apples. Stop doing this. You will be well in a couple of days."

Forgetting everything else the Mulla pursued the doctor out of the house. "Tell me, Doctor," he panted, "please tell me how you do it."

"It was quite simple, when you have experience to distinguish various situations," said the doctor. "You see, as soon as I knew that the man had a stomach-ache, I looked for a cause. When I got into the sick-room, I saw a heap of green apple cores under the man's bed. The rest was obvious."

Nasrudin thanked him for the lesson.

The next time he was visiting a friend it happened that the man's wife answered the door. "Mulla," she said, "we don't need a philosopher. We need a doctor. My husband has a stomach-ache."

"Don't think that the philosopher cannot be a physician, Madam," said Nasrudin, forcing himself into the presence of the patient.

The sick man lay groaning on a bed. Nasrudin went straight to it, looked underneath, and called the wife into the room.

"Nothing serious," he said; "he will be well in a couple of days. But you must make sure that he cuts down on this habit of eating saddles and bridles."[282]

At the end of this interrogation of Muslim Middle Eastern cultures, I am left asking whether I have misunderstood or misrepresented the societies about which I have written? Have I perhaps been too limited in focus to justify some of the broader inferences drawn? Or have I indulged too quickly in generalisation to permit the complexities and contradictions inherent in each specific theme to come across? My intention in writing has therefore to be only to offer, not to impose, a diagnosis. This book is proposed tentatively, for others' consideration.

Others' investigations

The suggestions proffered in these chapters, moreover, need to be placed in the context of other related offerings. Various investigators have attempted, from differing perspectives, to describe in overall, coherent terms the primary values, personality, ethos or worldview of peoples of the Middle East. Some of the more significant attempts are summarised in the following paragraphs. All of them have been consulted and considered in the writing of this book.

Sania Hamady, in a seminal book published in 1960, boldly delineated significant traits in Arab personality.[283] At the time of writing Hamady was an assistant professor in the department of human relations at the University of Miami. Her research provided materials for an analysis of the temperament and character of Arabs; indeed, her resulting book is entitled *Temperament and Character of the Arabs*. Hamady constructed her analysis around the themes of "feelings and reactions", "identifications and loyalties", "the Arab's outlook on life" and "the Arab mind". Hamady's presupposition was that Arabs had nothing of which to be ashamed in the world of newly-won independence from Western nations. Indeed they had a lot to offer. Her aim was eirenic, to promote better relations between Arab and Western nations through deeper exposure and comprehension of the psychological and social aspects of Arab life. She writes in a positive spirit and gives detailed examples of attitudes, including sayings and proverbs, to illustrate her conclusions.

Morroe Berger (a North American) wrote from a sociological

A glimpse of others

perspective, drawing broad conclusions from his study of Near Eastern culture generally in the 1950s and Egyptian society specifically in the 1960s.[284] His concern was to provide an answer to the question: "What kind of a person is the Arab?" He strove to discount the prevailing negative headlines in the Western media concerning Arabs, preferring to seek out how Arabs actually "live, work, marry, bear and rear children – how what they do makes them what they are".[285] Berger's research led him to identify certain hallmarks of Arab personality: namely, an exaggerated striving for self-esteem, a deep suspicion of others, an extreme adherence to tradition and an "infatuation with the ideal" that leads to frustration. Around these hallmarks Berger clustered his observations and conclusions.[286]

Raphael Patai, a professional anthropologist of Hungarian Jewish background, focused his suggestions about contemporary Arab ethos on an analysis of a few primary values inherited from the Bedouins.[287] He concluded that three "syndromes" function together to give substance to the values of Bedouin society. The "courage-bravery" syndrome consists in features such as the concern for kinship, loyalty and manliness. The "hospitality-generosity" syndrome is formed out of emphases on protection, generosity, raiding and blood-revenge. The "honor-dignity" syndrome has to do with "face", self-respect, female sexual purity and so on. Together, these interrelated syndromes comprise the major "Bedouin" concerns of the Arab ethos. They are complemented, in Patai's view, by the Islamic component which contributes a religious perspective on the totality of life. Patai went so far as to reduce his analysis to one primary observation. He felt that the preservation of self-respect was the characteristic of ultimate importance for Arabs, justifying a conclusion that "value" for Arabs is as much defined by the actions and attitudes of others as from any internal motivation.[288]

John Gulick, another anthropologist who has more recently researched Middle Eastern peoples, strove to discover an answer to the question "How *should* an Arab distinctively think, feel and act, in order to be genuinely Arab?"[289] His judgement was that the "good" Arab, the person striving for the "ideal life", is someone who subscribes to paternal dominance, fraternal solidarity and male superiority. At the same time, Gulick observed a conflict between the ideal and the real, illustrated in quarrels between parents and children, the lack of self-esteem in women (communicated via child-rearing habits to each new generation) and sibling rivalry. From such family stresses, Gulick concluded that suspicion of others tends to be projected by the individual Arab onto society at large. Gulick focused his research on the ensuing paradox of how the Middle Easterner can be both extremely group-oriented and strongly individualistic. He reckoned that in the realms of language, religion, ancestry, sex and territory there are major reasons for Arab insecurity. In each of these important realms where self-identity is achieved, there are major contradictions between the ideal and the real, between what should be the case and what actually is the case.

David Pryce-Jones, in his late 20th-century interpretative essay on the Arabs, speaks from the perspective of a journalist rather than as a social scientist.[290] His experience as a correspondent in the Sinai desert during the Six Day War of June 1967 provoked him to delve more deeply into the character of the Arabs. Pryce-Jones was stunned by the discrepancy between what was being done in the Arab world by its peoples at war and what was being said about the Arab situation in the West. He discovered in himself what he calls a "Eurocentric" reaction to the society which he was observing and he set out deliberately to lay that reaction aside and seek instead to understand Arab society on its own terms. His is a mainly historico-political approach, beginning with an analysis of tribal society and going on to describe the contradictions of that basic societal formation as it has become writ large in the nations of the Middle East. His analysis of careerism is particularly insightful and is in many ways the major theme of his book. Pryce-Jones argues that the Arabs are caught in a closed circle made up of overwhelmingly tenacious tribal, religious and cultural traditions. His sympathies obviously lie with the "masses". They provided the cannon fodder for the war Pryce-Jones observed. In his view, they remain chained to a non-democratic political reality, due to their leaders being "encircled" – that is, enmeshed in a particular worldview in which careerism is a primary factor.

The foregoing, and other, serious attempts to get to grips with Arab culture and personality are important contributions to understanding. For the most part they deliberately lay aside prejudice and seek some insider insight of a society foreign to the researcher. As such they are helpful models and offer a variety of avenues for an exploration of how Middle Eastern/Arab societies cohere.

The only "closed circle"?

Cultures evidently work as functional wholes. The complex component elements of them are interwoven in such a way as to reinforce
an implicit and deep-rooted ethos or worldview. The professional
social scientists referred to above have attempted in different ways
to "get a handle" on the Arab or Middle Eastern variety of human
socialisation. I am, to some extent, indebted to them for stimulating
my thinking about some of the cultural characteristics-in-tension
that I have outlined in this book.

To anyone who has crossed an ethnic or cultural boundary, it is
obvious that we human beings live in quite different ways. What is
customary for one group is strange to another. We have learned
different rules of life: how to discipline our children, whether to cry
in public or not, what sort of activity is beyond the pale and so on.
The German, for example, says to a wayward child: "Get in line!"
The Frenchman says: "Be wise!" The Britisher says: "Be good!"
Thus uniformity, wisdom and goodness are concepts taught as the
norm to the respective children in the process of their growing up.
We all make jokes about national neighbours based on the stereotyping of their attitudes and behaviour. A race's eccentricities allow
us to characterise and make fun of it. Appropriate cross-cultural
investigation takes seriously the fact that others' constructs of reality
are not simply to be laughed at or compared in a disparaging way
with our own. Rather, those constructs of reality are recognised as
channels for allowing the "soul" of each particular culture to find
expression.

Perhaps here would be an appropriate place to summarise some
of the motifs that have emerged from our investigation of Arab,
Middle Eastern and Muslim culture. Figure 21 lists them along with
contrasting, equivalent motifs from our own Western cultural background. There is no particular prioritising within the diagram. It is
easy to see that the points of contrast are considerable in number and
considerable in degree of difference.

Arising out of the assumptions about reality which form the bases
for these motifs, further assumptions are made concerning "normal"
approaches to living. In each cultural context, "what *is* the case"
gives rise to "what *should be*" our behavioural response. If human
beings are perceived as individuals with power to control both their

own destiny and the world in which they live, then life might well
consist in protecting individual choices and facilitating changes in

Figure 21
"East" and "West"

Important Motifs in Western Cultures	Important Motifs in Middle Eastern Cultures
reality-centred conceptual framework	value-centred conceptual framework
primacy of individual	primacy of the group
liberty to develop independent life	place in web of social relationships
equality of the sexes	differentiation of the sexes
task-oriented roles	gender-associated roles
achievement due to self-effort	honour from variety of sources
guilt: result of breaking law	shame: result of failing someone
emphasis on youth	emphasis on age
materialistic/humanistic in focus	theocentric/God-oriented in focus
love matches lead to marriage	status matches negotiated for marriage
rights of each individual paramount	duties towards family/clan paramount
open-ended attitude to economics	"limited good" attitude to economics
contract relationships important	oral/trust relationships important
public and private worlds separate	public and private worlds integrated
accumulation of private wealth lauded	generosity/hospitality on demand lauded
future-oriented	past-oriented
freedom-focused behaviour	status-focused behaviour
personal preference primary	conventional appearance primary
competition on basis of individual merit	advancement on basis of who you know

the world so that it better serves humanity. If human beings are perceived primarily as a creation of God, subject to a destiny imposed from above, then life might well consist in helping each human being to come to a place of submission and acceptance of his lot on earth. If reward comes from individual entrepreneurship and experimentation, then men or women will be set free to establish their own goals and achieve them, whatever anyone in their family may think. If honour is bound up with the maintenance of the group's reputation, then individuals will live and act in ways that gain and maintain that group's approbation: listening carefully to the past, to the elders, to the tradition.

The emerging normative assumptions – what *should be* humans' behavioural response – in turn determine the surface customs and behaviour of the respective peoples. In the instance of self-sufficient humanity, those structures and relationships will be encouraged which best help each individual fulfil his or her personal ambitions. In the instance of subservient humanity, those structures and relationships which best aid people in submitting to God will be promoted. What is on public view thus arises out of assumptions made corporately, at a deep level, by people within a common cultural background. It is little wonder that the motifs suggested as important to Western and Middle Eastern cultures respectively (Figure 21) are not only so different but also so deeply entrenched!

The truth many of us reading this book have to face is that the Westerner's "circle" is as much closed as the Middle Easterner's. The different components of each culture combine to reinforce unstated assumptions about the why and the wherefore of existence. It is just that the Western circle is different from the Middle Eastern variety!

Others' faithfulness

In the history of Christian mission to Muslim peoples there have been some Western missionaries, past and present, who managed to identify with the "soul" of Middle Eastern culture. One thinks of such exemplary men as Temple Gairdner, Charles Marsh, William Miller and Samuel Zwemer or such women as Lilias Trotter, to name but a few of the better-known gifted communicators of the gospel.[291] Theirs was an insight born of the Spirit and arising out of long-term residence amongst Muslim peoples in the Middle East and North Africa.[292]

My concern in these pages is to help the successors to such pioneers – especially Western Christians – to overcome prevalent psychological barriers of miscomprehension and fear. The negative stereotype accorded by Western society to Arabs, Iranians and North Africans in particular, and to Muslims in general, is quite blatant. Such negativism quickly spills over into evangelical concerns (proper concerns) for the salvation of those peoples. I still sometimes hear people amongst whom I have been ministering refer to Muslims as "Islams" or "Mohammedans". Islamophobia is a serious disease in the Western church as well as in Western society at large. The images we have of Muslims and the ways in which some of us talk about taking on this remaining "giant" tend to reflect a severe non-understanding of the Middle Eastern "soul". Colin Chapman concludes his essay on the biblical foundations of praying for Muslims with wistful words:

> I sometimes wonder what would happen if those who think simply in terms of "praying against" Islam were to turn their energy and enthusiasm into praying about all that goes to make up effective communication. It might mean, for example, thinking and praying about such mundane questions as whom to visit, when to tell stories and how to use graphics! And such a concern for communication leads us straight into the theme of rethinking and restating the gospel for the Muslim world.[293]

I have suggested that a "closed circle" is as much the Westerner's lot as the Middle Easterner's. It is a difficult process to break free from one's inherited mindset and learn to appreciate life from the perspective of an alternative culture. Ethnocentrism (a kind of innate tourist mentality) is strongly ingrained in us all. We so quickly judge others by the norms of our own inherited assumptions. We are normal; everyone else is strange or weird, even wrong.

The Bible is piercingly realistic in its appraisal of human culture. In the Wisdom literature of the Old Testament, a careful contrast is couched in two staggering phrases offered among "the words of the Teacher". On the one hand, human beings have "eternity in their hearts" (Ecclesiastes 3:11). What a wonderful phrase! All people are made in God's image, and the "circles" in which they conceptualise and prioritise values or norms are dim reflections – but still reflections – of how their Creator has made them to function. Each circle has a certain validity! On the other hand, there is "madness" in the hearts of human beings (Ecclesiastes 9:3). The image of God is marred in us all. As a consequence, our various societies sadly demonstrate that the creation, separated from its Creator, is warped, dysfunctional and deserving of judgement. The circles bind all of us to less than perfect creaturehood!

The only Person who dare differentiate between the intimations of eternity and the expressions of madness in each cultural expression is the Holy Spirit. He alone can break open the closed circles of self-contained, self-affirming worldviews. He alone can judge where Muslim or Christian ideals and Arab or Western cultures reflect eternity or proclaim madness. I am conscious that so often among the first disciples of Jesus, the primary, uncomfortable focus for conversion was in those disciples' view of others, especially "outsiders". Whether it was in wrongly wanting to call down fire on Samaritan villages or falsely halting a non-kosher exorcist or discovering through a Roman centurion that God loves Gentiles – as much converting went on in the disciples' hearts as in anyone else's! And they lived so close to Jesus! Christian missionaries today, agents of a Lord who seeks to redeem people enculturated in every variety of worldview, need deliberately to leave to the Holy Spirit the prerogative of deciding where each circle, including their own, might be broken open.

The Holy Spirit is also the Person best-equipped to help us mortals hear, from within constructs of reality different from our own, the all-pervasive music of lost humanity. Where "things fall apart" in a specific ethos is often where divine mending might begin.[294] We must learn to ask: where are the tensions in peoples' lives, where is the *angst* in changing societies, where is the Holy Spirit longing to say, "I am present to renew and change and mend"?[295] In cooperating with the Holy Spirit at such points of disintegration, Christian missionaries, servants of a sovereign creative Lord, need also to expect the unexpected – unexpected, that is, in terms of their own cultural understanding, though quite reasonable, maybe, from someone else's. Stuart Robinson relates a classic "missed opportunity" where a Christian leader failed to keep up with the Holy Spirit in what the latter was miraculously engineering in a community of Muslims:

In 1868 a group of Muslim mystics known as Shazlis met for two years in Damascus. An inner circle of leaders met at the home of Abd el Kadir to meditate and pray. On one occasion they all fell asleep and later awoke simultaneously. Each reported that they had dreamed of Jesus. Convinced of his reality and truth as recorded in the New Testament they were filled with joy.

Through a second similar supernatural event they became aware of an old white-bearded man who wore a coarse brown garment and held a lighted candle. After a three month search throughout Damascus they found the person of their dreams. He was a Spanish Franciscan monk, Fra Former.

Within a comparatively short time 25,000 Shalzlis were reportedly ready and willing to be baptised. The British consul in Damascus, Sir Richard Burton, proposed having all of them resettled in a purpose built, new community outside of the city. He sought the help of Archbishop Valerga of Jerusalem whom he assumed would organise a mass baptism. Instead Valerga reported developments to the Muslim Ottoman authorities. Twelve enquirers were killed. Fra Former died mysteriously. Sir Richard Burton was sacked.[296]

Many of us, probably, are responsible for less spectacular, but equally serious, failures in listening to the Holy Spirit.

How refreshing, then, to hear and close this chapter with Zubaidah's story – not an easy story, but one in which some British Christians listened well and hosted well:

Zubaidah came to Britain as a bride, but found that her in-laws disliked her. After three miserable years and a baby who died at three months, her husband divorced her under Islamic law and she was sent back to her family. Her father refused to take her in, because of the shame it would bring on him, so she was sent back to Britain – with no place to go and only temporary permission to enter the country. She found Christian friends who gave her a home, cared for her through a long period of depression, and helped her to get a work permit and a home of her own. One day, she asked them: "How can I follow your Jesus?" She is now following him, and finding that his acceptance of her heals all her previous rejections.[297]

Threshold of hope?

The chapters of this book represent a "doodling in the sand", a pause for reflection. They constitute a space for trying to understand some perspectives about Muslim people that are different from those that normally spring quickly to the Western mind. Instead of evaluations that are media-conveyed and fear-inspired, we are challenged to look again – to see from the insider's perspective.

Our deliberate hesitating needs to find conclusion in prayer to the Lord of all creation. In our seeking to obey his Great Commission, may we be quick to recognise the limitedness of our own worldview. Then might we seek his insight into cultures other than our own, his evaluation of their strengths and weaknesses and his inspiration for most faithfully representing him to them:

> Lord Jesus;
> You stretched out your obedient arms to shame on the hard
>   wood of the cross, that all men and women might come
>   within the circle of your saving embrace:
> Clothe us in your Spirit, that we, reaching beyond the known
>   and familiar and entering the unique worlds of our fellow
>   human beings, may bring those who know you not within
>   the clasp of your perfect salvation;
> To the glory of your holy name.
> Amen.

"Let us pray . . ."

Appendices

QUESTIONS FOR FURTHER STUDY

In this book I have painted a broad picture of some of the "themes in tension" that appear to function in contemporary Islamic cultures. It is important for each reader to evaluate the nature of the "mix" of tensions which apply to the people of the particular culture or subculture in which he or she is living and working.

In the paragraphs that follow, questions arising from the issues addressed within the various chapters of this book are posed. The aim, in asking such questions, is to suggest some avenues along which further localised inquiry might be made.

Chapter 1: To Save a Soul

In seeking to better understand people with a different faith from our own, it is important to study the fundamentals of their religious belief and experience. A grasp of some of the cultural issues, necessary for successful communication, is no substitute for the hard work of getting to know the faith of Islam in its essential expressions. Do you have a good awareness of the fundamentals of Islam? Have you read or listened to a presentation of the Islamic faith by a qualified Muslim – not just read about it in books by non-Muslims? Could you perhaps construct a list of some of the major facets of belief and practice in Islam and compare them with those of the Christian faith? What kind of view of Islam or Muslims colours your interaction with this faith and its adherents?

For what purpose are you seeking an understanding of cultural issues? In your own relating to Muslims, to what degree are you aware of differences in cultural upbringing between yourself and them? What has this led you to learn of your own cultural background? What unstated assumptions about life have you discovered in yourself through the process of getting to know people from a different cultural background? What have you come to enjoy in relating to Muslim friends? What have been points of frustration or clash? Has your appreciation of the Bible been enhanced by getting to know Muslims; if so, in what ways?

In the particular situation in which you live and work, how might a growing understanding of cultural themes and social structures be of importance for evangelism, church planting or any other involvement with local Muslims?

Chapter 2: Male and Female

This chapter has presented a fairly traditional view of the roles of male and female in Islamic cultures. In reality, all Islamic societies are in flux and attitudes tend to fluctuate (from conservative to more liberal or *vice versa*). The likelihood, also, is that Western Christians will meet Muslims who have at least been exposed to Western norms of relating across the sexes.

Amongst your Muslim acquaintances, what are the expected/accepted ways of interrelating for males and females? Do the males uphold traditional norms? Is there a difference in attitude and practice between the older and younger generations of males? How do the women interrelate? With whom, when and how do they socialise? What kind of interaction goes on within the family, in their own community and with the outsider, especially the Westerner? What are some of the points of tension over male/female issues in the society you are considering? Are there various codes of behaviour that are appropriated for different situations in that society? Even in Britain (or the West generally), is it appropriate for male or female Christians to witness to Muslims of the opposite sex? How do norms about male/female relating that arise from your own personal upbringing fit in with the answers to the previous questions? What changes of view and custom would you need consciously to make in order to accommodate the assumptions of your Muslim friends?

What might be some of the major characteristics of an emerging church that would best accommodate the norms of male/female relationships amongst the Muslims to whom you are ministering? What standards of church behaviour would need to be emphasised? How comfortable are you expecting to feel in such an emerging church?

Many Islamic cultures are status-oriented – appearances and roles are important to them. What is seen as modest dress and behaviour for males and females? Are you prepared to go along with changing your style of dressing and behaving in order to better communicate with Muslims? What kind of changes are required?

How can a Christian family best minister to a Muslim family? Think through the kind of appropriate visit you might make if a Muslim neighbour is ill. Would this include taking a gift? Would this involve you asking to say a prayer with them? If "yes", how are you going to sit/stand/kneel in order to pray? Is visiting your Muslim friend more appropriate than inviting your Muslim friend to visit you? Can you make a note of the feast days after Ramaḍân and the pilgrimage and keep them free to visit Muslim acquaintances with a card or gift?

What appropriate roles allow single expatriate women (missionaries) to validly relate to national Muslims? What messages are given out by your style of living, moving about in public, relating to Western men, and so on? Are there ways in which your preferred way of dressing/behaving might be giving the wrong message to Muslim acquaintances? What changes could you reasonably make so as not to give out a confusing message? How far along the "contextualisation axis" do you think it is appropriate for you to move in terms of your lifestyle when living among Muslims? Are all members of your family agreed about this?

Chapter 3: Family and Individual

To what degree is the bond of extended family being renewed or eroded in the community of Muslims amongst whom you live and work? Who makes what major decisions in life? Are the people you relate to at the heart or at the fringes of their culture? If a younger man seems responsive to the gospel, is it possible for you or an older male to approach his father or elder brother in order to discuss his interest in Christ with them? Should such a procedure be part of our strategy as responsible carriers of Christ's message of salvation? What risks would it involve? What do national believers think?

If we have to go the route of individual extraction (a Muslim becomes a believer and at the same time has to leave behind his natural links with his community), what are going to be some of the overwhelming needs (loneliness, grief, fear and so on) that will require to be immediately addressed in the new believer? Is his/her life in danger, or likely to become so? Does the new believer need to spend some time in a different environment (another city/country)? How will he/she be introduced to Christians there?

What sense of "family" is existing in the group of believers to whom the new believer becomes attached? Do they feel like family to him? If not, how can that sense be improved – what is missing and what needs to be developed? Is the new believer welcome in Christians' homes? How frequently? Just for meetings or at any time? Ask yourself whether your life and home is truly open or whether you are engaged rather in a program of meetings intended to evangelise and disciple Muslims. There is a big difference! What pattern of discipleship is being practised? One-to-one or shared ministry? Is the new believer developing dependency upon one Christian friend? Is that acceptable or wise?

Think through how you might help a wife who believes in Christ live out her faith before her husband and children in appropriate ways? Does she have to remain a secret believer? How might she behave in ways that are culturally acceptable to her own community and yet which could also be vehicles for sharing the gospel? Think this through similarly for a husband or a teenager or a young man.

Chapter 4: Honour and Shame

Family honour is a strong concept in many Muslim communities. Who are the people of honour in the community where you are living or working? What makes them people of honour? A reputation for purity and modesty enhances a group's sense of honour. How might such a reputation be sullied for individuals from a Muslim background in their associating with you? How might you accommodate some of your activities and customs so that the message received by others changes for the better?

What experiences have you had of blundering through the "saving face" mechanism amongst your Muslim friends? How would you behave differently in a similar situation in future?

Read through the book of Jeremiah and note how the idea of shame is conveyed by God in his dealings with a resistant people. Other searching questions about the prophecy of Jeremiah and its importance in the context of understanding and evangelising Muslims are asked by Colin Chapman.[298] In what other passages of Scripture is use made of honour/shame language? What assumptions about "normal" behaviour lie behind such passages?

Work through the contrasts between the guilt and shame axes as summarised from Helen Lynd's research in Figure 23 (page 286). Think about how you present the gospel. Is there a bias towards one of the two axes? Which one? In your own upbringing, which axis was most used by your parents/teachers/pastor? In some of the miscommunications that have taken place between yourself and Muslim acquaintances, has the difference between guilt-based and shame-based behaviour possibly been involved?

Can you identify other examples in the Bible or elsewhere where the appeasement of honour is presented as the means for the reclamation or renewal of relationship?

Chapter 5: Hospitality and Violence

What principles about offering and receiving hospitality need to become part of your attitude towards living amongst Muslims? Sometimes it seems that extrovert missionaries fit more naturally into a Muslim culture. Is this true? If it is, how might introvert missionaries order their lives so as to accommodate the hospitality/generosity priority and yet leave room for personal "aloneness" and space? How do you become a person who is bi-cultural – able to function healthily in your own and your host culture?

What is your home like? Who will feel at home in it? Are there rooms which accommodate the needs of Muslim visitors, and rooms which meet the needs of family or Western friends? Are there pictures or other artefacts on the walls? Are they appropriate to indigenous visitors or will your behaviour be seen as odd in displaying such things in your home? Will your visitor feel comfortable – emotionally? Who sits where and why?

What music do you listen to? Are you learning to appreciate indigenous art forms? Can you read some novels by national authors in order to get a feel for life from an insider's perspective? Are you able to appreciate this kind of learning as an adventure rather than a chore?

What kind of spiritual warfare are you engaged in? Do you have the prayer support you really need? Are there ways in which you can become more public in some of your praying? In your professional work, are you declaring that you are a man or woman of God there also? Do you say "grace" before eating – how do you do it? What are appropriate ways of praying with Muslim friends? Do you pray alone or with others – which situations might require team prayer as opposed to solo prayer? Can you identify at least one other person with whom you can work to "bind" and "loose" in prayer? Think through the importance of maintaining confidentiality in sharing details for prayer. Can you share, with integrity, by changing names?

The issue of violence is a sensitive one. What kind of "violence" is a fair reflection of the nature of God? What kinds of violence are distortions and misrepresentations of God's nature? Have you, or your Muslim friend, been involved in a war situation? Have you, or your Muslim friend, been subject to human violence in the name of God? Have you ever been on the receiving end of God's positive "violent" intrusion into your life? Could you share this with your Muslim friend? In being involved in ministry which has an element of "power encounter" in it, what care needs to be taken? What are the signs of manipulation in such encounters? How can they be avoided? Have you ever asked your Muslim friend about any experiences of dreams or visions or supernatural events which might have awoken him/her to God's desire to develop a personal relationship?

Chapter 6: Time and Space

How important is the clock in your life? Can you defuse its power a little? Many Western Christians find themselves caught in a tug-of-war between

Western sending agencies and bosses who demand the fulfilment of targets and quotas on the one hand, and national folk on the other, for whom time has a far more relaxed sense. How do you survive being in the middle? How strongly oriented towards the future are you? Does this contrast with Muslim friends of your acquaintance? Do you have some grasp of the history of relations between your nation and that of the people you serve? Is your own day punctuated by times of withdrawal for prayer?

How do you deal with the emphases of a value-focused culture (Jesus was a Muslim) compared with a reality-focused culture (Muḥammad lived after Jesus, so Jesus could not have been a Muslim)? How is time expressed or given significance in the Old and New Testaments? Is *kairos* rather than *chronos* a more strongly motivating concept of time in your own life?

Have you considered seriously the history and delicacy of Palestinian/Israeli relationships? What is your view about "Whose promised land"? How are you going to relate to people holding, perhaps, a different view from your own?

What messages are conveyed by the use of space in the area where you live (city, town, village), in the neighbourhood (avenue, road, alley) and in the housing? How do your Muslim friends view "space" within their homes? How does the balance between hosting space and private space work?

Are you *au fait* with concepts of space in the supernatural world? Have you experience in operating in such space with authority in Christ's name? What points do you think Jesus or Mark or the Holy Spirit is making through the double stories of exorcism and miraculous feeding at the beginning of Mark's Gospel?

What sort of personal space are you used to? How do you feel when that is invaded? How do you think that Muslim friends of yours feel about your use of space when interacting with them? Are there ways in which you can better demonstrate an integrated life – where faith is not simply personal, private piety but holistic, affecting every part of life? What messages would help convey that you, as a teacher, doctor, mechanic, businessman, politician, are also a person of prayer and trust in God?

Chapter 7: Language and Silence

What does the use of language reveal about the character/temperament of the people among whom you live and work? Are you communicating in their heart language or in a *lingua franca*? Are you familiar with proverbs and stories, set responses and songs of the Muslims among whom you live? Could you get to know some of those resources from children's books? Ask a Muslim friend to introduce you to the records or tapes of some of the famous singers and musicians of his/her country. Go and see some popular films, or watch the favourite soap opera on television. Of what are the local people ashamed? What is never spoken about? Who is allowed to comment on what? Are you familiar with some of the traditional poems and songs describing the human condition before a holy God?

What sort of emotion is it normally acceptable for you to display in public as far as your own culture is concerned? Does that coincide with the norm for the folk among whom you work? What does losing your temper convey to your Muslim friends? Are you a facts person or a feelings person? What about your Muslim associates? What do you conceal from your friends? What kind of things do they conceal from you?

Try retelling a parable of Jesus in modern Muslim guise, relevant to the people amongst whom you live and work. Vivienne Stacey suggests that Christian workers list some of the incidents (about women or men or sick people from the Scriptures) and main teaching themes (such as the resurrection, forgiveness, prayer, etc.) that they want to get across and then practise telling stories in appropriately embellished ways to hold the listener and engage his/her attention.

Chapter 8: Brotherhood and Rivalry

To what degree is the concept of "brotherhood" (the *'umma*) an important concept for the folk among whom you live and work? Do males pray regularly together? Is the fast of Ramaḍân kept by the majority of people? What respect is given to a person who has been on pilgrimage? Are there movements (Ṣûfî or Islamist or folk-Islamic) which offer opportunity for the expression of group togetherness? Is your Muslim friend involved in any of them? To what degree? What does he/she get out of that involvement?

How does the working out of righteousness find experience in your culture or among your Muslim friends? Do they pay the *zakât*? Anything more than that? What aspects of expressed solidarity are currently part of the norm for your Muslim friends?

Where are the limits to brotherhood currently being expressed in the Islamic culture with which you are familiar? What are some of the denials of brotherhood of which you are aware? Do these offer opportunity for Christian witness and work? Are you a person to whom a Muslim could admit a history of abuse by those in authority over him/her? What are some of the justice issues about which your Muslim friend feels passionate?

Are there ways in which the local Christian church, of which you are a part, could better demonstrate brotherhood in Christ? How has your own church dealt with matters of equality and justice in terms of its structures, values, ethos and *modus operandi*? What do you feel about the importance of fellowship as opposed to church meetings as the place for spiritual growth?

Chapter 9: Resignation and Manipulation

Have you discovered in your Muslim friend the tension of "resignation" versus "manipulation"? Where are the points of resignation – of giving over control? Is it possible for you to pray with your Muslim friend about these difficult matters? In what ways is your Muslim friend seeking to alter his/her life or destiny? Are there points of need being expressed that offer possibilities for you as a Christian to be involved? In what ways has your own trust in a sovereign involved God grown through knowing Muslims?

In what ways has your awareness of the "powers of darkness" grown? What part have dreams played, or might they play, in the sharing of the gospel? Are healing and exorcism ministries relevant among the people whom you are serving – are you equipped to get involved at this level? Can you seek help in growing in this area of ministry or is it theologically or psychologically off-limits for you? What do you think of Hiebert's exegesis of the "flaw of the excluded middle"? Does it describe your perspective?

Have you ever visited a Muslim shrine? Should a Christian visit a Muslim shrine? What do you think Scripture teaches about vow-making? How are Christians guided by God? How do Christians know God's purposes? What role does the Bible play in directing your life? Should the Christian from a Muslim background be expected to be in touch with God via dreams as well as through other means such as Scripture-reading, fellowship and prayer?

Chapter 10: Soul Music

What do you think are some of the primary values or themes of the Muslim people whom you know? How do they contrast with your own? Where do you think it is right to accept the values of your Muslim friend and where do you think they need challenging? Where have you discovered false ideas in your mind about Muslims or Islam? What have you found to be difficult concepts or practices or attitudes to accept?

How are you breaking down false stereotypes which the Muslim has of Western Christians? How might you do more to help the Muslim "hear" the gospel instead of the strident overtones of what he perceives to be Western Christianity?

What focus do you need to make in prayer arising out of the responses you have made to the questions posed in this appendix? Take time to pray now!

GLOSSARY

Words in the glossary following are transliterated from Arabic unless otherwise indicated:

abla: "elder sister"; Turkish
Abû: "father of so-and-so"; *Âb*: "father"
abûya: "my father"
ᶜadhrâ': "virgin"; from *ᶜadhara*, "to excuse, absolve from guilt"
aǧabey: "elder brother"; Turkish
agapê: from *agapao*, "to love" in a moral sense, hence especially God's love; Greek
ahl: "family, kin"; extended family
akhûya: "my brother"
ᶜaql: age of insight or rationality
al-Azhar: ancient university mosque in Cairo, Egypt
Alid: descendant of the Prophet's cousin and son-in-law ᶜAlî
amca: "uncle" (father's lineage); the relative towards whom respect must invariably be shown; Turkish
ammi: "my (paternal) uncle"
ana: (or *anne*), "mother"; Turkish
Anṣâr: "helpers"; the early converts to Islam from Medina who helped Prophet Muḥammad to victory
baba: "father"; Turkish
baraka: "blessing"; often thought of in terms of a kind of positive magic force available from holy people, places or objects
bint ammi: "daughter of *ammi*"
bint khalti: "daughter of *khalti*"
birr: appropriate actions of righteousness, hence charitable gifts
büyük anne: (or *ebe*), "grandmother"; Turkish
büyük baba: (or *dede*), "grandfather"; Turkish

chronos: a fixed time, hence chronology; Greek

çocuk: "child", strictly of ego or male *kardeş*; Turkish

Dâr al-Ḥarb: "the House of War"; territory not under Islamic law

dayı: "uncle" (mother's lineage); the familiar relative with whom one can joke; Turkish

deli: "insane"; Turkish

ḍiyâfa: "hospitality"

fatâ': "youth, adolescence"; *futûwa*: noble manliness, chivalry

gallabeya: *jallâbîya*; long dress worn by men and women in the Middle East

ḥadîth: (plural *aḥadîth*) "prophetic tradition"; a short account of some word or act of Muḥammad's. In its classic form it is passed on by one authority who has received it from another. The chain reaches back to an eyewitness

ḥâfiẓ: "a guardian"; a person who has memorised the whole of the Qur'ân

ḥajj: "setting out"; pilgrimage to Mecca and surrounding holy places

hala: "aunt" (father's lineage); Turkish

ḥamâsa: "bravery"

ḥarâm: "forbidden"

ḥasad: "envy"; in malevolent sense

Hashemite: descendant of clan of Hâshim into which Prophet Muḥammad was born

hijra: "migration", hejira; date of Muḥammad's flight from Mecca on the fourth day of the first month of AD 622. The Islamic calendar commences from the beginning of this year

ibn ammi: "son of *ammi*"

ibn khalti: "son of *khalti*"

idhn: "permission", authorisation (of God)

in shâ'a 'llâh: (*inshallah*) "if God wills"

intifada: "uprising", shaking off

ᶜirḍ: female sexual honour, chastity; can be lost by rape or abuse as well as by willed sexual intercourse

jâhilî: sphere of "ignorance"; Islamists speak of it in contrast with the separated, reformist cell where "true" Islam is adhered to

jamaᶜa: "assembly"; the community of the believers

jihâd: "a striving"; religious war by Muslims against unbelievers or apostates

jinn: species of spirit

kairos: an occasion or opportune moment; crisis time; Greek

kalama: to speak, address

kalm: a "wound" or "slash"

karâma: "miracle"; authenticating sign of a saint

kardeş: "younger brother/sister"; Turkish

khalti: "my (maternal) aunt"

khâtûn: socially prominent woman

kismet: "fate"; Turkish

kuttâb: stage of initial religious education of a child, Qur'ân school

mahram: "forbidden, taboo"; here in sense of unmarriagable

majnûn: "possessed by *jinn*"; generic term for state of being harmed by *jinn*, "mad"

maktûb: "written"; fate, predestination

marabout, murâbit: a man "attached" to God; as in the cult of saints in North Africa

marûf: "generosity"

mâ shâ'a 'llâh: (*mashallah*) "what God wills"; expression used to ward off the evil eye

mawlid: "birthday"; birthday of a prophet or saint

medina, madîna: lit. "town, city"; here in sense of shopping/business centre

mehr: dowry or bridal money; Persian

milla: "religious community"

mirat: "wife of . . ."

mirat ammi: "my father's brother's wife"

Mûhâjirûn: the "exiles"; those who accompanied Muhammad on *hijra*. They rank first in order amongst the Companions of the Prophet

murûwa: "manliness"; the ideal of manhood, hence sense of honour

nadhr: "vow"

nafr: (colloquial) "vow"

nasîb: "set-up"; descriptive word for fate

pirzade: sing. *pirzada*; descendants of saint (*pîr*); Urdu

purdah: lit. "curtain, veil"; Persian: the practice of secluding women from the sight of men and strangers

qadr, qadar: "measuring"; the divine determination of human events and actions

qarîna: f. of *qarin*, "the one united"; the spirit counterpart born into the supernatural world at the same time as the birth of the human baby

qawwâd: "pimp"

qisma: "dividing"; Turkish *kismet*: "lot, destiny, fate"

Ramadân: the fast during the ninth month of the Muslim calendar

rieh, rîh: "a spirit"; in folk-Islam a spirit of a bathroom or a toilet

rujula: "masculinity"

salât: ritual or liturgical prayer, performed five times a day

sandûq al-nudhûr: "vow-box"; where vows or vow-payments are deposited

shabâb: youth state

shahâda: "testimony"; the confession: "I bear witness that there is no deity but God, and that Muhammad is his apostle."

shaik, shaykh: "sheikh", Muslim religious leader

sharaf: "honour"; the core of *sharaf* is the protection of one's female relatives' *ᶜird*

Shîᶜa: "followers"; followers of ᶜAlî, first cousin of Muḥammad and the husband of his daughter Fâṭima

Ṣûfî: Sufi; a Muslim mystic, named after the early ascetics who wore garments of coarse wool

sunna: "a path, manner of life"; the custom, especially of Muḥammad, transmitted via the *ḥadîth* literature

Sunnî: those who accept the *sunna* and the historic succession of the caliphs, as opposed to the ᶜAlids or Shîᶜas; Sunnîs form the majority of the world-wide Muslim community

sûq: "bazaar"

sura: from *sûra*, "a row or series"; chapter of the Qur'ân

takâful: mutual or joint responsibility, solidarity

taklîf: age of legal responsibility when a person becomes *mukallaf* or obligated to observe the precepts of religion

taqîya: lit. "guarding oneself"; state of outward acquiescence in what is inwardly deplored

taqwâ: righteous living, godliness

teyze: "aunt" (mother's lineage); Turkish

thôhû: "formless"; Hebrew

torun: "grandchild", strictly child of *çocuk*; Turkish

ukhti: "my sister"

Umm: "mother"; "mother of So-and-so"

'umma: the "community" of Islam; the whole of the brotherhood of Muslims

ummi: "my mother"

veli: "a saint"; Turkish

vôhû: "empty, void"; Hebrew

wâgib: "obligation"

wajh: lit. "presence"; here "face" as in "saving face"

walî: "guardian"

waqf: religious endowment

wasîṭ: "mediator"

watan: "home, nation"

wazîr: "ruler, vizier"

Yahweh: "the Lord", the covenant name of God in the Old Testament; Hebrew

yiğin: (or *yeğen*), "nephew/niece", strictly child of *dayı*, *abla* or female *kardeş*; Turkish

yôm: "day"; Hebrew

zakât: "purification"; almsgiving, one of the five pillars

zâr: possessing spirit, not normally exorcised

zawja: "wife"; not used in speech because of its sexual connotations (it is derived from the verb meaning "to couple")

ziâra: *ziyâra*, "visitation"; visit to tomb of Muḥammad or grave of any saint

zoug khalti: "my mother's sister's husband"

NOTES

Introduction to the Second Edition

1. Samuel P. Huntington *The Clash of Civilizations and the Remaking of World Order*, Simon & Schuster: New York (1996).

Chapter 1: To Save a Soul

2. See William J. Lederer and Eugene Burdick *The Ugly American*, Cassell: London (1975) for a classic exposé of ethnocentrism and ill-judged international diplomacy .
3. For example, George Otis Jr.'s book *The Last of the Giants*, published by Revell (1991). The book is illustrative of the "giant" vocabulary, not of a pejorative view of Islam.
4. Jacques Jomier *How to Understand Islam*, SCM: London (1989), pp. 73–89.
5. Anne Cooper and Elsie Maxwell (eds.), *Ishmael My Brother: A Christian Introduction to Islam*, Monarch: London (2003), pp. 147–163.
6. See David Burnett *Clash of Worlds*, Monarch: London (2002), pp. 113–125 for a helpful introduction to the kind of cultural themes frequently found in Muslim societies. Burnett draws together his observations under the heading of "The Islamic Worldview".
7. For a good summary statement of a typical "Western" worldview, see Hiebert's contrast between the American worldview and the Indian worldview in Paul G. Hiebert *Cultural Anthropology*, J.B. Lippincott: Philadelphia (1976), pp. 358–362.
8. In using the term "Muslim cultures", I mean the cultures of Muslim peoples. I do not mean a single universal culture which can be described as specifically religious, namely "Muslim". I do, however, want to suggest that a fairly uniform construct of reality is common to many

Muslims, whether they are North African, Middle Eastern, from the Indian subcontinent or even Asian. In some situations, indigenous non-Muslims share many facets of that construct. Differences in some of the details of that construct do, of course, occur and can be considerable. Those differences are, however, beyond the scope of this book to explore. With regard to the ascriptions "Muslim" and "Arab", this book is open to the criticism that too little differentiation is made between the two terms. That is largely because I have in view more fundamental cultural themes; themes which are shared by nearly all Arabs, nearly all of whom happen to be Muslims. Interestingly, in their reviewing of this book in manuscript, one Middle Eastern critic frequently urged me to indicate that I was talking about "Muslim", not "Arab", while one Western critic periodically wanted me to limit my terms of reference to "Arab", not "Muslim". Anwar Moazzam addresses the issue of Islam as a faith and Islam as a culture in his essay "Islamic/Muslim Culture(s): A Study of Relationship between Uniformity and Variety" in "Emerging Patterns and Trends of Muslim Societies", *The Islamic Culture*, Islamic Culture Board: Hyderabad (1979), pp. 13–18.

9   I am concerned in this book to identify some basic norms of perception and behaviour, from which there may well be considerable degrees of development, especially in recent decades. Processes of secularisation, the influence of feminist activism, the ascendancy of the purist (Islamist) lobby each significantly affect how some of the themes delineated here might come to be reinterpreted, even eclipsed, in various current situations. Muslim culture is no more static than any other culture. My conviction, however, is that underlying such developments lies a basic construct of reality which remains largely intact and widely shared.

Chapter 2: Male and Female

10   Figure adapted from summary given by Muhammad Maᶜrûf al-Dawâlîbî, "The Emancipation of Women: A Continuing Priority" in Abdelwahab Bouhdiba (ed.), *The Different Aspects of Islamic Culture: The Individual and Society in Islam*, UNESCO: Paris (1998), p. 186.

11   Related by Ibn Ḥanbal; a similar conviction is passed on in the Hanifite school of Islamic law according to Tuhanni Negra in "A Delicate Balance: Rights, Responsibilities, Freedom" in Bouhdiba (ed.), 1998, pp. 68–69.

12   al-Dawâlîbî, *op. cit.*, pp. 188–189.

13   From A. Guillaume *The Life of Muhammad: A Translation of Ibn Ishaq's Sirat Rasul Allah*, Oxford University Press: Oxford (1955), p. 651. Ibn Ishaq was born in AH 85 and grew up in Medina; his is one of the

earliest full-length biographies of Prophet Muḥammad.

14 Seyyed Hossein Nasr *Ideals and Realities of Islam*, George Allen & Unwin: London (1975), p. 112.

15 Helen Watson *Women in the City of the Dead*, Hurst: London (1992), p. 184.

16 Fatima Mernissi *Beyond the Veil*, revised edition, Al Saqi Books: London (1985), pp. 18–19.

17 *Ibid.*, p. 19.

18 Haifaa A. Jawad *The Rights of Women in Islam: An Authentic Approach*, Macmillan Press: Basingstoke (1998), p. 38 where she quotes from M. Ulama *The Pious Woman*, Young Men's Muslim Association: Port Elizabeth, South Africa (1992), pp. 5–12.

19 Jawad offers Qur'ânic and *ḥadîth* support for her list of entitlements for women in Islam. Her list is summarised in Figure 22.

Figure 22
Rights of women in Islam according to Haifaa Jawad

Right	Support
to independent ownership	sura 4:31
to marry whom she likes and to end an unsuccessful marriage	*ḥadîth*
to education	sura 20:113
to keep her identity	*ḥadîth*
to sexual pleasure	*ḥadîth*
to inheritance	sura 4:7
of selection and nomination to political offices and of participation in public affairs	sura 58:1
to respect	*ḥadîth*

20 Concerning this verse, she says: "Balancing virtues and ethical qualities, as well as concomitant rewards, in one sex with the precisely identical virtues and qualities in the other, the passage makes a clear statement about the absolute identity of the human moral condition and the common and identical spiritual and moral obligations placed on all individuals regardless of sex." In Leila Ahmed *Women and Gender in Islam: Historic Roots of a Modern Debate*, Yale University Press: New Haven (1992), p. 65.

21 Ashghar Ali Engineer *The Rights of Women in Islam*, C. Hurst: London (1992), p. 10.

22 *Ibid.*, p. 147.

23 Quoted in Sana al-Khayyat *Honour and Shame: Women in Modern Iraq*, Saqi Books: London (1990), p. 216.

24 Jean P. Sasson *Princess*, Bantam Books: London (1993), p. 202.

25 Quoted in Sally Sutcliffe *Aisha My Sister: Christian Encounters with Muslim Women in Britain*, Solway: Carlisle (1997), p. 38.

26 Jan Goodwin *Price of Honour: Muslim Women Lift the Veil of Silence on the Islamic World*, Little, Brown and Company: London (1994), p. 16.

27 Abdelwahab Bouhdiba "Sexuality in Islam" in Ghoussoub, Mai and Sinclair-Webb, Emma (eds.) *Imagined Masculinities: Male Identity and Culture in the Modern Middle East*, Saqi Books: London (2000), p. 26.

28 From *Al-Afghani* by Salah al-Rizqi, quoted in Bouhdiba (2000), *op. cit.*, p. 27.

29 See the helpful summary "Childhood and Youth" by Chadly Fitouri in Bouhdiba (ed., 1998), pp. 203–228.

30 Julie Peteet "Male Gender and Rituals of Resistance in the Palestinian Intifada: A Cultural Politics of Violence" in Ghoussoub *op. cit.*, p. 107.

31 Haifaa Jawad, *op. cit.*, p. 57.

32 Nawal El-Saadawi (Sherif Hatata trans. and ed.) *The Hidden Face of Eve: Women in the Arab World*, Zed Press: London (1980), pp. 7–8.

33 Djanet Lachmet (Judith Still trans.) *Lallia (Le Cow-Boy)*, Carcanet Press: Manchester (1987), p. 40.

34 Fatemeh Moghadam "Commoditization of Sexuality and Female Labour Participation in Islam: Implications for Iran 1960–90" in M. Afkhami and E. Friedle (eds.) *In the Eye of the Storm: Women in Post-Revolutionary Iran*, I.B. Tauris: London (1994), p. 84.

35 See the case of Sultana's sister, Sara, in Sasson *op. cit.*, pp. 47–58.

36 Quoted in Sally Sutcliffe *op. cit.*, p. 84.

37 Frédéric Lagrange "Male Homosexuality in Modern Arabic Literature" in Ghoussoub *op. cit.*, pp. 169–198.

38 Alifa Rifaat (Denys Johnson-Davies trans.) *Distant View of a Minaret*, Heinemann: London (1983), p. 1.

39 In Arthur Jeffery (ed.) *A Reader on Islam: Passages from Standard Arabic Writings Illustrative of the Beliefs and Practices of Muslims*, Mouton: Gravenhage (1962), pp. 185–186.

40 Hanan Al-Shaykh (Peter Ford trans.) *The Story of Zahra*, Pavanne: London (1986), p. 10.

41 Lois Beck & Nikki Keddie (eds.) *Women in the Moslem World*, Harvard University Press: Cambridge, Massachusetts (1978), p. 18.

42 al-Khayyat *op. cit.*, p. 163.

43 Fatima Mernissi (Mary Jo Lakeland trans.) *Doing Daily Battle: Interviews with Moroccan Women*, The Women's Press: London (1988), p. 5.

44 Juliette Minces (Michael Pallis trans.) *The House of Obedience: Women in Arab Society*, Zed Press: London (1982), p. 41.

45 *Ibid.*, p. 44.

46 Christine Eickelman "Women and Politics in an Arabian Oasis" in Kazemi, Farhad and McChesney, R.D. (eds.) *A Way Prepared: Essays on Islamic Culture in Honor of Richard Bayly Winder*, New York University Press: New York (1988), p. 200.

47 See Saraya Altorki's analysis of élite families in Jiddah, Saudi Arabia written up in *Women in Saudi Arabia: Ideology and Behaviour Among the Elite*, Columbia University Press: New York (1986), and William Lancaster's account of a Bedouin tribe, recorded in *The Rwala Bedouin Today*, Cambridge University Press: London (1981) where, in a nomadic setting, he describes how women of the Rwala tribe play crucial roles not only in marriage arrangements but also in maintaining, increasing, and disseminating men's reputations (pp. 55–57, 63–66).

48 Hammudah Abdalati *Islam in Focus*, The Islamic Cultural Centre: London (1975), p. 184.

49 Fida Hussein Malik *Wives of the Prophet*, Sh. Muhammad Ashraf: Lahore (1979), p. 182.

50 Fâṭima was the beloved daughter of Prophet Muḥammad; ᶜÂ'isha, a wife of the Prophet, was a renowned scholar; Nafîsa was a theologian and jurist; Shuhda passed on significant *ḥadîth* knowledge; al-Khansa was a poet much admired by Prophet Muḥammad.

51 Andrea B. Rugh *Family in Contemporary Egypt*, American University in Cairo Press: Cairo (1985), p. 286.

52 See, for example, Nahid Toubia (ed., Nahed Al Gamal trans.) *Women of the Arab World: The Coming Challenge*, Zed Books: London (1988) for a modern feminist expression arising from the Arab Women's Solidarity Association Conference held in Cairo in September 1986.

53 Valerie Hoffman concludes that "vast segments of Middle Eastern society have been influenced by centuries of tradition that remain relatively untouched by modernization". In "The Christian Approach to the Muslim Woman and Family" in Don M. McCurry (ed.) *The Gospel and Islam*, MARC: Monrovia (1979), p. 584.

54 Fatima Mernissi *Women and Islam: An Historical and Theological Enquiry*, Blackwell: Oxford (1991), p. 1.

55 See John Bright's helpful summary of this period of Israel's experience in *The Kingdom of God*, Abingdon Press: Nashville (1953), pp. 31–35.

56 See G. Ernest Wright *God Who Acts*, SCM: London (1952), pp. 38–46.

57 The Hebrew language has no capital letters as such; the word "Adam" is used both as a generic term for humankind and as a personal name for the first male.

58 Genesis 2:24.

59 See the whole of Valerie Hoffman's helpful paper, *op. cit.*, pp. 581–593.

60 Charles R. Marsh *Too Hard for God?* Echoes of Service: Bath (1970), pp. 57–58.

61 Vivienne Stacey "The Practice of Exorcism and Healing" in J. Dudley Woodberry (ed.) *Muslims and Christians on the Emmaus Road*, MARC: Monrovia (1989), pp. 294–295.

62 Goodwin, *op. cit.*, p. 95.

63 Related in "Kazakstan" in *The 10/40 Window Reporter*, Fall 1997 and quoted in Stuart Robinson *Mosques and Miracles: Revealing Islam and God's Grace*, CityHarvest Publications: Upper Mt Gravatt (2003), p. 257.

64 Sally Sutcliffe *op. cit.*, pp. 16–17.

65 See the contributions of Hasan al-Ghazali and Donna Smith re. sharing the gospel in coffee houses and amongst women respectively in J. Dudley Woodberry (1989), pp. 198–200 and 201–204.

66 Christine Mallouhi *Miniskirts, Mothers and Muslims*, Monarch Books: Oxford (2004).

Chapter 3: Family and Individual

67 Ravone M'Baye "The Family Basis of the Islamic City" in Bouhdiba (ed.) 1998, p. 117.

68 Sasson *op. cit.*, p. 17.

69 Eickelman *op. cit.*, p. 200.

70 Theodore P. Wright, Jr "Kinship Ties among the Muslim Political Elite in India since Independence" to be found in "Emerging Patterns and Trends of Muslim Societies", *The Islamic Culture*, Islamic Culture Board: Hyderabad (1979), p. 130.

71 Minces *op. cit.*, p. 19.

72 Figure based upon that provided in Ernest L. Schusky *Manual for Kinship Analysis*, Holt, Rinehart & Winston: New York (1972), pp. 20, 81. See also Robert Murphy and Leonard Kasdan "The Structure of Parallel Cousin Marriage" in *American Anthropologist*, vol. 61 (1959), pp. 17–29.

73 Rugh *op. cit.*, p. 111.

74 See the detailed explanation in Joe E. Pierce *Life in a Turkish Village*, Holt Rinehart & Winston: New York (1964), pp. 80–81.

75 Nayra Atiya (ed.) *Khul-Khaal*, American University in Cairo Press: Cairo (1984), p. 149.

76   Naguib Mahfouz (Rasheed El-Enany trans.) *Respected Sir*, Quartet Books: London (1986), pp. 36–37.

77   *Ibid.*, p. 37.

78   As recounted in David Zeidan *The Fifth Pillar: A Spiritual Pilgrimage*, Piquant: Carlisle (2000), p. 90.

79   Extracted and adapted from W. Montgomery Watt *Muhammad at Mecca*, Oxford University Press: Oxford (1953), p. 7.

80   Jerome H. Neyrey *Honor and Shame in the Gospel of Matthew*, Westminster John Knox Press: Louisville, Kentucky (1998), p. 15.

81   Atiya *op. cit.*, pp. 48–49.

82   Sayyid Qutb, *Milestones*, The Mother Mosque Foundation: Cedar Rapids (n.d.), pp. 97–98. By "*jâhilî*" Qutb is referring to a state of ignorance, equivalent to the historical days before the onset of Islam via Prophet Muḥammad.

83   See the account of Father Zechariah's meetings given anonymously in the article "Obstacles in the Way of Winning Muslims" in *Evangelical Missions Quarterly* (1978), vol. 4, no. 3, pp. 178–183. Unfortunately Father Zechariah's public ministry was subsequently curtailed and he himself eventually forced to leave Egypt.

84   John Gulick *The Middle East: An Anthropological Perspective*, University Press of America: Lanham, MD (1983), p. 30.

85   Muhammad Karoui, *Les Temps Modernes*, September–October 1972, quoted in David Pryce–Jones, *The Closed Circle*, Paladin: London (1989), p. 396.

86   Al-Shaykh *op. cit.*, pp. 17–18.

87   Atiya *op. cit.*, p. 168.

88   A.A. Said "Precept and Practice of Human Rights in Islam" in *Universal Human Rights*, vol. 1, no. 1 (1979), p. 74.

89   See Ray Register on sharing the gospel through relatives in Woodberry *op. cit.*, pp. 209–210.

90   Related in Jean-Marie Gaudeul, *Called from Islam to Christ*, Monarch: London (1999), pp. 233–234.

91   Source protected.

Chapter 4: Honour and Shame

92   J. Pitt-Rivers *The Fate of Shechem or the Politics of Sex: Essays in the Anthropology of the Mediterranean*, Cambridge University Press: Cambridge (1977), p. 1.

93   This story is recounted by Nowal Messiri in her essay "The Sheikh Cult of Dahmit" in John E. Kennedy (ed.) *Nubian Ceremonial Life: Studies in Islamic Syncretism and Cultural Change*, University of California

Press: Berkeley (1978), p. 66.

94 Nawal El-Saadawi (Sherif Hetata trans.) *The Innocence of the Devil*, Methuen: London (1994), pp. 43–44.

95 Evelyn A. Early *Baladi Women of Cairo: Playing with an Egg and a Stone*, American University in Cairo Press: Cairo (1993), pp. 172–173.

96 Raymond Jamous "From the Death of Men to the Peace of God: Violence and Peacemaking in the Rif" in J.G. Peristiany & Julian Pitt-Rivers (eds.) *Honor and Grace in Anthropology*, Cambridge University Press: Cambridge (1992), pp. 167–192.

97 The suggested qualities are distilled from Johanna Stiebert "The Construction of Shame in the Hebrew Bible: The Prophetic Contribution", *Journal for the Study of the Old Testament*, Supplement Series 346, Sheffield Academic Press: London (2002), p. 20.

98 Raphael Patai *The Arab Mind*, Charles Scribner's Sons: New York (1973), pp. 101 and 105.

99 Duane Elmer *Cross-Cultural Conflict: Building Relationships for Effective Ministry* (pp. 100–102) as summarised in Sally Sutcliffe *op. cit.*, pp. 76–77.

100 Michael Fischer analyses this difference between a person's public face (*zâhir*) and that person's inner self (*bâtin*) in Iranian society. Michael M J Fischer "Aestheticized Emotions and Critical Hermeneutics" in *Culture, Medicine, and Psychiatry*, vol. 12, no. 1 (March 1988), p. 32.

101 See Kenneth Cragg *Jesus and the Muslim: An Exploration*, George Allen & Unwin: London (1985), pp. 280–281 for a fuller explanation of the philosophy behind *taqîya*.

102 Moghadam *op. cit.*, p. 85.

103 Leon Uris *The Haj*, André Deutsch: London (1985), pp. 560–561.

104 Muḥammad bin Ismâ'îl bin al-Mughîrah al-Bukhârî (Muḥammad Muhsin Khan trans.) *Ṣaḥîḥ*, vol. V, Kazi Publications: Chicago (1978), pp. 319–321.

105 Naguib Mahfouz (Ramses Awad trans.) *The Beginning and the End*, Anchor Books: New York (1985), p. 173.

106 Egyptian Gazette, 9 May 1981, quoted in Rugh *op. cit.*, p. 85.

107 Egyptian Gazette, 26 October 1980, quoted in Rugh *op. cit.*, p. 86.

108 *Age (Melbourne) Today Life and Times*, 26 April 2000, p. 7 and quoted in Stuart Robinson *op. cit.*, p. 266.

109 Donatella Lorch and Preston Meridenhall "A War's Hidden Tragedy" in *Newsweek*, 18 August 2000, pp. 83–84 and quoted in Robinson *op. cit.*, p. 266.

110 Nazik al-Malaika *A Tranquil Moment of a Wave* (Arabic, unpublished Beirut, 1957, p. 146), translated and quoted in al-Khayyat *op. cit.*, pp. 35–36.

111 Told in the biography of Anwar's younger brother Nabil as recorded in David Zeidan *op. cit.*, pp. 60–61.

112 Quoted from the complete letter, to be found in Jean-Marie Gaudeul *op. cit.*, Monarch: London (1999), p. 259.

Figure 23
"Guilt-axis" and "shame-axis" approaches to identity

Guilt Axis	Shame Axis
concerned with each separate act	concerned with the overall self
involves transgression of specific code	involves falling short, missing an ideal
process of deleting wrong acts and substituting right ones for them	involves a total response that includes insight
involves competition, measurement on a scale	involves acting in terms of the pervasive qualitative demands of oneself
exposure of a specific demeanour	exposure of the quick of the self
feeling of wrongdoing in specific act	feeling that may have loved wrong person
trust built on conception of no betrayal	trust slowly eliminating fear of exposure
emphasis on decision-making	ability to live with multiple possibilities
feeling of guilt toward someone who had denounced one for certain reason	feeling of shame toward someone whose trust one had not met
emphasis on content of experience	emphasis on quality of experience
surmounting of guilt leads to righteousness	transcending of shame may lead to sense of identity, freedom

113 For a full treatment of this parable from within a Middle Eastern perspective, see Kenneth E. Bailey *The Cross and the Prodigal*, Concordia: St. Louis (1973). For other, similar, treatments of New Testament texts, see the same author's *Poet and Peasant* and *Through Peasant Eyes: A Literary-Cultural Approach to Parables in Luke*,

Eerdmans: Grand Rapids (1976).

[114] Helen Merrell Lynd, in her book *On Shame and the Search for Identity*, Harcourt, Brace & World: New York (1958), produces an analysis of the "guilt-axis" and "shame-axis" approaches to identity. She summarises her findings in a diagram (pp. 208–209), edited and reproduced here (Figure 23).

One conclusion to be drawn from Lynd's work is that, within Western society, some individuals tend to function more on a shame axis than on a guilt axis. Nevertheless, in the declaring of the gospel by Westerners, "sin" is most usually equated with law-breaking rather than self-exposure; and the cancelling of guilt rather than the melting away of shame is emphasised in invitations to "convert".

[115] L.B. Huber "The Biblical Experience of Shame/Shaming: The Social Experience of Shame/Shaming in Biblical Israel in Relation to its Use as Religious Metaphor" PhD thesis, Drew University (1983). See concerning the Assyrians p. 93; the judicial system p. 101; the psalmist's shame p. 163; God's shame pp. 172–173.

[116] Johanna Stiebert *op. cit.*, p. 128.

[117] Barth L. Campbell *Honor, Shame, and the Rhetoric of 1 Peter*, Dissertation Series Number 160, Scholars Press: Atlanta (1998), p. 12.

[118] *Ibid.*, p. 28.

[119] In an appendix (p. 239), Campbell offers a suggested semantic field of honour and shame in 1 Peter. For each quality he proposes nouns, verbs and adjectives that convey a sense of honour or shame. I reproduce just the nouns here, by way of illustration (Figure 24).

Figure 24
Campbell's semantic field of honour and shame in 1 Peter

nouns conveying a sense of honour	grace, mercy, inheritance, praise, glory, honour, reverent fear, head of the corner, deference, credit, reverence, lord, Sarah's daughters, heirs, blessing, right hand [of God], gift, strength, crown of glory, power, kiss of love
nouns conveying a sense of shame	exiles, sufferings, evildoers, slander, ignorance, grief, cross, humble mind, evil, abuse, deceit, disgrace, murderer, thief, criminal, mischief-maker, sordid gain

[120] Neyrey (1998) *op. cit.*, pp. 35–36.

[121] See the helpful exegesis of this theme in Lowell L. Noble *Naked and Not Ashamed*, Jackson Printing: Jackson, Michigan (1975).

122 I have included in the bibliography (Appendix 4) a number of references to biblical studies that highlight the issues of honour and shame. Investigations of both Old and New Testaments are included.

123 Phil Parshall *New Paths in Muslim Evangelism*, Baker Book House: Grand Rapids (1980), p. 78.

124 Source protected.

125 David Arthur deSilva *Despising Shame: Honor Discourse and Community Maintenance in the Epistle to the Hebrews*, Society of Biblical Literature, 152, Scholars Press: Atlanta (1996), p. 2.

126 Neyrey *op. cit.*, p. 147.

127 Everrt Huffard "Culturally Relevant Themes about Christ" in J. Dudley Woodberry *op. cit.*, p. 172.

128 It is not my intention to minimise the difficulties of getting around traditional Muslim objections to the crucifixion. It is, however, to suggest that a shift away from intellectual argument towards a concern for the Muslim to be "shamed" into allowing God to be God is valid. After all, Paul knew that it was "word" and "power" together that convinced many of his hearers (1 Thessalonians 1:5) of the truth of his message. According to Luke, the story of Acts is really that of how Jesus *continued* from heaven, via his apostles on earth, to act and to teach – both aspects of proclamation going together (Acts 1:1).

Chapter 5: Hospitality and Violence

129 These traditions are recorded by Abû Dâwûd Sulaymân Ibn al-Ash^cath in his *Kitâb al-Sunan*, book 26, chapters 1, 4, and 14 respectively. They are quoted in Maulânâ Muḥammad ^cAlî *The Religion of Islam*, National Publication & Printing House: Cairo (n.d.), pp. 736–737.

130 See Ida Glaser & Shaylesh Raja *Sharing the Salt: Making Friends with Sikhs, Muslims and Hindus*, Scripture Union: Bletchley (1999) for an exposition of the importance of eating together in many cultures. It is in the act of sharing salt, they claim, that "friendships are bonded, deals are closed and settled disputes are celebrated" (p. 20).

131 *Ibid.*, p. 22.

132 *Ibid.*, p. 46.

133 Naguib Mahfouz (William Maynard Hutchins & Olive E. Kenny trans.) *Palace Walk*, Doubleday: London (1991), p. 339.

134 Yashar Kemal (Edouard Roditi trans.) *Memed, My Hawk*, Harvill: London (1961), pp. 350–351.

135 ^cUmar killed in AD 644; ^cUthmân murdered in AD 656; ^cAlî assassinated in AD 661.

136 Julie Peteet *op. cit.*, p. 109.

[137] Within a strict theological framework, of course, *jihâd* (literally "striving") has a variety of interpretations, not all of them violent. See Sarwar *op. cit.*, pp. 81–82.

[138] Faraj's pamphlet is entitled *Al-Farîḍa al-Ghâ'iba* and an English translation of it is given in Johannes J.G. Jansen *The Neglected Duty: The Creed of Sadat's Assassins and Islamic Resurgence in the Middle East,* Macmillan: New York (1986), pp. 159–234.

[139] See al-Bukhârî *op. cit.*, vol. VIII (1979), chapters 1–4, pp. 519–522.

[140] The abuse of the recently introduced law in Pakistan against blaspheming Prophet Muḥammad led to the death, imprisonment and persecution of Christian believers in the country until the legal procedures were eventually tightened up. In Iran, 1994 was a sad year for the church with the martyrdom, seemingly condoned by the authorities, of several leading churchmen. Christians who come from a Muslim background are still imprisoned and tortured in Egypt and Morocco for no other reason than that they have converted to Christ or are caught participating in a Bible correspondence course. See Patrick Johnstone *Operation World,* OM: Carlisle (1993), pp. 433, 305, 205, 393 for reports on respective countries.

[141] From Gamal al-Ghitani *The Events of Zaafarani Alley* as translated by Farouk Abdel Wahab (1992) and quoted from manuscript by Evelyn Early *op. cit.*, pp. 147–148.

[142] Maulana Ashraf Ali Thanvi in *Bahishti Zewar* (Heavenly Ornaments), p. 474 as quoted in Sally Sutcliffe *op. cit.*, pp. 85–86.

[143] Yashar Kemal (Thilda Kemal trans.) *The Sea-Crossed Fisherman,* Collins Harvill: London (1990), pp. 182–183.

[144] Brian Keenan *An Evil Cradling,* Random House: London (1992), pp. 146–147.

[145] Attia Hosain *Sunlight on a Broken Column,* Virago: London (1961), p. 59.

[146] Judges 19 and 20.

[147] Source protected.

[148] Source protected.

[149] Quoted in Sally Sutcliffe *op. cit.*, p. 155.

Chapter 6: Time and Space

[150] Ghassan Kanafani (Hilary Kilpatrick trans.) *Men in the Sun,* Three Continents Press: Washington (1983), pp. 49–50.

[151] al-Bukhârî *op. cit.*, vol. IX (1979), no. 382, p. 283.

[152] *Ibid.*, book no. 92, pp. 281–348.

[153] See Philip K. Hitti *The Arabs: A Short History,* Princeton University

Press: Princeton (1943), p. 21, for his comment on "lawful magic" as describing the effect of the rhythm, rhyme and music produced on listeners by orations in Arabic.

[154] Quoted in Richard P. Mitchell *The Society of the Muslim Brothers*, Oxford University Press: London (1969), pp. 86–87.

[155] Charles R. Marsh *Share Your Faith With A Muslim*, Moody Press: Chicago (1975), p. 60.

[156] Carlton S. Coon *Caravan: The Story of the Middle East*, Henry Holt: New York (1951), p. 6.

[157] Yusuf al-Qaradawi (Abu Maimounah Ahmad bin Muhammad Bello trans.) *Time in the Life of a Muslim*, Ta-Ha: London (2000), p. 14.

[158] Orhan Pamuk (Güneli Gün trans.), *The New Life*, Faber and Faber: London (1997), pp. 106–107.

[159] See Gershon Brin *The Concept of Time in the Bible and the Dead Sea Scrolls*, Brill: Leiden (2001) for an exhaustive analysis of the biblical words for, and concept of, time. His conclusions concerning the term *yôm* ("day") are found on p. 368.

[160] Simon J. DeVries *Yesterday, Today and Tomorrow: Time and History in the Old Testament*, SPCK: London (1975), p. 345.

[161] Brenda Deen Schildgen *Crisis and Continuity: Time in the Gospel of Mark*, Sheffield Academic Press: Sheffield (1998), p. 20.

[162] *Ibid.*, p. 17.

[163] See Michael Gilsenan on zones of "self" and "other", and other concepts of personhood as conveyed by the use of space, in *Recognizing Islam*, I.B. Tauris: London (1990), p. 171.

[164] Roy Mottahedeh *The Mantle of the Prophet: Learning and Power in Modern Iran*, Chatto & Windus: London (1986), pp. 34–37.

[165] See Muhammad Talbi's article "Everyday Life in the Cities of Islam" in Bouhdiba (ed.) 1998, pp. 379–460. He comments on the traditional layout of a *medina*, for example: "The manufacturer, the tradesmen and the craftsman all found in the *sûq* an organised space which allowed for easier control of goods, comparison of quality and prices, saving of time, and security as well since the market's gates were locked at night!" (p. 403).

[166] See George M. Foster "Peasant Society and the Image of Limited Good" in *American Anthropologist*, vol. 67 (1965), pp. 293–315 for a helpful explanation of the concept of "limited good".

[167] Stefano Bianca *Urban Form in the Arab World: Past and Present*, Thames & Hudson: London (2000), p. 38.

[168] *Ibid.*, p. 77.

[169] Mernissi (1985) *op. cit.*, p. 54.

[170] Evelyn Early *op. cit.*, p. 68, referring to the suburb of Boulaq in Cairo.

[171] Patricia Jeffery *Frogs in a Well: Indian Women in Purdah*, Zed Books: London (1979), p. 108.

[172] See Ira M. Lapidus *A History of Islamic Societies*, Cambridge University Press: Cambridge (1988), pp. 642–643 for an introduction to some of the delicate issues concerning Western involvement with Arabs and Jews in the first two decades of the 20th century. For the actual text of the MacMahon (and other contemporary) correspondence, see the appendices in George Antonius *The Arab Awakening: The Story of the Arab National Movement*, Hamish Hamilton: London (1938), pp. 413–458.

[173] Halim Barakat (Trevor Le Gassick trans.) *Days of Dust*, Three Continents Press: Washington (1983), pp. 163–164.

[174] Colin Chapman *Whose Promised Land?*, Lion: Oxford (2002), pp. 309–310.

[175] Tayeb Salih (Denys Johnson-Davies trans.) *The Wedding of Zein and Other Stories*, Heinemann: London (1969), p. 33.

[176] Hani Fakhouri *Kafr El-Elow: An Egyptian Village in Transition*, Holt, Rinehart & Winston: New York (1972), p. 72.

[177] Ched Myers *Binding the Strong Man: A Political Reading of Mark's Story of Jesus*, Orbis Books: New York (1988), p. 192.

[178] Sister Gulshan Esther (Nobel Din trans.) *The Torn Veil*, Marshalls: Basingstoke (1984), pp. 60–61.

[179] Source protected.

[180] Source protected.

Chapter 7: Language and Silence

[181] Ghulam Sarwar *Islam: Beliefs and Teachings*, Muslim Educational Trust: London (1987), pp. 33–34.

[182] Nasr *op. cit.*, p. 47.

[183] See, for example, this methodology as applied by Rashad Khalifa in *Miracle of the Qur'an*, Islamic Productions International: St. Louis (1973).

[184] Niloofar Haeri *Sacred Language, Ordinary People*, Palgrave Macmillan: New York (2003), p. 1.

[185] The term "Islamists" refers to contemporary Muslims who are primarily concerned for certain kinds of reform and renewal to take effect within the House of Islam. In the West they are often labelled "Muslim fundamentalists". For a detailed consideration of Islamist perspectives, see Bill A. Musk *Holy War: Why Some Muslims Become Fundamentalists*, Monarch Books: London (2003).

[186] Sayyid Qutb (M. Adil Salahi & Ashur A. Shamis trans.) *In the Shade of the Qur'ân*, vol. 30, MWH London Publishers: London (1979), p. 3.

Suras are classified as "Makkan" or "Madinan" according to whether they relate to Prophet Muḥammad's residence in Mecca or Medina.

187 Al-Thaᶜâlibî *Fiqh al-Lugha*, Cairo (1284), p. 3, quoted in Richard Tames *Approaches to Islam*, John Murray: London (1982), p. 22.

188 al-Bukhârî *op. cit.*, vol. IX, (1979), pp. 284–285.

189 Shahrokh Meskoob (Michael C. Hillmann trans.) *Iranian Nationality and the Persian Language*, Mage: Washington DC (1992), p. 11.

190 *Ibid.*, p. 10. The other contributors to the development of Iran's cultural identity he names as the pre-Islamic legacy, Shîᶜa Islam, and the bonds of people living in the same territory.

191 Idries Shah *The Sufis*, Anchor: New York (1971), p. 69.

192 *Ibid.*, p. 88.

193 See the many examples in Alan Dundes, Jerry W. Leach & Bora Özkök "The Strategy of Turkish Boys' Verbal Duelling Rhymes" in *Journal of American Folklore*, vol. 83 (1970), pp. 325–349.

194 See Simon Jargy *La Musique Arabe*, Presses Universitaires de France: Paris (1971) for a helpful introduction to Arab music. Constance Padwick comments on the contribution made by Temple Gairdner as "musician missionary" in recording Near Eastern airs and making them available for use in Christian worship. See Constance E. Padwick *Temple Gairdner of Cairo*, SPCK: New York (1929), pp. 123–125.

195 Jacques Berque *The Arabs: Their History and Future*, Praeger: New York (1964), p. 18.

196 Quoted in Pierce *op. cit.*, p. 97.

197 From Arthur Jeffery *op. cit.*, pp. 69–70.

198 For an English translation of this moving song see Süleyman Chelebi (F. Lyman MacCullum trans.) *The Mevlidi Sherif*, John Murray: London (1943).

199 *Ibid.*, pp. 38–39.

200 A. Yusuf Ali *The Glorious Qur'an: Translation and Commentary*, American Trust Publications (1977), p. 594. Ali's appendix to Sura 12 gives a detailed recounting and analysis of Jâmî's rendering of this allegorical poem.

201 *Ibid.*, p. 595.

202 *Ibid.*, p. 599.

203 An English translation of Shawqî's *Majnun Layla* was published by Luzac in 1933, the year that the great poet died. The sample quoted here is found in A.J. Arberry *Aspects of Islamic Civilization: The Moslem World Depicted through its Literature*, University of Michigan Press: Ann Arbor (1964), p. 371. See Doris Behrens-Abouseif's comments on Majnûn and Laylâ in *Beauty in Arabic Culture*, Markus Wiener: Princeton (1998), pp. 68–69.

[204] Watson *op. cit.*, p. 11.

[205] *Ibid.*, p. 14

[206] *Ibid.*, p. 202.

[207] Mariam Behnam recounts this story by Sheikh Saadi in *Heirloom: Evening Tales from the East*, Oxford University Press: Oxford (2001), pp. 312–314.

[208] Yashar Kemal (Thilda Kemal trans.) *The Legend of the Thousand Bulls*, Collins and Harvill: London (1976), pp. 234–235.

[209] Taha Hussein (E.H. Paxton trans.) *An Egyptian Childhood*, Heinemann: London (1981).

[210] Morroe Berger *The Arab World Today*, Weidenfeld & Nicolson: London (1962), p. 174.

[211] William O. Beeman "Affectivity in Persian Language Use" in *Culture, Medicine and Psychiatry* (Byron J Good ed.) vol. 12, no. 1 (March 1988), p. 16.

[212] *Ibid.*, p. 28.

[213] *Ibid.*, p. 21.

[214] Hamid Ammar *Growing Up In An Egyptian Village*, Octagon Books: New York (1973), p. 133.

[215] Sir Geoffrey Furlonge *Palestine Is My Country: The Story of Musa Alami*, Praeger: New York (1969), p. 152, quoted in Raphael Patai (1973), *op. cit.*, p. 51.

[216] Glaser & Raja *op. cit.*, p. 73.

[217] Afarin's story is found in Pauline Selby *Persian Springs*, Highland Books: Godalming (2001), pp. 87–106. Her first encounter with a Persian Bible is told on p. 101.

[218] Uris *op. cit.*, pp. 478–480.

[219] Martin Goldsmith *Islam and Christian Witness*, Hodder & Stoughton: London (1982), pp. 128–129. For another example of Goldsmith's parabolic preaching, see "Hadji Abdullah's Gift" as told in his article "Southeast Asia: Parable in Muslim Dress" for *Theology, News and Notes*, Fuller Theological Seminary: Pasadena (March, 1992), pp. 10–11.

[220] Sally Sutcliffe *op. cit.*, pp. 196–197.

Chapter 8: Brotherhood and Rivalry

[221] Quoted by Chadly Fitouri in "The Meaning of Islamic Brotherhood" to be found in Bouhdiba (ed.), 1998, pp. 229–249.

[222] Maulânâ Muhammad ᶜAlî *op. cit.*, pp. 382–383.

[223] Guellouz Ezzedine *Mecca: The Muslim Pilgrimage*, Paddington Press: London (1977), p. 108.

[224] "Agnatic" indicates descent reckoned by male links. "Polyandrous"

describes a woman with several husbands.

225 Lapidus *op. cit.*, pp. 35–36.

226 Fitouri *op. cit.*, p. 235.

227 Sayyid Jamal al-Din al-Afghani "Islamic Solidarity" in John J. Donahue & John L. Esposito (eds.) *Islam in Transition: Muslim Perspectives*, Oxford University Press: New York (1982), p. 21.

228 The lie was given to Afghani's ideal in various ways during the decades following independence, not least in the partition of India and the formation of Pakistan, and then in the splitting of the latter nation into West Pakistan and Bangladesh. In the political and civil upheavals accompanying those violent events, "ethnic origin" and "clan loyalty" counted for very much for many Muslims.

229 From *Al-Ahram* (4, 5 February 1966), translated and quoted by Emmanuel Sivan in *Radical Islam: Medieval Theology and Modern Politics*, Yale University Press: New Haven (1985), pp. 85–86.

230 David Burnett *World of the Spirits: A Christian Perspective on Traditional and Folk Religions*, Monarch Books: London (2000), p. 87.

231 Gerald Butt *The Arab World: A Personal View*, BBC Books: London (1987), p. 21.

232 Nawal El-Saadawi (Sherif Hetata trans.) *God Dies by the Nile*, Zed Books: London (1985).

233 Zechariah Tamer (Denys Johnson-Davies trans.) "A Lone Woman" in *Tigers on the Tenth Day*, Quartet Books: London (1985), pp. 47–51.

234 Summarised in Samuel P. Huntington *op. cit.*, p. 175.

235 *Ibid.*, p. 175.

236 Quoted in Pryce-Jones *op. cit.*, p. 39.

237 Pryce-Jones *op. cit.*, p. 112.

238 El-Saadawi (1985) *op. cit.*, p. 137.

239 Goodwin, *op. cit.*, p. 179.

240 Pryce-Jones *op. cit.*, p. 38.

241 Naguib Mahfouz (Philip Stewart trans.) *Children of Gebelawi*, Heinemann: London (1981).

242 *Ibid.*, p. 352.

243 Mahfouz's book has other dimensions as well. Most significantly, it calls into question whether a traditional belief in God is appropriate, given the realities of evil in human society. From the outset, *Children of Gebelawi* provoked a strong reaction: the novel's original serialisation angered orthodox Muslims. More recently, its celebrated author has been personally injured by Islamists who see him as denying the Islamic faith.

244 See John R.W. Stott *The Message of Acts*, Inter-Varsity Press: Leicester (1990), pp. 151–159 for a detailed treatment of the conversion and initiation of Samaritans as recorded in Acts 8.

245 Acts 10:44.

246 Acts 17:22–31.

247 See John's Gospel with its identification of Jesus as the pre-existent and divine *logos* or "word" and so on. Discussions about how far John was dependent upon Hellenistic as opposed to Jewish themes for his use of the *logos* idiom can be found in George Eldon Ladd *A Theology of the New Testament*, Eerdmans: Grand Rapids (1974), pp. 237–242 and in Ronald H. Nash *Christianity and the Hellenistic World*, Zondervan: Grand Rapids (1984), pp. 81–88.

248 Ephesians 2:14.

249 Philemon verse 17.

250 According to Jeremias, Jesus was the first Jewish rabbi to accept women disciples (cf. Matthew 12:46–50; Luke 8:1–3; 10:38–42). In post-resurrection days, the New Testament yields evidence of a female apostle and female ministers, prophets and elders in the early spread of the gospel and blossoming of "house" churches. This, despite the fact that most of the apostles/evangelists were people from a strongly hierarchical Jewish background and despite the fact that the ensuing Gentile church would largely take its structures from a hierarchical Roman worldview. See the exposition of the initial spread of the gospel as delineated in Edward Schillebeeckx *The Church with a Human Face*, SCM: London (1985). My personal view on the complimentariness of "brother" and "sister" in Christ is declared in these comments. I believe that the church should be on the cutting edge of abandoning a theology of hierarchical human relationships in which male is, by divine fiat, "head" over female in an "above/below" sense. I do not think that that theological perspective is sufficiently true to Scripture's concern for mutuality between the sexes. Nevertheless, I do not consider it appropriate for me to insist on such abandonment in a (Middle Eastern) culture which operates on a strongly hierarchical basis and in which I am a visitor. Although I disagree with Christine Mallouhi's theology (*op. cit.*, pp. 53–54), I agree with her conclusions for living as effective visiting advocates of the gospel within a culture where family structure already functions on a hierarchical basis.

251 Source protected.

252 Mallouhi *op. cit.*, p. 67.

Chapter 9: Resignation and Manipulation

253 Sarwar *op. cit.*, p. 23.

254 al-Bukhârî *op. cit.*, vol. VIII (1979), book 77, pp. 387–403.

255 *Ibid.*, pp. 387–388.

[256] Muhammad ᶜAbd al-Hâdî Abû Rîda in "Norms and Values", to be found in Abdelwahab Bouhdiba (ed.) *The Different Aspects of Islamic Culture: The Individual and Society in Islam*, UNESCO: Paris (1998), p. 46.

[257] Atiya *op. cit.*, p. 9.

[258] al-Khayyat *op. cit.*, p. 186. By "materialistic factors" al-Khayyat means tangible aspects of living, such as producing sons (for women) or providing wealth (for men). Al-Khayyat concludes that those "materialistic" kinds of contribution are of the greatest importance in determining how marriages develop. They eclipse any kind of mutual exploration of who the husband and wife might be in themselves.

[259] From "Bahiyya's Eyes" in Rifaat *op. cit.*, pp. 5–11.

[260] Atiya *op. cit.*, p. 177.

[261] Watson *op. cit.*, pp. 184–185.

[262] Alifa Rifaat "Degrees of Death" in *Distant View of a Minaret*, p. 112.

[263] See Paul G. Hiebert's whole article "The Flaw of the Excluded Middle" in *Missiology*, vol. 10, no. 1 (1982), pp. 35–47.

[264] My purpose in drawing this contrast is not to make a value judgement concerning Islam based on the suggestion that its popular "face" seemingly contradicts and undermines its theological affirmations. Rather, it is to bring to the forefront the tension that exists in many Muslims' lives. On the one hand, they perceive themselves to be faithful Muslims, however much they are involved in attempts to manipulate the spirit world. On the other hand, in many areas of their lives and for much of the time, they consider themselves hopelessly subject to what is determined for them from above. Incidentally, Paul Magnarella, in his study of tradition and change in Susurluk, Turkey, suggests that in other ways also, Turks, at least, prove to be anything but excessively fatalistic. He identifies the process at the end of World War I when a defeated country and people revitalised themselves under Atatürk into a secular nation-state as a strong example of Turks taking their destiny into their own hands. Similarly in 1950, voting power was used by ordinary Turks to displace a repressive government. His conclusion is that, for many Turks, at least, religiosity and fatalism do not necessarily go together. Paul G. Magnarella *Tradition and Change in a Turkish Town*, John Wiley and Sons: New York (1974), pp. 156–157.

[265] El-Saadawi (1994) *op. cit.*, pp. 177–178.

[266] See the sobering account of accurate predictions of respective marriage and remarriage for Sultana and her sister Sara through palmistry by Huda, their Sudanese slave, in Sasson *op. cit.*, pp. 144-148.

[267] Bill A. Musk *The Unseen Face of Islam*, Monarch Books: London (2003).

[268] Hoffman *op. cit.*, p. 588.

[269] Tayeb Salih "The Doum Tree of Wad Hamid" in (1969) *op. cit.*, pp. 11–13.

[270] Evelyn Early, *op. cit.*, p. 123.

[271] Messiri *op. cit.*, p. 65.

[272] Evelyn Early, *op. cit.*, pp. 124–125.

[273] Interview as recorded in Bill A. Musk *Popular Islam: An Investigation into the Phenomenology and Ethnotheological Bases of Popular Islamic Belief and Practice*, UNISA: Pretoria (1984), p. 384.

[274] See Robert A. and Elizabeth W. Fernea "Variation in Religious Observance among Islamic Women" in Nikkie R. Keddie (ed.) *Scholars, Saints and Sufis: Muslim Religious Institutions Since 1500*, University of California Press: Berkeley (1972), pp. 385–401. Robert and Elizabeth Fernea make the point that "as anyone knows who has been attentive to the patterns of behaviour and belief in Middle Eastern villages (or towns, or cities), these worlds are full of holy men and women, shrines, incarnate forces of good and evil, evil eyes, incantations, and ceremonies; all of which help to make up a cosmological outlook in which formal Islam plays an important but by no means exclusive role" (p. 387).

[275] Fatima Mernissi *Women, Saints and Sanctuaries*, Simorgh: Lahore (1987), p. 11.

[276] Bernard Collinson *Occultism in North Africa*, North Africa Mission: Aix-en-Provence (1977), p. 32. See also the experience of Said and Tétum (Example 16) who were professing believers living in Greater Kabylia. After enjoying a Christian marriage ceremony, they trekked to a distant saint's tomb for a "blessing" on their marriage. Collinson notes the tragic story of their marriage as it then unfolded and asks "Was the *baraka* of the Muslim saint a blessing or a curse?" *Ibid.*, p. 37.

[277] See Paul Hiebert's paper on "Power Encounter and Folk Islam" in Woodberry *op. cit.*, pp. 45–61.

[278] For the Greek words used in the Septuagint and the New Testament, see Heinrich Greeven on *euchomai, euchê, proseuchomai, proseuchê* in Gerhard Kittel (ed.) *Theological Dictionary of the New Testament*, vol. II, Eerdmans: Grand Rapids (1964), pp. 775–808.

[279] Donna Smith "Here is How I Share with Women in the East" in Woodberry *op. cit.*, p. 204.

[280] Jean-Marie Gaudeul, *op. cit.*, p. 193.

[281] *Ibid*, pp. 193–194.

Chapter 10: Soul Music

[282] Idries Shah "Cut Down on your Harness Intake" in *The Exploits of the Incomparable Mulla Nasrudin*, Picador: London (1973), p. 117.

283 Sania Hamady *Temperament and Character of the Arabs*, Twayne: New York (1960).

284 For his concentrated description of Egypt and Egyptians, see Morroe Berger *Islam in Egypt Today: Social and Political Aspects of Popular Religion*, Cambridge University Press: Cambridge (1970). For his exposition of the theme of Near Eastern "Arab", see Morroe Berger *The Arab World Today*, Weidenfeld & Nicolson: London (1962). Berger's conclusions are based on investigations conducted personally in Egypt, Syria, Lebanon, Jordan and Iraq.

285 Berger (1962) *op. cit.*, p. 15.

286 See Chapter 5 on "Personality and Values" in *ibid.*, pp. 154–185.

287 Patai (1973) *op. cit.* The central chapters of Patai's book deal with "The Bedouin Substratum of the Arab Personality" and "The Bedouin Ethos", pp. 73–83 and 84–117 respectively.

288 *Ibid.*, p. 310.

289 John Gulick *The Middle East: An Anthropological Perspective*, Goodyear: Pacific Palisades (1976).

290 David Pryce-Jones *The Closed Circle*, Paladin: London (1989).

291 For an examination of the thought and contribution of Gairdner, see Lyle L. Vander Werff *Christian Mission to Muslims: The Record*, William Carey Library: Pasadena (1977), pp. 200–224. For an analysis of the life and work of Zwemer, see *ibid.*, pp. 224–257. William McElwee Miller was a missionary of the Presbyterian Church in Iran from 1919 to 1962. He wrote his own account of his experience in *My Persian Pilgrimage*, William Carey Library: Pasadena (1989). Lilias Trotter's contribution is recounted in Patricia St. John's *Until the Day Breaks: The Life and Work of Lilias Trotter*, OM: Bromley (1990). Roger Steer and Sheila Groves (eds.) tell the story of Charles Marsh's life and ministry in *Love Will Find a Way: Charles Marsh*, OM: Bromley (1991).

292 I am not suggesting that these pioneers expressed their individual identification with their host peoples in identical ways, nor that they would necessarily agree with the approach taken in this book. However, in each of their ministries among Muslims there is evidenced a real awareness of Muslims as people enculturated in specific ways – ways different from their own inherited backgrounds.

293 Colin Chapman "Biblical Foundations of Praying for Muslims" in Woodberry *op. cit.*, p. 321.

294 Chinua Achebe applied the clause from W.B. Yeats' poem "The Second Coming" to summarise the processes he observed going on in Nigeria during the 1950s. Yeats' poem can be found in Philip Larkin (ed.) *The Oxford Book of Twentieth Century English Verse*, Oxford University Press: Oxford (1973), p. 79. Achebe's important novel is entitled

Things Fall Apart, Heinemann: London (1958).

[295] I have suggested some themes in tension for Muslim cultures in this book. Figure 25 summarises Michael Fischer's identification of "discourse" in Middle Eastern societies. His analysis is found in Fischer (1988) *op. cit.*, p. 35.

Figure 25

Fischer's summary of contrasting themes in Middle Eastern societies

Theme	Theme
public sphere	private sphere
masculinity	femininity
agonism	vulnerability
autonomy	dependence
stoicism	emotion
opportunity	constraint
honour	modesty

[296] Written up in "The Shazlis of Damascus", *ISIC Bulletin*, February/March 1996 and quoted in Robinson *op. cit.*, p. 249.

[297] Recorded in Ida Glaser & Napoleon John (1998) *op. cit.*, pp. 314–315.

Appendix 1

[298] Colin Chapman "The God Who Reveals" in Woodberry *op. cit.*, pp. 131–132.

AN INTRODUCTORY BIBLIOGRAPHY

Afghânî, Sayyid Jamâl al-Dîn al-. "An Islamic Response to Imperialism", in John J. Donohue & John L. Esposito (eds.), *Islam in Transition: Muslim Perspectives*, Oxford University Press: New York, 1982, pp. 16–19.

Afghânî, Sayyid Jamâl al-Dîn al-. "Islamic Solidarity", in John J. Donohue & John L. Esposito (eds.), *Islam in Transition: Muslim Perspectives*, Oxford University Press: New York, 1982, pp. 20–23.

Afkhami, M. and E. Friedle (eds.), *In the Eye of the Storm: Women in Post-Revolutionary Iran*, I.B. Tauris: London, 1994.

Ahmed, Leila. *Women and Gender in Islam: Historic Roots of a Modern Debate*, Yale University Press: New Haven, 1992.

ᶜAlî, Maulânâ Muḥammad. *The Religion of Islam*, National Publication & Printing House: Cairo, n.d.

Altorki, Saraya. *Women in Saudi Arabia: Ideology and Behaviour Among the Elite*, Columbia University Press: New York, 1986.

Ammar, Hamid. *Growing Up In An Egyptian Village: Silwa, Province of Aswan*, Octagon Books: New York, 1973.

Atiya, Nayra. *Khul-Khaal: Five Egyptian Women Tell Their Stories*, American University in Cairo Press: Cairo, 1982.

Aydin, Mehmet. "The Concepts of Man and Society in Islam", in *Newsletter* (Centre for the Study of Islam and Christian–Muslim Relations, Selly Oak Colleges, Birmingham): no. 17/18 (1987), pp. 9–23.

Bailey, Kenneth E. *The Cross and the Prodigal*, Concordia: St Louis, 1973.

Barakat, Halim (Trevor Le Gassick trans.), *Days of Dust*, Three Continents Press: Washington DC, 1983.

Bechtel, L.M. "Shame as a Sanction of Social Control in Biblical Israel: Judicial, Political, and Social Shaming", in *Journal for the Study of the Old Testament*, vol. 49 (1991) pp. 47–76.

Bechtel, L.M. "What if Dinah is not Raped? (Genesis 34)" in *Journal for the Study of the Old Testament*, vol. 62 (1994), pp. 19–36.

Beck, Lois & Nikki Keddie (eds.), *Women in the Moslem World*, Harvard University Press: Cambridge, Massachusetts, 1978.

Beeman, William O. "Affectivity in Persian Language Use", in *Culture, Medicine and Psychiatry* (Byron J. Good ed.), vol. 12, no. 1 (March 1988), pp. 9–30.

Behnam, Mariam. *Heirloom: Evening Tales from the East*, Oxford University Press: Oxford, 2001.

Behrens-Abouseif, Doris. *Beauty in Arabic Culture*, Markus Wiener: Princeton, 1998.

Berger, Morroe. *The Arab World Today*, Weidenfeld & Nicolson: London, 1962.

Berger, Morroe. *Islam in Egypt Today: Social and Political Aspects of Popular Religion*, Cambridge University Press: Cambridge, 1970.

Bianca, Stefano. *Urban Form in the Arab World: Past and Present*, Thames & Hudson: London, 2000.

Bouhdiba, Abdelwahab (ed.), *The Different Aspects of Islamic Culture: The Individual and Society in Islam*, UNESCO: Paris, 1998.

Bowen, Barbara M. *The Folklore of Palestine*, Eerdmans: Grand Rapids, 1940.

Bukhârî, Muḥammad bin Ismâ‘îl bin al-Mughîrah al- (Muḥammad Muhsin Khan trans.), *Ṣaḥîḥ*, vols. I–IX, Kazi Publications: Chicago, 1976–1979.

Burness, Margaret. *What Do I Say to my Muslim Friends?* Church Missionary Society: London, 1989.

Burnett, David. *Clash of Worlds*, Monarch: London, 2002.

Butt, Gerald. *The Arab World: A Personal View*, BBC Books: London, 1987.

Campbell, Barth L. *Honor, Shame, and the Rhetoric of 1 Peter*, Dissertation Series Number 160, Scholars Press: Atlanta, Georgia, 1998.

Carmichael, Joel. *The Shaping of the Arabs: A Study in Ethnic Identity*, George Allen & Unwin: London, 1967.

Chapman, Colin. *Cross and Crescent: Responding to the Challenge of Islam*, IVP: Leicester, 1995.

Chapman, Colin. *Whose Promised Land?* Lion: Oxford, 2002.

Chapman, Colin. *"You Go and Do the Same": Studies in Relating to Muslims*, CMS, BMMF and IFES: London, 1983.

Chelebi, Süleyman (F. Lyman MacCullum trans.), *The Mevlidi Sherif*, John Murray: London, 1943.

Christensen, Jens. *The Practical Approach to Muslims*, North Africa Mission: Marseille, 1977.

Cline, Walter. "Proverbs and Lullabies from Southern Arabia", in *American Journal of Semitic Languages and Literature*, vol. 57 (1940), pp. 291–301.

Coon, Carlton S. *Caravan: The Story of the Middle East*, Henry Holt & Co.: New York, 1951.

Cooper, Anne and Elsie Maxwell (eds.), *Ishmael My Brother: A Christian Introduction to Islam*, Monarch: London, 2003.

Cragg, Kenneth. *The Arab Christian*, Mowbray: London, 1991.

Cragg, Kenneth. *The Call of the Minaret*, Oxford University Press: New York, 1964.

Cragg, Kenneth. *The Pen and the Faith: Eight Modern Muslim Writers and the Qur'ân*, George Allen & Unwin: London, 1985.

Daube, D. "The Culture of Deuteronomy" in *Orita*, vol. 3 (1969), pp. 27–52.

Dearden, Ann (ed.), *Arab Women*, Minority Rights Group Report, no. 27: London, 1975.

DeSilva, David Arthur. *Despising Shame: Honor Discourse and Community Maintenance in the Epistle to the Hebrews*, Society of Biblical Literature, no. 152, Scholars Press: Atlanta, 1996.

DeVries, Simon J. *Yesterday, Today and Tomorrow: Time and History in the Old Testament*, SPCK: London, 1975.

Dretke, James P. *A Christian Approach to Muslims: Reflections from West Africa*, William Carey Library: Pasadena, 1979.

Dundes, Alan, Jerry W. Leach & Bora Özkök. "The Strategy of Turkish Boys' Verbal Duelling Rhymes", in *Journal of American Folklore*, vol. 83 (1970), pp. 325–349.

Early, Evelyn A. *Baladi Women of Cairo: Playing with an Egg and a Stone*, American University in Cairo Press: Cairo, 1993.

Eickelman, Dale F. *The Middle East: An Anthropological Approach*, Prentice-Hall: Englewood Cliffs, NJ, 1989.

Engineer, Ashghar Ali. *The Rights of Women in Islam*, C. Hurst: London, 1992.

Esther, Sister Gulshan (Noble Din trans.), *The Torn Veil*, Marshalls: Basingstoke, 1984.

Fakhouri, Hani. *Kafr El-Elow: An Egyptian Village in Transition*, Holt, Rinehart & Winston: New York, 1972.

Faruki, Kemal A. "Common Concerns and Values for Family Life", in *Encounter*, no. 145–146 (1988), pp. 3–9.

Fernea, Elizabeth Warnock. *Guests of the Sheik: An Ethnography of an Iraqi Village*, Doubleday: New York, 1965.

Fischer, Michael M J. "Aestheticized Emotions and Critical Hermeneutics", in *Culture, Medicine and Psychiatry* (Byron J. Good ed.), vol. 12, no. 1, (March 1988), pp. 31–42.

Foster, George M. "Peasant Society and the Image of Limited Good", in *American Anthropologist*, vol. 67 (1965), pp. 293–315.

Foster, George M. *Traditional Societies and Technological Change*, Harper and Row: San Francisco, 1973.

Fuller, Anne H. *Buarij: Portrait of a Lebanese Village*, Harvard University Press: Cambridge, MA, 1961.

Gaudeul, Jean-Marie. *Called from Islam to Christ*, Monarch: London, 1999.

Gaudeul, J.-M. "Women in Islam", in *Encounter*, no. 19 (1975), pp. 1–7.

Geertz, Clifford. *Islam Observed: Religious Development in Morocco and Indonesia*, Yale University Press: New Haven, 1968.

Ghoussoub, Mai and Sinclair-Webb, Emma (eds.), *Imagined Masculinities: Male Identity and Culture in the Modern Middle East*, Saqi Books: London, 2000.

Gilsenan, Michael. *Recognizing Islam: Religion and Society in the Modern Middle East*, I.B. Tauris: London, 1990.

Glaser, Ida & John, Napoleon. *Partners or Prisoners? Christians Thinking About Women and Islam*, Solway: Carlisle, 1998.

Glaser, Ida & Raja, Shaylesh. *Sharing the Salt: Making Friends with Sikhs, Muslims and Hindus*, Scripture Union: Bletchley, 1999.

Goldsmith, Martin. *Islam and Christian Witness*, Hodder & Stoughton: London, 1982.

Good News in Our Times: The Gospel and Contemporary Cultures, Church House Publishing: London, 1991.

Goodwin, Jan. *Price of Honour: Muslim Women Lift the Veil of Silence on the Islamic World*, Little, Brown and Company: London, 1994.

Gowler, David B. *Host, Guest, Enemy and Friend: Portraits of the Pharisees in Luke and Acts*, Emory Studies in Early Christianity, no. 2, Peter Long: New York, 1991.

Guellouz, Ezzedine. *Mecca: The Muslim Pilgrimage*, Paddington Press: London, 1977.

Gulick, John. *The Middle East: An Anthropological Perspective*, Goodyear: Pacific Palisades, 1976.

Haeri, Niloofar. *Sacred Language, Ordinary People*, Palgrave Macmillan: New York, 2003.

Haleblian, Krikor. *Worldview and Evangelization: A Case Study on Arab People*, ThM project, Fuller Theological Seminary: Pasadena, 1979.

Hamady, Sania. *Temperament and Character of the Arabs*, Twayne: New York, 1960.

Hanson, K.C. "'How Honorable! How Shameful!': A Cultural Analysis of Matthew's Makarisms and Reproaches", in *Semeia*, vol. 68 (1996), pp. 81–111.

Hosain, Attia. *Sunlight on a Broken Column*, Virago: London, 1961.

Huber, L.B. "The Biblical Experience of Shame/Shaming: The Social Experience of Shame/Shaming in Biblical Israel in Relation to its Use as

Religious Metaphor", PhD thesis: Drew University, 1983.

Huffard, Evertt W. "Culturally Relevant Themes about Christ", in J. Dudley Woodberry (ed.), *Muslims and Christians on the Emmaus Road*, MARC: Monrovia, 1989, pp. 161–174.

Hussein, Taha (E.H. Paxton trans.), *An Egyptian Childhood: The Autobiography of Taha Hussein*, Heinemann: London, 1981.

Ismael, Jacqueline S. and Tareq Y. *Civil Society and the Oppressive State in the Arab World*, Ankara Paper 2, Frank Cass: London, 2001.

Jamous, Raymond. "From the Death of Men to the Peace of God: Violence and Peacemaking in the Rif", in J.G. Peristiany & Julian Pitt-Rivers (eds.), *Honor and Grace in Anthropology*, Cambridge University Press: Cambridge (1992), pp. 167–192.

Jansen, Johannes J.G. *The Neglected Duty: The Creed of Sadat's Assassins and Islamic Resurgence in the Middle East*, Macmillan: New York, 1986.

Jawad, Haifaa A. *The Rights of Women in Islam: An Authentic Approach*, Macmillan: Basingstoke, 1998.

Jeffery, Arthur (ed.), *A Reader on Islam: Passages from Standard Arabic Writings Illustrative of the Beliefs and Practices of Muslims*, Mouton: Gravenhage, 1962.

Jeffery, Patricia. *Frogs in a Well: Indian Women in Purdah*, Zed Books: London, 1979.

Jennings, George J. "Cultural Features Important to Christian Missionaries in Lebanese Villages", in *Practical Anthropology*, vol. 19, no. 2 (1972), pp. 59–82.

Jennings, George J. "Islamic Culture and Christian Missions", in *Practical Anthropology*, vol. 18, no. 3 (1971), pp. 128–144.

Jennings, George J. "The Arab Ethos: A Key for International Understanding and Rapport?" Xeroxed copy (1977).

John, Patricia St. *Until the Day Breaks: The Life and Work of Lilias Trotter*, OM: Bromley, 1990.

Jomier, Jacques. *How to Understand Islam*, SCM: London, 1989.

Kanafani, Ghassan (Hilary Kilpatrick trans.), *Men in the Sun and Other Palestinian Stories*, Three Continents Press: Washington DC, 1983.

Kateregga, Badru D. and David W. Shenk. *Islam and Christianity: A Muslim and a Christian in Dialogue*, Eerdmans: Grand Rapids, 1980.

Kazemi, Farhad and McChesney, R.D. (eds.), *A Way Prepared: Essays on Islamic Culture in Honor of Richard Bayly Winder*, New York University Press: New York, 1988.

Kearney, Michael. *World View*, Holt, Rinehart & Winston: New York, 1976.

Keenan, Brian. *An Evil Cradling*, Random House: London, 1992.

Kemal, Yashar (Edouard Roditi trans.), *Memed, My Hawk*, Harvill: London, 1961.

Kemal, Yashar (Thilda Kemal trans.), *The Legend of the Thousand Bulls*, Collins and Harvill: London, 1976.

Kemal, Yashar (Thilda Kemal trans.), *The Sea-Crossed Fisherman*, Collins Harvill: London, 1985.

Khalifa, Rashad. *Miracle of the Qur'an: Significance of the Mysterious Alphabets*, Islamic Productions International: St Louis, 1973.

Khayyat, Sana al-. *Honour and Shame: Women in Modern Iraq*, Saqi Books: London, 1990.

Lachmet, Djanet (Judith Still trans.), *Lallia (Le Cow-Boy)*, Carcanet Press: Manchester, 1987.

Laffin, John. *The Arab Mind: A Need for Understanding*, Cassell: London, 1975.

Lancaster, William. *The Rwala Bedouin Today*, Cambridge University Press: London, 1981.

Lapidus, Ira M. *A History of Islamic Societies*, Cambridge University Press: Cambridge, 1988.

Lederer, William J. and Eugene Burdick. *The Ugly American*, Cassell: London, 1975 (originally Victor Gollancz: London, 1959).

Lenning, Larry G. *Blessing in Mosque and Mission*, William Carey: Pasadena, 1980.

Lynd, Helen Merrell. *On Shame and the Search for Identity*, Harcourt, Brace & World: New York, 1958.

McCurry, Don M. (ed.), *The Gospel and Islam*, MARC: Monrovia, 1979.

Magnarella, Paul J. *Tradition and Change in a Turkish Town*, John Wiley and Sons: New York, 1974.

Mahfouz, Naguib (Olive E. Kenny trans.), *Wedding Song*, Doubleday: New York, 1984.

Mahfouz, Naguib (Philip Stewart trans.), *Children of Gebelawi*, Heinemann: London, 1981.

Mahfouz, Naguib (Ramses Awad trans.), *The Beginning and the End*, Anchor Books: New York, 1985.

Mahfouz, Naguib (Rasheed El-Enany trans.), *Respected Sir*, Quartet Books: London, 1986.

Mahfouz, Naguib (Trevor Le Gassick trans.), *The Thief and the Dogs*, Anchor Books: New York, 1984.

Mahfouz, Naguib (William Maynard Hutchins & Olive E. Kenny trans.), *Palace Walk*, Doubleday: London, 1991.

Mallouhi, Christine. *Miniskirts, Mothers and Muslims: A Christian Woman in a Muslim Land*, Monarch Books: Oxford, 2004.

Marsh, Charles R. *Share Your Faith With A Muslim*, Moody Press: Chicago, 1975.

Marsh, Charles R. *Streams in the Sahara*, Echoes of Service: Bath, 1975.

Marsh, Charles R. *Too Hard for God?* Echoes of Service: Bath, 1970.

Masood, Steven. *Into the Light*, Kingsway: Eastbourne, 1986.

Matheny, Tim. *The Communication of Religious Innovations among the Transitional Arabs: An Evangelistic Strategy for the Churches of Christ*, thesis presented to Harding College Graduate School of Religion: Memphis, Tennessee, 1977.

Meghdessian, Samira Rafidi (compiler). *The Status of the Arab Woman: A Select Bibliography*, Mansell: London,1980.

Mernissi, Fatima. *Beyond the Veil: Male–Female Dynamics in Muslim Societies*, Al Saqi Books: London, 1985.

Mernissi, Fatima (Mary Jo Lakeland trans.), *Doing Daily Battle: Interviews with Moroccan Women*, The Women's Press: London, 1988.

Mernissi, Fatima. *Women and Islam: An Historical and Theological Enquiry*, Blackwell: Oxford, 1991.

Mernissi, Fatima. *Women, Saints and Sanctuaries*, Simorgh: Lahore, 1987.

Meskoob, Shahroth (Michael C. Hillmann trans.), *Iranian Nationality and the Persian Language*, Mage: Washington DC, 1992.

Messiri, Nowal. "The Sheikh Cult of Dahmit", in John G. Kennedy (ed.), *Nubian Ceremonial Life: Studies in Islamic Syncretism and Cultural Change*, University of California Press: Berkeley, 1978, pp. 61–103.

Miller, William M. *A Christian's Response to Islam*, Presbyterian and Reformed Publishing: Nutley, 1977.

Minces, Juliette (Michael Pallis trans.), *The House of Obedience: Women in Arab Society*, Zed Press: London, 1982.

Mitchell, Richard P. *The Society of the Muslim Brothers*, Oxford University Press: London, 1969.

Molteno, Marion. *A Language in Common*, The Women's Press: London, 1987.

Mottahedeh, Roy. *The Mantle of the Prophet: Learning and Power in Modern Iran*, Chatto & Windus: London, 1986.

Moucarry, Chawkat Georges (David Monkcom trans.), *Islam and Christianity at the Crossroads*, Lion: Tring, 1988.

Moxnes, Halvor. "Honour and Righteousness in Romans", in *Journal for the Study of the New Testament*, no. 32 (1988), pp. 61–77.

Murphy, Robert & Leonard Kasdan. "The Structure of Parallel Cousin Marriage", in *American Anthropologist*, vol. 61 (1959), pp. 17–29.

Musk, Bill A. *Holy War: Why Some Muslims Become Fundamentalists*, Monarch: London, 2003.

Musk, Bill A. *The Unseen Face of Islam: Sharing the Gospel with Ordinary Muslims*, Monarch: London, 2003.

Nasr, Seyyed Hossein. *Ideals and Realities of Islam*, Allen & Unwin: London, 1975.

Nazir-Ali, Michael. *Islam: A Christian Perspective*, Paternoster Press: Exeter, 1983.

Neyrey, J.A. "'Despising the Shame of the Cross': Honor and Shame in the Johannine Passion Narrative", in *Semeia*, vol. 68 (1996), pp. 113–37.

Neyrey, J.A. (ed.), *The Social World of Luke-Acts*, Hendrickson: Peabody, MA, 1991.

Neyrey, Jerome H. *Honor and Shame in the Gospel of Matthew*, Westminster John Knox Press: Louisville, Kentucky, 1998.

Nida, Eugene A. *Customs and Cultures: Anthropology for Christian Missions*, William Carey Library: Pasadena, 1954.

Noble, Lowell L. *Naked and Not Ashamed: An Anthropological, Biblical and Psychological Study of Shame*, Jackson: Michigan, 1975.

Padwick, Constance E. *Temple Gairdner of Cairo*, SPCK: London, 1930.

Pamuk, Orhan (Güneli Gün trans.), *The New Life*, Faber and Faber: London, 1997.

Parshall, Phil. *New Paths in Muslim Evangelism*, Baker Book House: Grand Rapids, 1980.

Patai, Raphael. *Golden River to Golden Road: Society, Culture and Change in the Middle East*, University of Pennsylvania Press: Philadelphia, 1962.

Patai, Raphael. *The Arab Mind*, Charles Scribner's Sons: New York, 1973.

Peristiany, Jean G. (ed.), *Honor and Shame: The Values of Mediterranean Society*, University of Chicago Press: Chicago, 1966.

Pierce, Joe E. *Life in a Turkish Village*, Holt, Rinehart & Winston: New York, 1964.

Pryce-Jones, David. *The Closed Circle: An Interpretation of the Arabs*, Paladin: London, 1989.

Qutb, Sayyid (M. Adil Salahi & Ashur A. Shamis trans.), *In the Shade of the Qur'ân*, vol. 30, MWH London Publishers: London, 1979.

Rifaat, Alifa (Denys Johnson-Davies trans.), *Distant View of a Minaret and Other Stories*, Heinemann: London, 1983.

Rugh, Andrea B. *Family in Contemporary Egypt*, American University in Cairo Press: Cairo, 1985.

Saadawi, Nawal El- (Sherif Hetata trans.), *God Dies by the Nile*, Zed Books: London, 1985.

Saadawi, Nawal El- (Sherif Hetata trans. and ed.). *The Hidden Face of Eve: Women in the Arab world*, Zed Press: London, 1980.

Saadawi, Nawal El- (Sherif Hetata trans.), *The Innocence of the Devil*, Methuen: London, 1994.

Said, A.A. "Precept and Practice of Human Rights in Islam", in *Universal Human Rights*, vol. 1, no. 1 (1979), pp. 64–79.

Saleh, Nabil. *Outremer*, Quartet Books: London, 1998.

Salih, Tayeb (Denys Johnson-Davies trans.), *The Wedding of Zein and Other Stories*, Heinemann: London, 1969.

Sarwar, Ghulam. *Islam: Beliefs and Teachings*, Muslim Educational Trust: London, 1987.

Sasson, Jean P. (ghost-writer). *Princess*, Bantam Books: London, 1993 (originally Doubleday: London, 1992).

Scarce, Jennifer. *Domestic Culture in the Middle East: An Exploration of the Household Interior*, National Museums of Scotland: Edinburgh, 1996.

Schildgen, Brenda Deen. *Crisis and Continuity: Time in the Gospel of Mark*, Sheffield Academic Press: Sheffield, 1998.

Schusky, Ernest L. *Manual for Kinship Analysis*, Holt, Rinehart & Winston: New York, 1972.

Shah, Idries. *The Sufis*, Anchor: New York, 1971.

Shaykh, Hanan Al- (Peter Ford trans.), *The Story of Zahra*, Pavanne: London, 1986.

Sheikh, Bilquis. *I Dared to Call him Father*, Kingsway: Eastbourne, 1978.

Shouby, E. "The Influence of the Arabic Language on the Psychology of the Arabs", in *The Middle East Journal*, vol. 5 (1951), pp. 284–302.

Shushtery, A.M.A. *Outlines of Islamic Culture*, Bangalore Printing & Publishing Co.: Bangalore, 1954.

Sivan, Emmanuel. *Radical Islam: Medieval Theology and Modern Politics*, Yale University Press: New Haven, 1985.

Stacey, Vivienne. *Christ Supreme Over Satan*, Masihi Isha'at Khana: Lahore.

Stacey, Vivienne. *Practical Lessons for Evangelism Among Muslims*, Interserve: London, 1988.

Stacey, Vivienne. "The Practice of Exorcism and Healing", in Woodberry *op. cit.*, pp. 291–303.

Stiebert, Johanna. "The Construction of Shame in the Hebrew Bible: The Prophetic Contribution", in *Journal for the Study of the Old Testament*, Supplement Series 346, Sheffield Academic Press: London, 2002.

Sutcliffe, Sally. *Aisha My Sister: Christian Encounters with Muslim Women in Britain*, Solway: Carlisle, 1997.

Tamer, Zakaria (Denys Johnson-Davies trans.), *Tigers on the Tenth Day and Other Stories*, Quartet Books: London, 1985.

Thackston, Wheeler McIntosh. *The Tales of the Prophets of al-Kisa'i*, Twayne: Boston, 1978.

Uris, Leon. *The Haj*, André Deutsch: London, 1984.

Watson, Helen. *Women in the City of the Dead*, C. Hurst: London, 1992.

Westermarck, Edward. *Wit and Wisdom in Morocco: A Study of Native Proverbs*, George Routledge: London, 1930.

Wikan, U. "Shame and Honour: A Contestable Pair", in *Man*, vol. 19 (1984), pp. 635–652.

Woodberry, J. Dudley (ed.), *Muslims and Christians on the Emmaus Road*, MARC: Monrovia, 1989.

Zenner, Walter P. "Ethnic Stereotyping in Arabic Proverbs", in *Journal of American Folklore*, vol. 83 (1970), pp. 417–429.

Zwemer, Samuel M. *Islam: A Challenge to Faith*, Student Volunteer Movement for Foreign Missions: New York, 1907.

INDEX